the
legacy guide

2006

1
05/29/2007

FROM

_____

TO

_____

Let this book be your guide
as you record your life and legacy.

Allow us to know you as a person.
Help us learn from your experience.
Tell us how you became the person we love.

the legacy guide

CAPTURING THE FACTS, MEMORIES,

AND MEANING OF YOUR LIFE

carol franco AND *kent lineback*

JEREMY P. TARCHER / PENGUIN
a member of Penguin Group (USA) Inc.
NEW YORK

JEREMY P. TARCHER/PENGUIN
Published by the Penguin Group
Penguin Group (USA) Inc., 375 Hudson Street, New York, New York 10014, USA • Penguin Group
(Canada), 90 Eglinton Avenue East, Suite 700, Toronto, Ontario M4P 2Y3, Canada (a division of Pearson
Penguin Canada Inc.) • Penguin Books Ltd, 80 Strand, London WC2R 0RL, England • Penguin Ireland,
25 St Stephen's Green, Dublin 2, Ireland (a division of Penguin Books Ltd) • Penguin Group (Australia),
250 Camberwell Road, Camberwell, Victoria 3124, Australia (a division of Pearson Australia Group Pty Ltd) •
Penguin Books India Pvt Ltd, 11 Community Centre, Panchsheel Park, New Delhi–110 017, India •
Penguin Group (NZ), Cnr Airborne and Rosedale Roads, Albany, Auckland 1310, New Zealand (a division
of Pearson New Zealand Ltd) • Penguin Books (South Africa) (Pty) Ltd, 24 Sturdee Avenue,
Rosebank, Johannesburg 2196, South Africa

Penguin Books Ltd, Registered Offices: 80 Strand, London WC2R 0RL, England

Most Tarcher/Penguin books are available at special quantity discounts for bulk purchase for sales promotions, pre-
miums, fund-raising, and educational needs. Special books or book excerpts also can be created to fit specific needs.
For details, write Penguin Group (USA) Inc. Special Markets, 375 Hudson Street, New York, NY 10014.

Library of Congress Cataloging-in-Publication Data

Franco, Carol, date.
The legacy guide: capturing the facts, memories, and meaning of your life / Carol Franco
and Kent Lineback.
p.   cm.
Includes bibliographical references.
ISBN-13: 978-1-58542-516-7
ISBN-10: 1-58542-516-8
1. Autobiography—Authorship.   2. Biography as a literary form.   3. Legacies.
I. Lineback, Kent L.   II. Title.
CT25.F715   2006   2006022201
929'.1072—dc22

Printed in the United States of America
1   3   5   7   9   10   8   6   4   2

BOOK DESIGN BY JUDITH STAGNITTO ABBATE/ABBATE DESIGN

While the authors have made every effort to provide accurate telephone numbers and Internet addresses at the time
of publication, neither the publisher nor the authors assume any responsibility for errors, or for changes that occur
after publication. Further, the publisher does not have any control over and does not assume any responsibility for
author or third-party websites or their content.

PERMISSIONS

AND CREDITS

To our beloved families

Carol

My parents Ruth and Ed
My brother Allen and his wife Wei
My sister Toby

Kent

My parents Ethel and Frank
My children Eric, Lauren, Lesley, and Rich
My grandchildren Ted, Phoebe, and Hadley
My sister Marcia and her husband Robert

CONTENTS

PREFACE

When I was barely a teenager, I saw on my father's dresser a note he had obviously written to himself and placed where he would see it at the beginning and end of each day. In his neat, distinctive hand that was half script, half printing, the note said, "When you get to the end of your rope, tie a knot and hang on." Well, being a typical adolescent, I thought that was the dumbest thing I'd ever heard. (Never mind my father meant it only for himself.) Years, decades, later, after struggling through my own trials as a grown-up, I came to appreciate the wisdom of what he wrote. But only after my dad was buried did I begin to wonder what provoked him to write that note and put it on his dresser. Something did. Some pressure, some fear, some personal demon. I'll never know.

—Kent Lineback, personal story

Both of us, Carol and Kent, have lost parents. We didn't realize until they were gone just how much of their lives remained a mystery to us.

Ironically, the degree of mystery didn't depend on how much contact we'd had with them. All his adult life, Kent lived on the East Coast, while his parents lived on the West. They saw each other only on occasion. Carol, on the other hand, saw her parents often and talked to them every day through the many last years of their lives. She and they shared the details of each other's daily activities. Yet after they died, she realized what vast gaps remained in her knowledge of their lives, even about simple details. It wasn't for lack of interest, but somehow in spite of their close relationship and daily contact, the holes and mysteries never got resolved. Learning someone's life story, she discovered, doesn't happen casually.

Both of us wish, in particular, that we had learned to know our parents as people. We saw them for decades in their roles as parents. Not until we became mature adults ourselves did they become in our minds ordinary people struggling with the same life challenges we all face. Sometimes we find ourselves playing a little game: when we remember a key moment in our own lives, we figure out how old Mom or Dad was then. It's often a shock to realize he or she was younger at that time than we are now. That realization changes how we see them and immediately brings to mind questions about their lives then—lives which, we now realize, probably were not too different from our own. "Tie a knot and hang on." Our questions, sadly, will remain questions forever.

We wrote this book to help loved ones recall and record the stories of their lives, for we know now that telling those stories won't happen by chance. We particularly wanted to create a simple but comprehensive tool a child or grandchild could give to a parent or grandparent. Our aim was to provide a guide for either the storyteller or someone interviewing the storyteller.

We hope you find *The Legacy Guide* useful and rewarding. We wish we'd had it to give to our own parents.

—CAROL FRANCO and KENT LINEBACK

THE GREATEST GIFT

What will be your legacy? What will you leave for the benefit of your children, their children, and all the children who follow them?

Perhaps you think only of money and property when you think of legacy. But, important as those can be, there's an even greater gift you can leave those who follow you . . . and give yourself in the process. That gift is the story of your life.

Think of someone in your family whom you know little about—perhaps a parent, but more likely a grandparent or great-grandparent or even someone further back. Think of some face staring out at you from an old family photo, an interesting face perhaps full of character or humor, the kind of face that compels you to wonder, Who was that? What was he or she like? Perhaps that face looks a little like yours.

You wish you knew more about this person. After all, you came from him. His existence led directly to you. The conditions of his life helped create the circumstances of yours. Some of your genes—who you are—came from him.

Imagine being able to read this person's story—perhaps it was a woman—the key events of her life, the choices and challenges she faced, the details of her days, and, perhaps most interesting, her thoughts and feelings about what she did and what happened to her. Imagine reading her memories of people, places, events, and moments, and understanding the forces that shaped her life. Imagine being able to hear her stories told in her own words.

Now imagine another person, the child of the child of your grandchild, looking at your face gazing out from some family photo. Imagine this future man or woman wondering about you and curious to know *you* as a person and the story of *your* life. Wouldn't that person, the offspring of your offspring, be as interested in you as you are in your ancestors? Wouldn't all those who follow you want to know the key events of your life, the choices and challenges you faced, the details of your days, your feelings?

Of course they would. They come from you. To know you is to know themselves. There's no greater gift, no more generous legacy, that you could give.

How often have you thought back on some time in your life and said to yourself, I wish I'd known then what I know now? But you can't go back. Time only moves in one direction. A moment comes, you make a choice, large or small, then time moves on and you live with the consequences.

In the process, you learn something. But what is it, exactly, that you learn? It's not like learning to bake bread or drive a car. It's more that you come to *understand* life—how everything fits together, what counts, what you need to focus on, what's important.

This is what you want to pass on, but what's the best way to do that? It's hard to express outright this kind of "knowledge," and, when you try, it usually sounds trite—Work hard, Be patient, Tell the truth, Keep your promises. Reduced to such simplicity, your lessons become clichés—not to you, because you learned them with sweat and tears—but to the listener, who will roll his eyes and think, Sure, Dad, or You bet, Grandma. Your pithy lessons, though true, will make little difference to anyone else. You say, "When I was a child . . ." and eyes glaze over, as did yours when someone years ago said those words to you.

It's a mistake most people make. You *tell* when the better way is to *show*. Those who follow you don't want your advice. They want your *experience*. They want to understand your life, your *story*, so they can learn from it, too. They want to know what you did and why. How did you make choices? What was important to you? What happened after you made those choices? How did you reach the place you did in life? It doesn't matter where that is, how humble or exalted. What matters is how you got there. "Tell us about your *journey*!" they say. "What was your *journey* like?" Isn't that what you'd like to know about that ancestor you recalled a few moments ago?

So it's your experience, the details of your journey, that's your real legacy. If you tell your children and grandchildren, "Never give up," it will mean virtually nothing. If you tell the story of your life, a life in which perseverance paid off, it will change how they live their lives. That's why there's no greater gift than telling your story.

It's a gift you give to yourself, as well.

To remember a life is to journey back through time. But unlike time, which always marches forward, memory is free to roam down the corridors of the past. With it you can revisit the events and people and occasions that made a difference. Dwelling in memory on a wonderful moment can be one of life's great pleasures.

Not every moment was wonderful, you might protest. That's true, of course, but you're a different person now. As you remember, you can apply the understanding you lacked earlier, the knowledge and insight you've accumulated since then. A childhood incident, for example, that embarrassed you deeply can now be seen as simply a part of growing up. For now you have a much larger context, an entire lifetime, in which to view such moments.

As you journey back in memory, you'll see your life whole. What may have felt at the time like a series of disconnected and chance events will take on a flow and coherence that only the passage of time could reveal. You're able now to see how the consequences of a choice, perhaps made casually, rippled through the years that followed. You can see now how a chance event led to other events that shaped your entire life. Memory, in short, can reveal the links, the connections—the story—of your life.

It's hard to exaggerate the satisfaction this kind of insight can produce. It's the satisfaction of feeling that your life, whatever happened in it, made sense.

We hope you'll tell the story of your life. Let the children of your children know you as a person, so they can know themselves. Let them learn from your experience. Let them benefit from what you've worked so hard to understand. And, not least, give yourself the satisfaction of seeing your life whole.

When you're done with this book and all it guides you to do, you will hold in your hand your own book filled with the facts, memories, stories, people, and feelings that made up every step of your unique journey. You'll be able to say, "This is what I did. This is what happened to me. This is my story, my legacy."

I'M NOT SURE
I CAN DO THIS!

If you're ready and eager to tell your story, you can skip this part. If you have doubts and questions, as many people do when they think of recording their life stories, read on.

"But I can't write."

Yes, you can. Can you write a simple declarative sentence? Something like, "Jim fell off the porch." If you can do that, you can record your legacy. You don't need to be an accomplished writer. You only need to write out one memory at a time in simple sentences. You don't need to write a book. You're creating a mosaic, a picture composed of small pieces that combine to create a complete image.

"But I don't know enough."

Yes, you do. You're an expert in at least one subject, and that subject is you and your life. All that's required is that you put down what you know as that expert. It will require some work and thought and diligence, but you can do it with the help you receive from this book, which will guide you every step of the way. You'll start with the simple facts—what you did, where you lived, and so on. These will trigger memories and stories of people and places and events. Finally, you'll talk about what it all meant to you and how you felt about it. Step by step, fact by fact, memory by memory, you'll build up that mosaic of your life.

"But I didn't do anything in my life."

Yes, you did. You probably mean you didn't do anything you consider interesting or noteworthy. But that's only your opinion. In the eyes of those you're writing for—your family, the child of your child of your child—your life is automatically noteworthy, because it led to them. It's a way for them to know where they came from. Whenever you're tempted to think you did nothing of interest in your life, think of that ancestor of yours you'd like to know more about. Do you care that he or she didn't change the world?

"But no one cares what happened to me."

Yes, they do. Your family, the people who love you, all want to know. They want to know how you got to be the person you are. They want to learn from your experience. You have a guaranteed audience. All you have to do is put down what happened to you, your memories, the events that shaped your life, your choices, and how you made them. You'll have a guaranteed audience for generations to come.

"But I can't remember anything."

Yes, you can. We chuckle when someone says this, because invariably that person within minutes is recounting something from their past. Unless you have some actual mental impairment, we guarantee you can remember the past. Perhaps you really mean, "I can't remember much." We understand how it can seem that way. But we will take you through a series of steps that encourage and facilitate remembering. Try this experiment. Think of the home where you lived as a child. Spend a few moments reflecting on that physical place. See it in your mind's eye. Imagine yourself walking through its rooms. *Recall the colors, the furniture, the light. What was the kitchen like? The bedroom? The living room? Put yourself in each of those rooms, one by one. Who else is there with you? What is he or she saying? What's happening? Who were the neighbors? What were they like?* You get the idea. You're probably filled with memories of that home now and the people in it and the events that happened there. That's how this process works. We start you with a simple fact—the home where you lived—and use that to trigger more memories. You'll remember far more than you ever thought possible.

"But there's too much! How can I make sense of it all?"

You will. Don't worry. We help you break your life into stages and then guide you to recall the details and memories and feelings that compose each stage. We lead you to recall your life in pieces and parts, which in the end will add up to your life story. How long you make your story is entirely up to you. You can choose to recount your childhood, for example, in only ten or twenty memories, or you can do it in two hundred, or as many as you want. And there's no deadline. You're free to take as much time as you want. It's all under your control.

"But I don't want to remember some things!"

We understand. Every life contains painful and private moments. Perhaps there were some events you wish hadn't occurred, or incidents you'd like to do over, or some moments you'd just like to forget. Must you include those in your life story? Not at all. What you include is entirely up to you.

Having said that, we do encourage you to be candid in telling your story. No one wants to read a story in which everything is wonderful. Some rain falls in every life. If you exclude the bad weather, no one will believe or learn from what you do say. Be yourself. Reveal who you were and are. Hard times and difficult situations can be the best teachers. Failure is human. If you're open and honest about your life, it might help others avoid the pain you suffered. In the end, though, you're free to put in or keep out whatever you want.

HOW *THE LEGACY* GUIDE WORKS

Perhaps you're a little intimidated. The book you're holding has lots of pages and questions and suggestions. It probably looks complicated. If you feel that way let us assure you right away: there are indeed lots of questions and suggestions, but the *process* is simple. It's *simple!*

Imagine you've just walked into a huge department store, with many floors, each crammed with goods to buy. You feel overwhelmed. Where do you go? You're about to give up and leave when you see a sign that says, *"1st Floor: Women's Clothing; 2nd Floor: Men's Clothing; 3rd Floor: Children's Clothing; 4th Floor,"* and so on. You're relieved because now you understand how it works. You go to the floor you want and there you find the same thing: everything's arranged in logical groups—suits, jackets, shoes, underwear, and so on.

The Legacy Guide uses the same twofold approach that makes it easy to know where you are and what you're doing. Here's how it works.

First, *The Legacy Guide* breaks life into the natural stages that all of us pass through, stages such as childhood, adolescence, young adulthood, and so on. Recalling a life becomes easier if approached through such natural phases or eras.

Second, in each stage we guide you to recall your life through a process we call *facts to memories to meaning*. This approach will help you remember what hap-pened, and not just what happened but how it felt and what it meant to you.

These two approaches—stages and *facts to memories to meaning*—make up the heart of *The Legacy Guide* process. They provide a simple, flexible, and pow-erful framework for composing the story of your life.

THE STAGES OF LIFE

Philosophers and storytellers have spoken about the "Ages of Man" for hundreds and thousands of years. Aesop, Aristotle, Solon, Ptolemy, Ovid, Shakespeare are only some of the writers and sages who've described the stages of life. In our own time, Erik Erikson wrote extensively on the subject, and, of course, the whole idea came to public attention through Gail Sheehy's book *Passages* and Daniel Levinson's books *The Seasons of a Man's Life* and *The Seasons of a Woman's Life*.

Everyone passes through roughly the same life stages, but that hardly means everyone's lives are all the same. In each stage everyone faces the same life prob-lems and tasks, but the ways each individual responds to those problems and per-forms those tasks are uniquely his or her own. Every face includes two eyes, a nose, and a mouth, yet every face looks distinctly different.

The human life span seems to fall naturally into twenty-year eras. There are five such eras for those who live into old age. Growing up extends from birth to roughly twenty. We all establish our places in the adult world from twenty to forty. The middle years extend from forty to sixty, the later years from sixty to eighty, and the elder years from eighty onward. Obviously these time frames can only be rough, with some variation in the life of each individual. For example, adoles-cence, the latter stage of childhood, often extends into the twenties. Some seventy-year-olds seem elderly and some ninety-year-olds remain sprightly. Still, the periods and ages seem roughly right. Think about life at ten, thirty, fifty, and seventy, the midpoints of the eras. Don't those ages feel sharply different? Each seems distinct from the others, with its own unique set of problems, tasks, goals, and pleasures.

In *The Legacy Guide* we use seven stages, instead of five, because we split each of the first two twenty-year eras into roughly decade long stages. If you think

about the first twenty years of your life—when you were growing up—it's clear
that childhood and adolescence were truly distinct. They felt different as you
lived through each, and each feels different now in memory. In the second era,
approximately twenty to forty, the two processes of first becoming an independent
adult, and then making a place for yourself in the world through family and work,
also seem distinct enough to deserve separate treatment.

THE SEVEN STAGES OF LIFE

Stage 1	*Childhood*	*Birth to roughly 11–13*
		(the beginning of puberty)
Stage 2	*Adolescence*	*Roughly 11–13 to 20*
Stage 3	*Young Adult*	*Roughly 20–30*
Stage 4	*Adult*	*Roughly 30 to 40–45*
Stage 5	*Middle Adult*	*Roughly 40–45 to 60*
Stage 6	*Late Adult*	*Roughly 60–80*
Stage 7	*Elder*	*Roughly 80 plus*

Stages offer more than a handy way to think about your past. People connect
with each other around common experiences. Old soldiers trade war stories.
Mothers talk of childbearing. Life stages are life experiences everyone has in common. They represent points of connection and learning between your life and the
lives of those who follow you. Readers of your story can apply, for example, what
you learned facing the challenges of young adulthood, when you were trying to
find a place in the world, to the same challenges in their own lives.

Two features of life stages deserve some explanation. First, chronological age
is *not* what moves you from one stage to the next. The stages are age-correlated,
but not age-driven. Life events, what you've learned, a shifting set of personal desires and needs, a sense of aging (as opposed to age alone) propel you from one
stage to the next. For each stage is defined by the specific and unique life tasks
and challenges it holds for those passing through it.

Second, the passage from any stage to the next can be tumultuous. In *The
Legacy Guide,* this time of turmoil and transition is considered part of the new,

oncoming stage. The previous stage ends when you begin to question your life in it—what you want, whether your life can be satisfying in its current form, where it's ultimately taking you. This questioning begins a process of change that can be subtle or dramatic, quiet or loud, external or virtually all internal. Such a transition can take as much as four or five years before you finally emerge into the more stable and placid portion of the new stage. When you do, you're most likely to find your life different in key ways (new work, new goals, new or different relationships) from the previous stage.

FACTS TO MEMORIES TO MEANING

Within each stage, *The Legacy Guide* will take you through a three-step process—*facts to memories to meaning*—of recalling and recording your life.

Facts

You'll be guided to record the basic facts of your life—such as where you lived, the work you did, schools you attended, and so on. Don't underestimate the importance of facts. Not only will they spur memories, but the reader of your story will find them fascinating all by themselves. Many who've lost their parents realize only too late, and to their sorrow, that they don't know all the basic facts of their parents' lives. So if you give this book to parents or grandparents, you might even suggest that they do only the facts if you think they'll be reluctant to do more. Odds are they'll go on and do more because facts always seem to elicit memories.

Memories

Next, you'll be guided to recall memories around the facts you recorded. *Memories* is a catchall word for remembered events, occasions, places, moments, people, and, not least, stories. Using facts to evoke memories is the heart of this approach because memories come to mind through association. One thing triggers another. First, facts bring memories to mind and then memories themselves spawn more memories. In fact, you'll probably have more memories than you know what to do with. You can record all of them, if you want, or only the ones with special meaning.

You'll record each memory on a separate sheet of paper (or sheets, for those memories that require more space). Because each memory is recorded individually, you'll be able to arrange your memories in any sequence you want when you're done.

Meaning

Finally, you'll be guided to think about the meaning of each stage and all the facts and memories associated with it. Meaning has to do with what shaped you, made you the person you are. It has to do with highlights, key moments, turning points—all the things that set the subsequent course of your life. It has to do with what mattered most to you and what you learned, consciously or unconsciously. It has to do with helping others and serving some higher purpose. Suggestions and questions in a few areas—*Defining Moments, Values, Love, Learning and Wisdom,* and *Summing Up*—will help you extract the real significance and meaning of each period in your life.

What you'll have when you're done

The result of all this work will be a three-ring notebook entitled *My Life Story* which holds the facts, memories, and meaning of your life, stage by stage. The reader of your story will start with your childhood and then go on to your adolescent years, followed by young adulthood, adulthood, and so on.

A note about stages and sequence

We hope by now you understand what we meant when we said this process is simple. Once you've set up your *My Life Story* notebook, you will have complete freedom as to the sequence in which you recall the facts, memories, and meaning of your life. You can work through your life story in chronological order, if you choose. That's how most people prefer to do it, and that's how *The Legacy Guide* is organized, because it takes you through your life the way you lived it.

But you don't have to do it that way. You can proceed through your life stages in whatever order you want. Start, for example, with your current stage, and then do, say, childhood, followed by your adult stage. If you get stuck in one stage, you can simply go to another, and return to the first later.

Within a stage, it's natural to go from facts to memories to meaning. Facts trigger memories, and meaning rises out of facts and memories. But you're free to change that sequence as well. You can go straight to memories in each stage, and go back and do facts later. You can even do all the fact sections in all the stages first, if you want, before doing any memories. You can answer the questions and suggestions about meaning first, though we think your answers will be richer for having worked through at least a few of your key memories.

Finally, you can always return and add memories to any stage at any time, or expand your thoughts about meaning, or insert facts you couldn't remember earlier. Having the simple framework of stages and *facts to memories to meaning* will keep everything you do in the right place.

GETTING STARTED

CREATE YOUR *MY LIFE STORY* NOTEBOOK

The actual life story you create will be gathered in a separate three-ring notebook, which we call your *My Life Story* notebook. That is where you'll place all writing and other materials related to your life story. This book, *The Legacy Guide,* is your manual, your how-to guide. The actual work you produce will go into the notebook.

To make that notebook, you'll need two items, which you can find at virtually any stationery or office-supply store.

- A standard *three-ring notebook* or *binder*, the kind into which you can insert three-hole paper
- A set of 8 three-hole *dividers with tabs*

Insert the tabbed dividers in the notebook and label them with the following titles, in the order given:

Family Information

Stage 1—Childhood

Stage 2—Adolescence

Stage 3—Young Adult

Stage 4—Adult

Stage 5—Middle Adult

Stage 6—Late Adult

Stage 7—Elder

You ultimately may find that one notebook can't hold everything. If so, get more notebooks and spread the dividers and the materials you prepare among them.

Here are some suggestions that may make your notebook easier for others to read and follow.

Sample *title* page for *My Life Story* notebook:

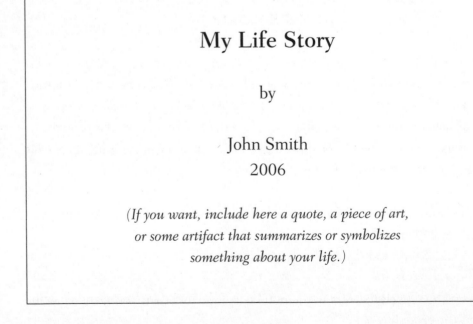

My Life Story

by

John Smith
2006

*(If you want, include here a quote, a piece of art,
or some artifact that summarizes or symbolizes
something about your life.)*

Start each stage with a title page that identifies the stage. Add, if you want, the years that opened and closed the stage, and your ages at the beginning and end. Add, too, some words—say, of key events in the stage—that capture the essence of that time in your life.

Sample *stage* title page for *My Life Story* notebook:

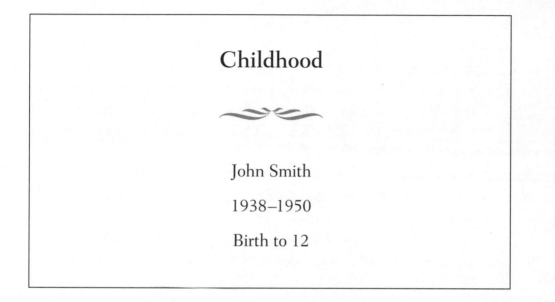

Childhood

John Smith

1938–1950

Birth to 12

As you record the facts in a stage, record them on separate pages for each segment of the stage—e.g., a page for work facts, another page for facts about the places you lived, and so on. Try inserting all these fact pages at the beginning of each stage in your notebook. That way, the reader will cover all the facts of your life in that stage first. Those facts will give her or him a good overview of your life at that time and create a context for reading your memories. As you record your facts, in response to the directions and questions in *The Legacy Guide,* include enough information to make clear what and why you're recording. Label the page on which you list your friends, for example, with the heading "Friends and Other Memorable People." Otherwise, the reader may not understand why you're listing and describing these people. Here is a sample page for facts about the places you lived.

Sample *facts* page for *My Life Story* notebook:

Young Adult FACTS

Home

1965–1966—Kenmore, New York. After graduating from college, Jane and I lived for a year in this little northside suburb of Buffalo. We rented a frame duplex in a quiet residential neighborhood. It had a half-basement, a small kitchen, and living/dining room on the first level, a bath halfway upstairs, and two bedrooms on the second floor.

1966–1970—Charlesbank Road, Newton Corner, Massachusetts. We lived in this small two-level town house on Charlesbank Road while I was in graduate school and in my first job after school. It was a busy road in a crowded neighborhood with easy access to Boston.

1970–1972—Leighton Road, Wellesley, Massachusetts. Our first house and we were house poor! A four-bedroom, single-bath Colonial built early in the century. Nice neighborhood not far from Wellesley College and Wellesley Center. House needed a lot of work . . .

You'll also record your memories for each stage, one by one, on separate pages. That way you can arrange your memories in any sequence you want. If you follow our suggestion above, to place all fact pages first in the stage, then you would follow those with your memory pages. We suggest you head each memory page with something like "Adult Memories," or "Childhood Memories," or Adolescent Memories," depending on the stage. We especially recommend for each memory that you include in the heading a title for the memory, the location of the memory, and the year it occurred.

Sample *memory* page for *My Life Story* notebook:

Childhood MEMORIES

Title: Favorite hiding place
Year: 1952   Location: Owego, New York

My favorite hiding place was under the dining room table. It wasn't so secret since everyone could see me. But once under the dark wood table, fenced in by six chairs, all I could see were feet and legs moving about from room to room, so I was convinced I was invisible. I felt safe, alone, and independent. I remember the thrill of learning my first written word—"the"—especially since I was afraid I'd never learn to read. I took a book down from our library shelf, crawled under the table, and spent the afternoon locating every "the" in Theodore Dreiser's 800-page *An American Tragedy*. I could read!

In the same way, we recommend that you respond to each of the meaning segments—such as "Defining Moments" or "Learning and Wisdom"—on separate pages. Head each of those pages with the appropriate title—again, such as "Defining Moments," and so on.

Sample meaning page for *My Life Story* notebook:

Middle Adult MEANING

Defining Moments

One day, shortly after my divorce and following much reflection on my life, I was vacuuming my apartment and a long-ago memory came to mind.

It was Sunday morning and I'd just returned from Sunday service at the Baptist church. Mom emerged from the bedroom, a serious look on her face. "I have to ask you something," she said. "Do you think Daddy is a Christian?" It was somehow clear to me that she and Dad had been talking and now she was his intermediary. He's the one who wanted to know. I forget my answer but it was something to the effect, No, I don't think so. In fact, I said in so many words, I thought he was some form of inferior person.

I put the vacuum aside and sat down. There was something big here.

I was struck as a middle-aged man by how cruel I'd been in what I said as a 12- or 13-year-old. I was struck by an insight both obvious and beyond my emotional capability until this moment: My father cared what I thought of him. It mattered to him. That was followed by a second insight: He believed I was rejecting him. . . .

In short, as you prepare pages for your *My Life Story* notebook, keep the reader in mind and provide whatever guideposts you think will keep that person clear at all times as to what and whom you're talking about and why. On every page include the life stage involved and, if appropriate, the year and location.

USING THE WEB SITE: THELEGACYGUIDE.COM

For those of you who use the Web, we have provided electronic files containing all the forms for each stage, including the title, fact, memory, and meaning pages described above. Just go to TheLegacyGuide.com. You can download the forms, print them out, and fill them out by hand or on a typewriter. Or you can download them, fill them out on your computer, and print them out to create truly finished-looking pages.

The Web site also contains supplemental information and material. There are references and links to such Web locations as genealogical sites (information on researching your ancestors), historical sites (news events by year), and other sources of help in pulling together your life story. We will add new links and sources of more useful information as we learn of them.

GATHER LEGACY MATERIALS

In every stage, we suggest you start by pulling together photographs, letters, files, items with family members' handwriting, scrapbooks, yearbooks, clippings, and any other items or memorabilia related to your family and your life. When you do this, don't be too picky. Don't worry about what to include; you can decide later which items you'll actually use. And don't feel you must gather absolutely everything all at once. You can add new items and memories at any time. As you go through the stages of your life, the various items will transport you to those earlier times and help trigger memories. Some, like photos or letters, can be placed, if you want, in your *My Life Story* notebook.

SET UP A LEGACY ROUTINE
AND GO TO WORK

If possible, set aside a permanent place to work where you won't have to pick up materials at the end of every work session. This should be a place where you can just sit down and resume the work where you left off without having to find and lay out your materials anew every time. If you cannot do that, get a portable file from any office-supply store and keep everything there. Even if you have to spread out and pick up materials for every work session, you'll at least have everything together.

Work on whatever schedule is best for you. Take a month or year or decade to finish. Whatever your schedule, establish regular work habits. If you're an early riser and mornings are your best time of day, work on your life story then. Whatever time you choose, mark it in your calendar, just like a meeting or appointment. Then sit down faithfully at the appointed time and do the work.

USING *THE LEGACY GUIDE* WITH SCRAPBOOKING OR WRITING A MEMOIR

Perhaps you've already decided to tell your life story, or parts of it, through writing a memoir or putting together scrapbooks. Interest in memoir writing is growing, and scrapbooking is turning into a real phenomenon of our times, with sales of scrapbooking products rising to the billions of dollars and scrapping clubs popping up everywhere.

Following the course laid out in *The Legacy Guide* will naturally complement and support both scrapbooking and writing your life story as a memoir.

SCRAPBOOKING

Both scrapbooking and your interest in telling your life story spring from the same human impulse—the desire to collect, preserve, and communicate the important moments, the meaning and feelings, of the life you've lived.

The Legacy Guide focuses on getting that life down with words on paper, but it also encourages you to incorporate photos, letters, and memorabilia, too. Scrapbooking simply extends this step by creating attractive pages that capture both the facts and feelings of some important moment.

If there's a difference, it's this: *The Legacy Guide* seeks to collect and record ALL the important moments in your life. Scrapbooking may or may not be so ambitious; it will depend on you, the scrapper. Scrapbooking an entire life would be a large job, but you may want to do it.

However, scrapbooking and *The Legacy Guide* don't need to be combined entirely. They can supplement each other wonderfully. Use scrapbooking techniques on selected moments in your life story. Treat the pages you create on those moments as scrapbook pages. Scrapbooking will let you add one more element of personal creativity to telling your story. Or, if your focus is on scrapbooking, select pieces of writing from your life story and drop them into scrapbooks you're creating. They couldn't be more natural partners.

WRITING A MEMOIR

A memoir is like a traditional book. It starts talking, so to speak, on page one and keeps talking in a continuous voice about a continuous story, your life, until it stops on the last page. It's a single flow or sequence all the way through, like a novel.

The Legacy Guide, on the other hand, will tell your story too, but it does the job in pieces—facts, memories, statements of meaning—and all those pieces fit together, as we've said before, like the pieces of a mosaic, to create one overall story in the eye and mind of the reader.

Both approaches can communicate your life story. However, creating a memoir requires much more writing ability and storytelling skill. Finding the right "voice" and maintaining it through, say, two hundred pages is a great challenge.

If you do choose to write a memoir, there's no better preparation than *The Legacy Guide*. To write a good memoir, you must know the facts of your life. Even if you don't put them all in, you still need to have them straight in your mind— what happened when. The memories you write out for *The Legacy Guide* will be the raw material from which you create your memoir. And your descriptions in *The Legacy Guide,* of how you felt and what was important to you, will become the themes that meld the parts of your memoir into a continuous story. In short, doing *The Legacy Guide* will give you an understanding of how all the parts of your life fit together.

Think of writing a memoir as taking one step beyond *The Legacy Guide.* In that one step, you'll select and arrange the pieces (memories, meaning) developed in *The Legacy Guide* and then write the links tying them all together, incorporating whatever facts you need to include. That's not a small task but it's straightforward and infinitely easier than writing a memoir from scratch, without the foundation created by *The Legacy Guide.*

TIPS AND ADVICE

As *you begin to write* down the memories and meaning of your life, keep in mind these tips.

USE MORE THAN WORDS

It's worth repeating: add photographs, letters, memorabilia, artifacts (ticket stubs, programs, and so on) to your *My Life Story* notebook. If objects fit, include them in the actual notebook. If they don't, put them in a specific storage place, like a small box, and label them by stage. If you're interested in scrapbooking, turn some of the more memorable moments into lovely scrapbook pages that combine text, photos, other memorabilia, and beautiful design to capture the facts and feelings of that memory.

CARRY A PEN AND PAPER

Once you start recalling memories, you'll find they come to mind almost any time and any place. Something you see in the supermarket or on the street will spark a memory. You may think you'll remember it, but why take a chance? Make a note of it right away, something brief that will bring it back to mind. Carry pen and notepaper with you at all times for this purpose.

SOME WRITING ADVICE

You'll soon be writing out memories. Here is some simple writing advice that many people have found useful.

First, be yourself and don't take yourself too seriously

It's possible to take your writing—finding the right word and worrying what others will think, for example—so seriously that you're paralyzed. You should have fun doing this project. At times it will feel like work, but overall it should give you pleasure. No one expects you to be a wonderful writer. They just want to know about you. So be yourself. Tell *your* story in your own voice and have fun.

Write about yourself

Don't try to write about world or national events or social trends or scientific developments—unless, of course, you were personally involved, or your life was touched by them directly. For example, don't write about John Kennedy's assassination just because you happened to live through that time. But *do* describe, if it was important to you, what you were doing when you heard of Kennedy's death in Dallas, or how it touched your life directly (if it did). Your readers will enjoy hearing what it was like to be around when something momentous happened. But describe it in terms of you and your life. Focus on yourself. You're the subject of this story. Don't stray or wander. In the same way, if various individuals were important to you, do describe them and what they did, but focus on their personal connections with you and their influence on *your* life.

Write a little sticky note that says, "This is about Me!" and place it where you'll see it as you work. Then make sure everything you write is about that topic (you!). Don't be shy.

Write with someone in mind

As you write, imagine you're talking to some specific individual you love—a child or grandchild or niece, for example—and write as you would speak to that person. Make it personal, warm, and friendly. If you want, imagine you're simply writing a letter to this person, who should be someone you trust and with whom you can be candid and natural.

Include specific detail to make your writing come alive

Write about specific, tangible things, rather than generalities or vague descriptions.

My mother took up two new hobbies: riding a bicycle and playing piano. The piano I didn't mind, but the bicycle drove me crazy. It was a huge old clunker, blue with white trim, with big fat tires, huge fenders, and a battery-powered horn built into the middle of the frame with a button you pushed to make it blow. . . . She would ride in slow motion across our street, Murdock Avenue in the St. Albans section of Queens, the only white person in sight, as cars swerved around her and black motorists gawked at the strange, middle-aged white lady riding her ancient bicycle.

—JAMES MCBRIDE, *The Color of Water*

Concrete, specific detail will make the events you describe seem real. That bicycle James McBride described is so real you could ride it yourself, and maybe you did (or one like it) as a kid. Concrete details create a world more easily imagined by the reader. If you don't remember every detail, that's fine. You only need a few of the right ones. But you do need them.

Don't be discouraged

If you find writing difficult, don't conclude, "I can't write." You might be surprised to learn that almost all professional writers find the act of writing fearsomely difficult. They write because they need to write and because they love to *have written*—like having mowed the lawn or washed the dishes. But almost to a person, they find writing painful and hard. It requires enormous courage. So don't be discouraged. You're in good company. The British have a saying something like this: "Hard writing makes easy reading and easy writing makes hard reading."

Speak your memories, if you prefer

If writing is just too tough for you, there's an alternative. You can speak your answers into a tape recorder and have your words transcribed. Some people find it easier to talk, and that's fine. You'll have to find someone to do the typing, and you probably will need to edit what you said (or have someone with editorial skills do it for you).

Take it a step at a time

Finally, if you ever feel overwhelmed, don't panic.

> *Thirty years ago my older brother, who was ten years old at the time, was trying to get a report on birds written that he'd had three months to write, which was due the next day. We were out at our family cabin in Bolinas, and he was at the kitchen table close to tears, surrounded by binder paper and pencils and unopened books on birds, immobilized by the hugeness of the task ahead. Then my father sat down beside him, put his arm around my brother's shoulder, and said, "Bird by bird, buddy. Just take it bird by bird."*
>
> —ANNE LAMOTT, *Bird by Bird:*
> *Some Instructions on Writing and Life*

A couple of writer's tricks

It's difficult to write regardless of how you feel, but that's what professional writers do. If you wait until you're in the mood, you'll find yourself writing less than you want. Two writer's tricks can help you get going each time you sit down to work.

Start each work session by reading over what you did or wrote at the previous session. It's easy to do, it will focus your mind, and it usually leads directly into writing new material.

Never stop writing when you don't know what to write next. It's tempting to stop when you're stuck. You think, I'll go back to it when my mind is fresh. But that only creates anxiety at the thought of going back. Always end a work session when you're confident of what to say or do next. Make a note to yourself about that next step, and then read the note at the start of the next session. Knowing exactly what you're going to do, or write about, will give you the courage to get going.

FAMILY
INFORMATION

No life story can begin without first considering your family. Who were your parents? Who were their parents? Did they have brothers and sisters? Do you? Who's in your extended family? Those who read your story will want to know.

> *My mother married my father largely, it seems, to help him out with his five motherless children. Having any herself was a secondary consideration. But first she had a girl, then she had another girl, and it was very nice, of course, to have them, but slightly disappointing, because she belonged to the generation and tradition that made a son the really important event; then I came, a fine healthy child. She was forty at my birth; and my father forty-nine. Four years later she had another son, and four years later still another son. The desired preponderance of male over female had been established, and twice five made ten. I found the gap of two generations between my parents and me easier, in a way, to bridge than a single-generation gap. Children seldom quarrel with their grand-parents, and I have been able to think of my mother and father as grand-parents. Also, a family of ten means a dilution of parental affection; the members tend to become indistinct: I have often been called: "Philip, Richard, Charles, I mean Robert."*
> —ROBERT GRAVES, *Good-bye to All That*

We've divided the work of recording family information into two steps because families vary in their interest in ancestors and in the amount of genealogical information they possess.

Step 1—Everyone: Create a basic family tree for your family (see the diagram on page 31), at least through your grandparents and, if possible, your great-grandparents. Record that information to the best of your knowledge. But don't get bogged down now trying to gather information you don't already possess. Put down what you know or can easily find out and get on with telling your own story. You can always add more family information later, as you have a chance to look up information or ask family members who know.

Step 2—Optional: The second step consists of three parts, of which you can do all or only one or two.

- First, extend your family tree beyond the "Basic Family Tree" by either deepening it (going further back in time) or broadening it (by including relatives further removed than cousins and aunts and uncles). In fact, create as large a family tree as you want.
- Second, include more factual information about specific ancestors or relatives, such as where they came from, what they did, and what happened to them.
- Third, include any family lore—stories, true or not, about ancestors or relatives that have been passed down in your family. These are stories that do NOT include or involve or touch you personally; if they do, they should appear in your own memories and life story.

Remember, as with all parts of *The Legacy Guide* and the *My Life Story* you create, you can always go back later and put in additional information as you recall or find it.

BASIC FAMILY TREE

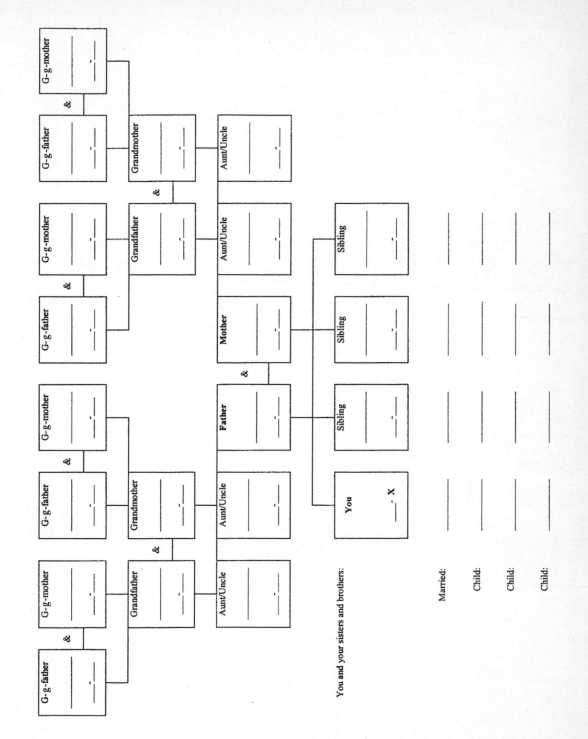

STAGE I

_____

childhood

Extending from birth until the beginning of puberty and our teen years, childhood was something of a paradox for many of us.

We look back at that time in our lives fondly. The world was small and our needs basic. Compared with the trials and tribulations of being grown up, our problems then can seem trivial and silly now. Recalling them makes us smile for how large they seemed at the time. The snub of a friend, striking out in baseball, not knowing the answer when called on in class, being teased for what we wore . . . all felt world-shattering. Every earache, every upset stomach, every cold we thought would last forever. Now, as an adult, we can put all those distant problems in perspective. Seen through adult eyes and the haze of intervening decades, childhood assumes a nostalgic glow.

Truth is, childhood for most of us was a time both magic and awful, a string of delightful moments mixed with terrifying challenges. We lived in the care of a comforting mother, assuming she existed solely for us, and then learned we had to share her with others. We left a sheltering home for the frightening world of school. We learned to read and write, add and subtract, and talk and act and play so as to fit in and avoid the ridicule of others. We forget what emotional savages young children could be—what cruel things we did and said to each other—and how distressing that made this time in our lives. One psychologist has defined personality as the "strategy people develop for getting out of childhood alive." For most of us in the developed world, childhood was rarely a matter of life and death. It just seemed that way at times.

On the one hand, childhood truly was serious business. It was then we formed our fundamental understanding of the world—how it works and how we fit into it—an understanding that for most of us persists to this day in subtle ways. As a child, we began to develop a sense of who we were (a never-ending task that has continued through all our lives since). It was a time of powerful and basic emotions, which we as children were ill-equipped to understand. Some of these deep, primordial feelings took shape before we even had words to express and comprehend them, and so they rippled forward, unspoken and inexplicit, through succeeding years. Each of us carries pieces of childhood through the rest of life. If we want someone to understand us and who we are, what do we usually do? We tell them of our families and our growing up. Childhood may not set our characters and personalities for life, but it was a powerful influence for most of us.

Yet, for all its importance in shaping our lives, childhood could be profoundly fun, too. In ways we would never fully appreciate until later, it was wonderfully carefree. We had no responsibilities to speak of, certainly not like our burdens as adults. We knew the thrill of exploring and learning about a new, strange, and often wonderful world. In our child's mind everything was possible. We would be able to fly, like Superman, hit stupendous homeruns, like Babe Ruth or Mickey Mantle, and deflect speeding bullets, like Wonder Woman. And even when we outgrew that kind of magical thinking, we still daydreamed about the kind of adult we would become. We had heroes—real people like sports stars, movie stars, world leaders, explorers, scientists on the frontier of knowledge, conquering generals—and we imagined our lives would be like theirs.

Everyone's childhood falls to a different place between the poles of magic and awful. For some of us it was a time more wonderful than not. Others of us feel lucky, for good reason, to have survived.

Wherever your childhood landed on that spectrum, your goal here should be to capture all of it, the joy and delight, the fear and anxiety, the comfort and distress of your first, small world and the excitement and trepidation with which you ventured into a wider world.

FACTS AND MEMORIES FROM YOUR CHILDHOOD

Here your journey back into childhood begins. The pages ahead will lead you to explore that time in its many segments—school, home, sports, religion, family, interests, and so on. In each segment, you'll be asked first to record the facts. Then, using those facts as a base, you'll be guided to recall memories.

As you begin the actual work of remembering facts and conjuring up memories, let us anticipate some questions you're likely to have.

Does the sequence in which you recall or write out your memories matter?

No. The sequence of remembering is unimportant. If you're in the "School" segment and you recall something about your mother, unrelated to school, simply record the memory. Don't worry about organizing your memories by segment. The only purpose of segments is to help you recall memories. Think of each memory as a snapshot you've taken. For the moment, you're simply tossing each snapshot in a box, to be arranged later in an album *in whatever order you want.*

Do you need to remember everything from childhood now?

Not at all. It's not possible to remember everything, and it's certainly impossible to remember everything all at once. Childhood memories are likely to keep popping up long after you've gone on to later life stages. When and if they do, that's fine. If a childhood memory comes to you a year from now, simply record it and put it in the childhood section of your *My Life Story* notebook with your other childhood memories.

Do you need to record every memory?

Absolutely not. If you don't want to write out a memory, for whatever reason, then don't. It's entirely up to you. That's why we suggest you may want to recall and record memories in two steps. First, simply list the memory as it occurs to you, using only enough words to remind yourself of it later. Then, at some later time, write out the memories, but only the ones *you want to record.*

The memory sections of each life segment contain a lot of detailed questions and suggestions. Must you respond to or answer all of them?

Emphatically no. Do respond to each of the fact directions that precede the memory prompts. But the questions and suggestions in each memory section are only there to stir up memories. Think about them. Ponder them. But respond only to those that elicit memories for you.

Suggestion: As you write a memory, you'll often be tempted to extend the story forward beyond childhood. Say you developed a serious illness as a child and didn't recover fully until you were eighteen or twenty-five. In remembering the illness in childhood, you may want to explain that it went away years later. *Resist that temptation.* Write here about your childhood only. If you reveal how something got resolved later in life, after childhood, it's like giving away the punch line of a story in the beginning or middle, instead of the end. You as a child didn't know until later how that illness came out. Why should your reader know more than you knew? This is part of what pulls readers through life stories—the desire to find out ". . . and then what happened?" Let the reader know what you knew as you went through life. Let your life unfold for the reader as it unfolded for you. Take them with you on your journey.

You as a Child

You were just beginning to be "you" in childhood. Who were you and how were you different as a child? What were your moments and occasions of deepest feeling? What did you daydream about? How did others see you? Start with the facts and then go on to memories.

FACTS ABOUT YOU AS A CHILD

❦ Note when and where you were born and the facts of your birth—for example, your parents rushed to the hospital, or there were problems with your birth.

❦ Note the origin of your name, if you know. Were you named after a relative or some prominent figure, for example? Did you have a nickname? If so, where did it come from?

❦ Without a lot of thought or effort, simply list the key moments and highlights of your childhood—illnesses, accidents, something that happened to your parents that changed your life, anything that felt important to you.

❦ Note your age at the end of childhood (e.g., when the body changes of puberty began for you), and describe yourself at that time—height, weight, hair color, eye color, general physical description.

MEMORIES OF YOU AS A CHILD

What is your earliest memory? Think of each sense—sight, sound, taste, touch, smell—and your earliest memory of it. What is the earliest *object* you remember? A toy or a pet? Who is the earliest *person* you can recall? Your mother? Your father? What is the earliest *place* you recall? Think of all those hazy, stream of consciousness kinds of moments and semi-moments.

What stories were told of you as a very young child? Were you ever told stories about yourself before you had your own distinct memories—stories of what you did or said or looked like or liked to do or refused to do?

What did you look like? Imagine looking in the mirror as a child. Describe the person you saw there. Did you look like anyone else in your family—say, your father? If so, how did you feel about that? Were you big or small for your age? What kinds of clothes did you wear? What did your hair look like? Did your teeth come in straight? What part of your body most pleased you, or concerned you? How would someone describe you as a young child? Did you ever wish you were different? Bigger, smaller, taller, shorter, prettier?

What did you dream, daydream, or fantasize about? Was it about owning something, like a horse? Was it about doing something, like playing a sport? Did you ever make up stories, out loud or in your mind, about yourself and your life and family?

I did, however, have a fantasy when I was about ten. It wasn't a dream that crawled into my sleep but a day-to-day fantasy that persisted during my waking hours. I thought I was born a king. Not of America, not of any country, but a king of some vast domain that existed in my mind. In the fantasy, the entire world knew of my noble birth, but they were sworn to secrecy not to reveal to me the truth of my majestic lineage for fear of spoiling me.

—NEIL SIMON, *Rewrites*

What were your strengths and weaknesses? Was there anything, some talent, you thought you were really good at in childhood, that made you feel good about yourself? Why did you think this? Did anyone, such as your mother, tell you that you were good at something? How about weaknesses? Did you have any that you recognized or others told you about? Did you feel unique or somehow different from everyone else because of these strengths or weaknesses?

What kind of person were you? Did you prefer being alone or spending time with others? Were you excited by new things? Or did you prefer the familiar and tried and true? Did you worry or "go with the flow"? Did you make lists? Did you like games and other forms of competition? Were you a collaborator? A peacemaker? Self-confident, or unsure of yourself? Were you quiet and withdrawn, or loud and boisterous? Were you a good child, careful to stay out of trouble? Or were you always getting in hot water?

Did you struggle to be you? Were there any times or occasions when you struggled to have your own, separate identity—for example, to be different from friends or from brothers and sisters?

Did you encounter discrimination? Were you ever treated differently or unfairly because of *what* you were—female, black, short, skinny, or something similar?

Were you a stepchild? Did that affect what you did or how you thought about yourself? Did you ever feel you were treated differently?

Were you adopted? Did that change the way you acted or how you thought about yourself? Were you ever treated differently? When did you learn you were adopted? Did you meet, or try to meet, your biological parents?

Did you have a sense of destiny? Did you believe that your life was foreordained to take a certain path in some way, or that you would play a certain kind of role, or accomplish something important? Where do you think that sense of fate came from?

What did you want to be when you grew up? What made you want to do that? Were there occasions (e.g., watching firemen put out a fire) or role models (e.g., a teacher or baseball player) associated with your dream? Did you play fantasy games about what you would do, or the abilities you would have, when you grew up? What people made you say to yourself, I want to be like him or her? What did you think you'd be able to do when you grew up that you couldn't do as a child? What did you *not* want to do or be? Was there a moment when you discovered or realized what you were going to do in your life?

My sister, being not merely the only woman in the family after our mother died but also the eldest of us children, was allowed the privilege of a bath by herself and to herself. We three males, father, elder and finally younger son, had no such luxury but seemingly were required to pay for our sister's privilege by jumping into the same water one after the other: Father first, of course, then my elder brother, Dickie, and finally me. By this time the water had got into such a state that it could hardly be described as a cleansing agent. . . .

However, on the particular evening . . . there were only two in the bathroom, not the customary three. My father and I had that morning accompanied my beloved brother to Waterloo [station] to see him off to be a rubber planter in India for possibly nine years. . . .

Lowering myself into the water . . . I snatched the hot tap on for the allotted number of seconds, and, after a minute or so I asked my father how soon I might reckon on being allowed to follow Dickie to India. My father's answer was so astonishing that it gave me a deep shock: "Don't be such a fool; you're not going to India, you're going on the stage." "Am I?" I stammered lamely. "Well, of course you are," he said. . . .

And that is how it was that, as I sat in two or three inches of lukewarm water which was none too clean, on the order of an eccentrically surprising father, my fate was sealed.

— LAURENCE OLIVIER, *Confessions of an Actor*

What were your most intense moments as a child?

- Do you remember a time when you *laughed* so hard your stomach ached and your face hurt?
- Were you ever deeply *embarrassed*? Did you ever do anything truly dumb?
- What was the *happiest* moment you remember?
- When did you feel deeply *ashamed*?
- Did you ever feel wildly *angry*? Did your feelings get you in trouble?
- Was there a time when you *grieved* or *cried* inconsolably?
- Did you ever feel *jealous* or *envious*? Who was the object of your jealousy and who or what caused you to feel jealous?
- When did you feel most *proud*, of yourself or someone in your family?
- What was your biggest *disappointment*? Did you want or expect something and not get it?

- What times or occasions were your *feelings hurt* deeply? How did you express your pain?
- Were you ever *surprised* as a child? Did anything *shock* or *amaze* you? Were you ever *awestruck*?
- Did you have a moment of wild *abandon* and *joy*?
- When and where were you deeply *frightened*? Did your fear come true?

I lay alone and was almost asleep when the damned thing entered the room by flattening itself against the open door and sliding in. It was a transparent, luminous oblong. I could see the door whiten at its touch; I could see the blue wall turn pale where it raced over it, and see the maple headboard of Amy's bed glow. It was a swift spirit; it was an awareness. It made noise. It had two joined parts, a head and a tail, like a Chinese dragon. It found the door, wall, and headboard; and it swiped them, charging them with its luminous glance. After its fleet, searching passage, things looked the same, but weren't.

I dared not blink or breathe; I tried to hush my whooping blood. If it found another awareness, it would destroy it.

Every night before it got to me it gave up. It hit my wall's corner and couldn't get past. It shrank completely into itself and vanished like a cobra down a hole. I heard the rising roar it made when it died or left. I still couldn't breathe. I knew—it was the worst fact I knew, a very hard fact—that it could return again alive that same night.

Sometimes it came back, sometimes it didn't. Most often, restless, it came back. The light stripe slipped in the door, ran searching over Amy's wall, stopped, stretched lunatic at the first corner, raced wailing toward my wall, and vanished into the second corner with a cry. So I wouldn't go to bed.

It was a passing car whose windshield reflected the corner streetlight outside. I figured it out one night.

—ANNIE DILLARD, *An American Childhood*

- Do you have any vivid recollections around *sight, sound, smell, taste,* or *touch*?

Did you ever tell a lie? Not an innocent white lie, but a real, out-and-out untruth. What happened to make you do it and what happened afterward? Did you ever get in trouble for telling the truth?

Were you ever treated badly by playmates or family or others? Did anyone ever treat you unfairly, or lie to you or cheat you or hurt you or say hurtful things to you? Did people you thought were friends ever abandon you? Did any group ever ignore you or refuse to let you join them or play with them? Did you ever feel out of place, unwanted? Did you ever treat someone else in a way that hurt them?

Did you have a special place? Did you have a safe haven, a private and perhaps secret place you loved to go? Imagine yourself back in that place.

Did you suffer any illnesses or other health problems as a child? Recall specific memories—moments, events, people, places—of any serious illnesses or physical limitations. What were they, where did they come from, and how were they diagnosed and treated? Did they have any effect on your daily life or the lives of others, such as your parents? If you were born with a physical problem, recall when you first realized you were different. Do you have any memories of recovery? Also, recall your experiences with any of the common childhood illnesses. Were you ever injured? What kind of treatment did you receive and how long was the recovery? What did you do during your recovery? Did you miss school?

Did you ever have to cope with a period of hardship as a child? Was it economic hardship? Physical pain? A time of being alone or far away? A time of extraordinary duress?

It was around 3:00 p.m., June 10th, 1944. Suddenly Anatoli, Russian war prisoner, who was escaping with me, and I were left alone in almost total darkness inside of the tire of a shot down American bomber. The Russians who hid us there, and covered the tire with broken airplane wings and fuselages from the area, left to work in a different area of the commando. This was done in order to avoid any suspicion that they were in any way part of the escape conspiracy.

We did not utter a single word to each other. We just lay there, inside the large tire still mounted on its metal rim, and looked aimlessly into flickering lights penetrating through the small opening. . . .

Within a half hour we could hear the SS guards with their dogs and the capos yelling and screaming, asking us to give ourselves up. Several times I heard dogs barking and sniffing above me. At such times we tried to hold our breath. The dogs had no access to the tire opening. And the smell of the urine left by over twenty Russians in this area overwhelmed, detracted and disoriented the smell ability of these dogs. Around us, we could hear the prisoners pressed into the search parties, lifting wings and skeletons of broken planes hoping to find us hiding under them.

The search extended over the wide area where other commandos were working. Perhaps we walked away and we hid somewhere else, away from our commando. Fortunately, a tire on the bottom of a gully, covered by many plane parts, did not raise any suspicion. No one could possibly hide there.

—JOHN R. SAUNDERS, "The Perfect Prisoner"

When and how did you learn about the facts of life? Where did you think babies came from? Did someone tell you the facts? What was the occasion and how was it done? Did you discover the facts by yourself, say, on a farm watching animals? Did you ever play "Show me" with friends? Did you sneak peeks at books or magazines you weren't supposed to see?

When did you first encounter life and death? Did you see something, like kittens, being born? What was your first experience of death? Perhaps a pet died or was killed, or a friend or relative died. How did it affect you?

Family

When you were a child, your life probably centered around your family. It shaped you in fundamental ways. It was the focal point of deep feelings and sharp memories. Much of who you are began there.

If you were adopted, answer or consider the questions and suggestions below for the family in which you grew up. You may wish to consider any questions that apply to your biological parents and siblings.

If you were a stepchild, consider the questions and suggestions for both your stepparent and your biological parent, and for stepsisters, stepbrothers, and original siblings.

FACTS ABOUT YOUR FAMILY

❦ List the people who lived in your family household.

❦ Describe your mother briefly: how old was she when you were born? Did she work? If so, what did she do? Where did she grow up? What education did she have?

❦ Describe your father briefly: how old was he when you were born? What work did he do? Where did he grow up? What education did he have?

❦ Name any sisters and brothers and note the years they were born.

❦ Name any grandparents alive in your childhood and note their ages and where they lived.

❦ Name any members of your extended family—aunts, uncles, cousins—who were an important part of your childhood.

❦ Note briefly any milestones during your childhood in the lives of these family members such as illness, divorce, accident, change of fortune, and so on.

❦ Describe briefly your family's economic circumstances. Were you more or less well off than most others in your community? More or less well off than your friends and their families?

Recall any memories that capture your father. What did he look like? What impression did he create? Was he quiet or outspoken? What memories do you have of his work? What interested him most? Did he have any specific talents? What kind of parent was he? What were the best conversations you ever had with your father, a time when you felt you really connected? Were there difficult times with your father? Recall moments with him that revealed who he was—things he did or said. What one story or stories capture for you who your father was?

> *One rainy Sunday morning my father and I headed out a little later than usual to pick up the Sunday* New York Times. *Reading the paper was a Sunday ritual for him.*
>
> *Because we got going late, the place he usually bought it was sold out. So was the next place. And the next. Finally, at the one remaining local store, he bought the last copy.*
>
> *As we left the store to return to our car, we started to cross the street, and I reached for my father's hand, as I had been taught to do.*
>
> *The timing was perfect: I knocked the paper out of his hand and into a huge puddle!*
>
> *I froze. Uh-oh, I thought. I looked up at him, expecting him to chew me out. He looked at the soggy paper. He looked at me. And then he burst out laughing like it was the funniest thing that had ever happened to him. He laughed all the way home.*
>
> —RICH SHEARER, personal story

Recall any memories that capture your mother. What did she look like? What impression did she create? Was she quiet or outspoken? What memories do you have of her work? What interested her most? What talents did she have? What kind of parent was she? What were the best conversations you ever had with your mother, a time when you felt really close? Were there difficult times with your mother? Recall moments with her that revealed who she was—things she did or said. What one story or stories capture for you who your mother was?

What was your parents' upbringing like? Recall what you were told about the upbringing of each of your parents. Where did each grow up? What of significance happened to each as the two were growing up? Did their lives turn out as they hoped—did each end up doing what he or she had wanted to do as a child? If not, why not? What effect did their upbringing have on you and your family life? What did they bring into their own home from the homes they grew up in?

If you were a stepchild or adopted. What effect did that have on your family and your place in it? Did you feel a strong sense of belonging, or were you ever treated differently? By parents or siblings?

Think about your brothers and sisters. One by one, bring each of your siblings to mind. What did each look like as children? What kind of personality did each have? What special moments come to mind that reveal who each was then? Did you ever feel especially close to any of them? Did you ever experience sibling rivalry? Did they tease you, or you them? What did you do together? Were there times they helped and supported you? Did any of them ever let you down? What moments or incidents reveal each as a person and the kind of relationship you had?

Think of other household members. One by one, bring to mind anyone else who was part of your household as a child. What did each look like? What kind of personality did each have? Why were they there? What was your relationship with each of them?

Jenny, our wonderful cook, was a miracle. Much later in life I wondered how she made it for 40 years. She came from Algiers, across the Mississippi River, and got to our house [in New Orleans] to give Daddy his breakfast at 7:00 a.m. She stayed after dinner to clean up leaving around 8:00 p.m. All of this meant taking a bus, the ferry, and the streetcar. Impossible, but she did it for 6½ days a week, serving us a big Sunday lunch before Shangra La was built. I'll always wonder what she was paid. It couldn't have been enough, probably around $25.00 a week, with all that travel and cooking three meals a day for different numbers of people but at least 3–6 for dinner each night and everything from scratch of course. No wonder she never let me touch anything in the kitchen. I remember her listening to The Guiding Light *on the radio when I was small.*

> *When Jenny was dying in Charity Hospital, I remember Mother going to her to get the recipes for coconut cake, sugar cookies, and marrons (chestnuts). She never got the recipes. Perhaps it was Jenny's revenge.*
>
> —JANE BUCHSBAUM, personal story

Recall your grandparents. If you knew your grandparents in childhood, bring them each to mind. Recall any moments spent with them. What were they like when you were a child? What did each look like? Describe their homes and lives when you knew them. Did they live with you? Did you know the stories of their lives—where they grew up, what they did, what happened to them, and so on?

Think about your extended family who were part of your childhood—aunts, uncles, cousins. What did each look like? What moments do you remember of each? What were the highlights in his or her life? Did any of these people help you or your family? What was your relationship with any of them at this time? Did you spend time together? Were you close?

What can you remember of your parents' relationship? How did they meet? Why were they attracted to each other (in your opinion, if they never said)? Were their personalities and interests similar, or different, or even at odds? Was their relationship close, loving, and warm or not? How did they demonstrate their feelings for each other? Recall any moments or occasions that revealed something about them as a couple. If your parents separated or divorced, what specific memories do you remember about that time?

What did your family usually talk about? Was your family talkative or not? Was good conversation valued? Did your family encourage or discourage the expression of feelings and emotions? Was there anything *not* talked about in your family? Money, sex, politics, other people, relatives?

Were there any family secrets? What facts, aspects, features of your family life were never discussed outside the family, or in the family? How did you find out about them? Did you ever tell anyone?

"They must have had a fight last night," I whisper to him. "Because I woke up this morning, and my father was in my bed." I say it in this joking way just in case it really is funny. I watch Buddy closely for a reaction. "Oh yeah?" he says.

"Pam." My mother has that edge to her voice that she always uses for dogs and sometimes for me. It means come here, fast, now. She has heard me talking to Buddy. I go into the kitchen, where she is standing at the stove. She turns to me, and in a voice bristling with hostility but whispered in a way that Buddy can not possibly hear, she says, "I'm only going to tell you this once." She jabs at the air between us with a spatula. "Don't you ever tell anyone about anything that goes on in this family. Is that understood?" I nod. In that moment, waking up with my father beside me is no longer wrong. The thing that is wrong was the telling about it.

— PAM LEWIS, "A Little Death"

What were the milestones in the lives of family members when you were a child? Illnesses or accidents, births or deaths, divorce, or changes at work, for example. Did any of these milestones touch your life directly?

What did your parents hope for, and expect from, you? Do you have any memories of your parents' hopes and/or expectations for you and what you would do with your life? Any memories of what they expected from you as a child—in sports, in school, in your social life? Do you remember times when you pleased them? Times when you disappointed them?

What talents did family members have? Did any family member demonstrate a specific talent—athletic, academic, verbal, and so on? What talents were most prized in your family? Did you have any of those talents?

Do any holidays or special times stand out in your memory? Were there any special days or occasions or rituals in your family? Any holidays that you specially celebrated as a family, like the Fourth of July or Christmas or Passover? Do you recall receiving any special gifts, say, for a birthday?

Was food important in your home? Were there any meals or dishes your mother (or anyone else) prepared that you remember as special? Did food in general receive special attention in your home? Was eating particularly important to any family members?

What was the general atmosphere in your home? Was it quiet, restrained, boisterous, unruly, happy, stern, free? Do you have any memories that reveal the social dynamics in your family? Imagine you're eating dinner with your immediate family. Who usually said and did what? Were these good times? Were there favorites among the children? Who talked to whom? Who dominated? Who always went along (if anyone)? How did each of you children try to get what you wanted?

> *One of my most vivid memories of that time was sitting in silence at the dinner table in that spooky house on the hill—Peter, Grandma, Mother, and me. Through the window I could see the gray March landscape. Mother, at the head of the table, was crying silently into her food. It was spinach and Spam. We ate a lot of canned food in those days, as though the war and food rationing were still going on. I used to wonder about this, but now I know that Mother was terrified of running out of money and not receiving anything from Dad in the divorce.*
>
> *No one said anything about the fact that Mother was crying. Maybe we feared that if one of us put words to what we saw and heard, life would implode into an unfathomable sadness so heavy the air wouldn't bear it. Not even after we left the table was anything said. Grandma never took us aside to explain what was happening. Perhaps if "it" was not named, "it" would not exist. Peter and I went to our rooms as always, to do our homework. The dinner scene got buried in a graveyard somewhere next door to my heart, and the habit of not dealing with feelings became embedded in another generation.*
>
> —JANE FONDA, *My Life So Far*

What was discipline like in your home? Were there specific family or household rules? Did you ever break the rules? How were you disciplined? Who was the disciplinarian? Was there anything you were forbidden to do that you wanted to do? Did you ever do it?

Did you have to do any chores or other work around the house? Put yourself back into the time when you were doing them, and where you were. What kind of worker were you? Hardworking, dependable, or lazy? Recall any jobs or work you did for money.

What was your family's place or role in your community? Were your parents respected, active members, or did they basically keep to themselves? Recall any occasions or moments when family members took part in community work. What clubs or other groups did each of them belong to? Did your parents hold any positions in local government or social organizations? Were they ever recognized? Did they have many friends? Do you recall any times that your parents entertained?

Think about your family's economic standing in the community. Was there a time or moment when you realized you and your family had more (or less) than others (or your friends specifically)? Did your family and you ever suffer economic hardship?

When was the first time you were away from home overnight? Where were you? At camp? At a friend's house? At a slumber party? How did you feel? Were you afraid? Homesick? Did you call home, or did the whole experience make you feel grown up?

Did you ever run away from home? Did you ever want to run away but didn't? Why?

One day I decided to run away from home, being enraged at my mother about something or other. I stomped into the kitchen and announced my intentions. "Oh, OK," said Mom. It was dead-cold winter. I packed a tiny suitcase that I loved that had a dancing Spanish lady on the front (it held about 5 pairs of underwear) and put on my coat. I had a little red woolen head scarf that tied under the chin. Problem: I didn't know how to tie it. That meant having to trudge out to the kitchen and ask my mother to do it. Well, there was no help for it. I remember standing next to her by the sink, speechlessly pointing to my neck. She tied the scarf and I went to the kitchen door. Problem: I was too short to open the door. This gives you an idea of how young I was. "Would you please open the door?" I managed to snarl. Mom was quite obliging. Then I was out in the snow. At that moment I realized exactly what the "away" part of running away necessarily entailed. It was, almost literally for someone my age, unthink-

able. The effects of cold on the bladder were also making themselves felt. We had a few acres around our house. I wandered around at the perimeters of the backyard for a while (probably all of about 5 minutes, and completely within eyeshot of the kitchen windows), and went back inside. Fortunately, Mom was just as obliging about letting me in as out, and smart enough to keep her mouth shut about the whole pathetic affair.

—TONI SCIARRA POYNTER, personal story

Home

So much of childhood is bound to a place—the home and neighborhood and community where you grew up. In these early years, it was your world.

FACTS ABOUT YOUR CHILDHOOD HOME

❦ List the address or location of each place you lived in childhood.

❦ In a few words, describe the house or building in which you lived, the neighborhood, and the town or city, all as they were when you were a child.

❦ Identify any of your neighbors or other townspeople who stand out in your memory of childhood.

MEMORIES OF YOUR CHILDHOOD HOME

Think about each house or building where you lived as a child.

- *Recall how it looked.* What memories does standing outside and looking at it bring to mind? Imagine the house at different times of day and in different seasons of the year.
- *Now you're walking into your home.* Recall the layout, what rooms were where, interesting features or objects. What was most distinctive about this place? How did it feel? What made it feel that way?
- *Remember people, moments, and events linked to each room or place.* Who

would you normally find there? What were they doing? What were you doing?

- *Where was your space—where you slept and kept your things? Did you share this space? Where was your parents' space?*

As a twin, I grew up sharing a bedroom with my sister. Our room was on the lower level of the house while our other sisters' and parents' rooms were upstairs. I think our bedroom walls were orange. We had bunk beds. What I remember well was that both of us wanted to sleep on the top bunk. So each month we would switch.

At night, if she couldn't sleep, my twin would ask me to tell her a story. I seem to recall that this was often when I was on the top bunk. Her favorite story was one I made up about a girl without a belly button. In this story, the girl without a belly button met a fairy princess who promised to give her a belly button if she did three good deeds. I don't remember exactly what three deeds she did—or if the deeds changed each time I told the story—but it always ended with the girl getting a belly button and my sister drifting off to sleep.

— DEBORAH OGAWA, personal story

- *How was this home different from homes today, or other homes then?* For example, was it heated by wood stove only, or did it have well water instead of running water, or an outhouse instead of inside bathrooms?

Think about your yard, the land around each place where you grew up. Now imagine yourself walking around the outside of your home, through the yard, if there was one. What happened there? Is this where you played?

Imagine yourself back in your neighborhood. Look at the houses or buildings next to your home. Who else lived in the same building with you? Who lived next door? Do you recall any interactions with neighbors? What were they like? Now imagine walking along the street where you lived. What else was there? Who lived there? Were there any interesting objects nearby? A statue? A cliff? A river? An old building or house? What about the socioeconomic status of the neighborhood? Was it working class? Middle class? Well-off? Were there any rivalries be-tween your neighborhood and others? Did you have to be careful where you went?

Think about the town or city where you grew up. Imagine now going to the various places around your town or city—downtown, the library, school, etc. What do you see as you travel to these places? What objects or buildings? What people? What kind of town or city was it? A factory town? A suburb? A farm town? A country town? If a small place, what larger towns or cities were nearby? Did you ever go there, say, to shop? Was there a local fair, festival, or circus where you grew up? How did you get around your town (bus, on foot, bike)?

What did you like most—and least—about the places where you grew up? Did you have a favorite place (or places)? Did you have any hated or dreaded places? What happened there?

> *The family home of Rock Hill [Sri Lanka] was littered with snakes, especially cobras. The immediate garden was not so dangerous, but one step further and you would see several. The chickens that my father kept in later years were an ever greater magnet. The snakes came for the eggs. The only deterrent my father discovered was ping-pong balls. He had crates of ping-pong balls shipped to Rock Hill and distributed them among the eggs. The snake would swallow the ball whole and be unable to digest it. There are several paragraphs on this method of snake control in a pamphlet he wrote on poultry farming.*
>
> *The snakes also had the habit of coming into the house and at least once a month there would be shrieks, the family would run around, the shotgun would be pulled out, and the snake would be blasted to pieces. Certain sections of the walls and floors showed the scars of shot. My stepmother found one coiled asleep on her desk and was unable to approach the drawer to get the key to open the gun case. At another time one lay sleeping on the large radio to draw its warmth and, as nobody wanted to destroy the one source of music in the house, this one was watched carefully but left alone.*
>
> *Most times though there would be running footsteps, yells of fear and excitement, everybody trying to quiet everybody else, and my father or stepmother would blast away*

not caring what was in the background, a wall, good ebony, a sofa, or a decanter. They killed at least thirty snakes between them.

— MICHAEL ONDAATJE, *Running in the Family*

Was there a vacation home or location you regularly visited in childhood? If so, where was it? Revisit it in your imagination, as you did above with your childhood home or homes.

Religion or Spirituality

Were you raised in a religion or set of religious or spiritual beliefs from earliest childhood? If you were, or if religion or spirituality played some part in your growing up, consider these questions and suggestions.

FACTS ABOUT YOUR RELIGIOUS OR SPIRITUAL BELIEFS

❦ Note what religion, if any, your family observed.

❦ Note what beliefs you professed as a child.

❦ Note what religious or spiritual practices you followed as a child—attending Sunday School or church, praying, serving as altar boy, or something similar.

❦ Describe briefly any personal religious experiences you had as a child.

MEMORIES OF YOUR RELIGIOUS OR SPIRITUAL BELIEFS

Think about your family's religious beliefs and practices. What memories do you have of religious events, observances, and holidays in your family? Did you as a child ever question your family's beliefs or practices?

I remain unaware of anyone talking to us about our feelings after our father died. What I (and my brother Morrie) do remember, though, is that for one year after his death we were required to say Kaddish—the mourner's prayer for the dead in the Jewish religion. What this meant was that daily, for many months (Morrie's recollection is that it was twice a day!), I had to attend a service—at the Temple or at someone's home—where at least ten men would gather to say prayers. We then would recite the Kaddish. So here I was, several months as a nine-year-old and then another many months as a ten-year-old, saying these absolutely meaningless Hebrew words. There was no grieving process; there was no catharsis. There was no feeling. What there was for me as a young child was senseless ritual, and I believe that this experience was a major factor leading to my lifelong disdain for religious dogma and formalized religion in general.

—Stephen K. Blumberg, A Satisfying Life

What do you recall of any formal religious instruction? When and where did this occur? Who taught you? Were you ever confirmed, baptized, or otherwise inaugurated into religious maturity?

Recall any religious roles you played. Did you ever play any kind of formal role at your place of worship, such as singing in the choir? Were any of those moments memorable?

Recall any religious experiences you had as a child. Were you "saved"? Did you think you saw or heard anything—a religious vision?

How did your beliefs and practices change or affect your daily life? Did they lead you to do something you might not have done otherwise? Did you ever break these rules? Did your religion or beliefs make you feel different or apart from other people? Did you like that or not?

Recall your religious practices. Recall entering your place of worship. What services did you attend? What practices did you follow? Did you observe religious holidays? Did you follow any religious or spiritual practices at home, such as daily prayer, scripture reading, and so on?

When I was in the sixth grade, I got pretty seriously involved in a local Baptist church. I was saved and went to Sunday evening services and, on occasion, Thursday Prayer Meetings. Not to mention Bible Camp and going door-to-door handing out pamphlets (I absolutely hated that). I'd even get up early in the morning, which nearly killed me but I did it, to pray and read the Bible. I probably read the Bible, at least the New Testament, several times over in that period. I also memorized many, many Bible verses. It was around all these beliefs that a peculiar need I had first appeared. It was the need to reduce ideas to their essence and say them with great pith. In fact, it was my goal to reduce the entire teachings of the New Testament to a few words whose letters and spaces totaled no more than 24. Why 24? Because that's how many letters and spaces would fit on an aluminum luggage tag I could stamp out on a machine in the Greyhound bus station in Redding, a nearby little city. The makers of that machine, who intended it for travelers wanting some durable ID for their suitcase, surely never thought a 12-year-old kid would be summarizing all of Christianity on it. But I was. I not only had to get the ideas simmered down to their purest essence—"Grace made real by faith alone" (Darn! Too long!) was the kind of thing I was writing—but I had to express them on something fairly eternal, like a piece of metal. I'd get a set of words figured out that excited me and I'd pester Mom to take me to Redding so I could squeeze out one of those eternal disks for 25 cents, which I would carry in my pocket and look at whenever I began to feel uncertain about what I believed. I probably made a pocketful of those little disks and never did get one that kept me happy for long.

— KENT LINEBACK, personal story

Was religion part of your social life too? Did you participate in social activities at your place of worship? How important was this social aspect of religion in your life? Did you restrict your real friendships to people who shared your beliefs?

Were any people from this part of your life memorable? When you think of the religious groups you were in, were there any special individuals who stand out—such as a rabbi, minister, priest, teacher, or someone in the congregation? Did any make a difference in your life, positive or negative?

School

As you grew older in childhood, school probably played an increasingly important role in your life. Indeed, childhood and school were most likely inseparable.

FACTS ABOUT SCHOOL

❦ Name the schools you attended—school name, dates, location.

❦ Describe briefly how you did in school.

❦ Identify your favorite subject. Your least favorite.

❦ Name your favorite teachers and your least-liked teachers.

❦ Name your friends and memorable classmates.

❦ Name any school clubs or groups you belonged to.

❦ Note any recognition or awards you earned in school.

❦ Name the school social group or clique you were considered a member of, if any (jocks, cool kids, bookworms, bandies, eggheads, dweebs, nerds, and so on).

❦ Note any classes or training, like piano or dance, that you took outside regular school.

MEMORIES OF SCHOOL

Going off to school. Recall when you first left home and spent your days at school. Was that difficult? Can you recall your first day? Were you ever "the new kid" at school?

My first day at the Walley set the tone for all the years to follow. Still as timid about leaving the country of the blue-eyed as I had been when I was taking catechism lessons, I tagged after Ruthie. She ushered me through the squirming crowd at the entrance marked "Girls" and through the dreary corridors and up to the big square classroom. But once in my seat—last one in the first row—I was on my own. And the first thing I did was insult the teacher.

I corrected her spelling. "It's not p-s-l-a-m, Miss P——," I said of the word she'd written on the blackboard. "It's p-s-a-l-m. You've spelled it puh-slam." I giggled, thinking she'd see the joke. Miss Fritzi would have. "Don't you be so smart, Mary Lee Cantwell," Miss P—— snapped, and her eyes were a basilisk's.

An hour or so later the music teacher, a barrel of a woman with a chin you could wrap your hand around, bustled into the room. She chalked some notes on the blackboard with short, vicious strokes, then went around the room, asking each student to read aloud those she jabbed at with her pointer. When she got to me I rose from my desk and said, "I'm sorry, Mrs. D——, but I haven't been taught how to read music." "I'm sorry, Mrs. D——," she replied in perfect mimicry, "but I haven't been taught how to read music." I sat down, my eyes hot and my stomach melting. Till then I had believed that all rooms would brighten because I entered them.

—MARY CANTWELL, *Manhattan Memoir*

Did your family value and support education in your home? Did your parents encourage you, help you with homework or projects? Where did you do schoolwork at home? Did your brothers and sisters do well in school? What effect did that have on you? Did they help you with schoolwork? Was doing well important to you? In general, did you like or dislike school as a child? What happened to create or reinforce this feeling?

For each school you attended, use the following questions and suggestions to recall important moments.
- *Imagine yourself back in that school building.* Walk through its corridors, offices, classrooms. What memories of people and events and moments do these places bring to mind?

- *How did you do in this school?* Did you get good grades? How hard did you work?

- *Recall your most memorable classmates (not necessarily your friends).* Recall any moments or occasions involving each. Did you wish you were like any of these people? Did you want to be their friend? Were there people you avoided?

- *What was social life at this school like?* Imagine it's recess or lunch hour or after school. Walk through your school yard, playground, and playing fields. Let those places and spaces bring to mind the people, events, moments, and stories of what happened there. What did you play? With whom? Were you popular, liked by many or most of your classmates? Did you feel like an insider or outsider? What group or clique did you belong to? Did you want to be part of this group? Did you spend time and effort inviting or excluding others from your clique? Were you a "mean girl" or a tough guy? Were you a victim of such people? Did you try to join a clique and were denied? What were the other groups? How did you feel about them? Were there any bullies, physical or emotional, at school? Were there any times they bothered you? Were you ever the bully? Did you ever get in a fight?

- *Recall your favorite and least favorite subjects. Favorite and least favorite teachers.* What subjects did you like best? Imagine yourself back in each of those classes. Imagine yourself back in each of the subjects you liked least. Recall the teachers you liked best. What moments or occasions do you remember of each of them? Did you have a crush on any of them? What teachers did you like least? Recall each of them and what happened to make you dislike them. Recall some moment in school when you did well. When you didn't do well.

[The Governess and I] continued to toil every day, not only at letters but at words, and also at what was much worse, figures. Letters after all had only got to be known, and when they stood together in a certain way one recognized their formation and that it meant a certain sound or word which one uttered when pressed sufficiently. But the figures were tied into all sorts of tangles and did things to one another which it was extremely difficult to forecast with complete accuracy. You had to say what they did each time they were tied up together, and the Governess apparently attached enormous im-

portance to the answer being exact. If it was not right, it was wrong. It was not any use being "nearly right." In some cases these figures got into debt with one another: you had to borrow one or carry one, and afterwards you had to pay back the one you had borrowed. These complications cast a steadily gathering shadow over my daily life.

—WINSTON CHURCHILL, My Early Life

- *Recall the clubs and groups you belonged to.* What memories do you have of those meetings and events? Did you participate in something like a school play or other public event? What role did you play in each group?
- *What was your personal reputation in this school?* Did anything happen to give you that reputation? Did anything happen because of your reputation? Did you try to change your reputation? Did your reputation come, at least in part, because of your family, or your brothers or sisters?
- *Did you ever receive any recognition, positive or negative?* What did you do to earn awards? Did you ever get in trouble? Were you punished?
- *Recall any memorable school events.* Visitors? Field trips? Games? Did your parents ever come to school? Did they attend any of your school events or games?
- *Did you take classes outside school?* Music? Dance? Art? Were they important to you?

Friends and other memorable people

Friends were no less a part of life in childhood than they would be in later stages. Perhaps they were even more important here because the world was new and we felt particularly vulnerable.

FACTS ABOUT FRIENDS AND OTHER MEMORABLE PEOPLE

❧ List the names of your best childhood friends. Describe each very briefly and note when and where each was a friend.

❦ If you had a childhood boyfriend or girlfriend, note his or her name, when you were friends, and, briefly, what the relationship was like.

❦ If you ever had an imaginary friend, describe this "friend" and when and where and how he or she was part of your life.

❦ Name the people besides family and friends who were important in your childhood. Note his or her relationship with you and what made this person memorable.

❦ Name other people or social groups you tended to hang out with.

MEMORIES OF FRIENDS AND OTHER MEMORABLE PEOPLE

Think of your best childhood friends, one by one. How did you meet? What drew you together? What did you typically do together after school, on weekends, and during vacations? Hark back to the places you did things together—a home, a yard, a playground, some woods—and recall any incidents with the friend that occurred there. What are your fondest memories with this friend? Did you have any secrets, or secret places? Did you ever fight? Did you compete? Did something happen to end the friendship?

Pam McGavin was my best friend in elementary school. We walked to school together every day, had lunch together in the playground, and reunited after school at the point where our two backyards connected. We were inseparable. One day, while in second grade, we overheard French being spoken by several visitors to our school. We were fascinated by the sounds, and even more intrigued by the fact that it was possible to have a public conversation that no one else could understand. At lunchtime we decided we would speak French to each other. So for the next hour, we strode around the playground making nonsensical warbling sounds pretending to our classmates that we could have a private conversation in French, and that not a single one of them could possibly understand us. I don't think they cared a whit. Nor could we understand each other. We never did it again.

—CAROL FRANCO, personal story

Did a friend ever betray or disappoint or let you down? Recall what happened, and why. Did you ever let a friend down yourself?

Did a childhood friend suffer some illness or other misfortune? What happened and how were you involved? Did it change you in any way?

Think about your childhood sweetheart(s). How did you know this person? Why did you like him or her? Recall any times you spent together. Did others know about your relationship? What happened to end it?

Did you have a crush on anyone? A crush was a one-way love relationship with someone who was usually beyond reach, like a teacher, an actor, an older person. Was it on someone your age? Someone older? Did this person ever discover your feelings? If so—how and what happened? What was it you liked about this person? Did you ever make your feelings known to this person? Did anyone have a crush on you?

On a bicycle I traveled over the known world's edge, and the ground held. I was seven. I had fallen in love with a red-haired fourth-grade boy named Walter Milligan. He was tough, Catholic, from an iffy neighborhood. Two blocks beyond our school was a field— Miss Frick's field, behind Henry Clay Frick's mansion—where boys played football. I parked my bike on the sidelines and watched Walter Milligan play. As he ran up and down the length of the field, following the football, I ran up and down the sidelines, following him. After the game I rode my bike home, delirious. It was the closest we had been, and the farthest I had traveled from home.

(My love lasted two years and occasioned a bit of talk. I knew it angered him. We spoke only once. I caught him between classes in the school's crowded hall and said, "I'm sorry." He looked away, apparently enraged; his pale freckled skin flushed. He jammed his fists in his pockets, looked down, looked at me for a second, looked away, and brought out gently, "That's okay." That was the whole of it: beginning, middle, and end.)
— ANNIE DILLARD, *An American Childhood*

Who else was important to you? What did each look like? How did each act? Where did you meet? What happened between you? What made them stand out in your childhood? What events or moments or occasions happened that involved them?

Other social groups. If there were places you tended to go to be with others your age, note the places, the people who were generally there, and what would happen.

Sports

For many children, organized games—sports—were a crucial part of growing up. How important were they for you?

FACTS ABOUT SPORTS IN CHILDHOOD

❦ Name the sports you played. For each sport, note where and when you played—along with any other factual information, such as your position or role, how you or your team did, and your contribution.

❦ Describe your level of athletic skill as a child in each of the sports you played.

❦ Name the pro, college, or local teams that you followed and how they did.

MEMORIES OF SPORTS IN CHILDHOOD

Think of each sport that you played. What were they? Were you passionate about any one of them? Were there any moments you recall with pride, that you play over and over in your mind? Any moments you recall with embarrassment, that you'd like to do over, or wish hadn't happened?

You begin by bouncing a ball—in the house, on the driveway, along the sidewalk, at the playground. Then you start shooting: legs bent, eyes on the rim, elbow under the ball. You shoot and follow through. Let it fly, up, up and in. No equipment is needed beyond a ball, a rim, and imagination. How simple the basic act is. I'm not sure exactly when my interest turned to passion, but I was very young, and it has never diminished.

— BILL BRADLEY, *Values of the Game*

Did you or your team win any awards or championships? What was that like and what memories do you have of the games or matches you won?

What memorable people did you know in playing sports? Teammates? Coaches? What incidents or events made each person memorable? Recall other players you remember for their athletic ability, or for some other reason. Try to recall any events that illustrate why they stood out.

Did you have any dreams of playing sports professionally? What were your fantasies and dreams? Did anything happen to make you think you could realize those dreams? Recall any sports heroes—an older player in your school or town, or a player for a pro or college team—you followed.

Recall any sports you followed as a fan. Did you follow any particular teams—pro, college, or local—avidly? Recall any memorable games or events. Were there any stars on the teams you particularly followed? Did you go to any games?

Interests and Activities

Childhood was full of interests and activities as you explored a strange and brand new world. As you got older, your childhood interests probably assumed more focused forms, like hobbies. Perhaps you took on some part-time work or chores for money, played music, and tried a variety of other activities.

FACTS OF CHILDHOOD INTERESTS

❦ Name and briefly describe any pets that you or your family kept.

❦ Describe your favorite toy, if you had one.

❦ Note what games you liked to play at various stages in your childhood.

❦ Identify any childhood objects you saved and why.

❦ Name any favorite stories that you read (or were read or told to you).

❦ Name any movies that you particularly remember.

❦ Name any favorite television or radio programs from childhood.

❦ Note any work you did for money outside your family as you got older, such as a paper route or mowing lawns or babysitting.

❦ Note any hobbies or collections that you pursued.

❦ Name any groups you belonged to and what they did (e.g., Brownies, Cub Scouts).

❦ Note any memorable trips, or times and occasions you spent away from home.

❦ Describe anything you did musically—play an instrument, sing, dance, etc.

❦ Note any honors or distinctions you earned as a child. How were you recognized or awarded?

MEMORIES OF CHILDHOOD INTERESTS

Recall each pet your family kept. How important were pets in your life or your family's? Did you have a set of chores around caring for a pet? What did you most like doing with your pet? Did any pet suffer an injury, or die? Did you want a pet you couldn't have?

I don't recall exactly how old I was when I got Tweety. I remember reading that it is easier to teach a male to talk, so I chose one with blue coloring on the upper part of his beak since that was the indicator; females are brown. I also remember buying a record with someone speaking the words that talking birds are supposed to know so it could be put on the record player and play all day. I don't remember when I gave up on that endeavor, but in any case it was a failure. Perhaps he was simply a male parakeet with a learning disability. The one sound he did master was my father's sneeze. It was so precise it would elicit a gesundheit from people outside the living room if my father and the bird were in there together.

Tweety had the run of the house, to my father's dismay. When I came home from school, one whistle would cause a rush of wings and then a dutiful perching on my shoulder. When I watched TV at night, Tweety would crawl around chewing on my hair and earlobes. He would often prowl the floor looking for morsels of chocolate chip cookies that we kids might have dropped. Often this would elicit a calico streak as the family cat would attack, and Tweety would dart to the heavens . . . more precisely the ceiling, squawking loudly. I never knew if he was frightened or just taunting the old cat.

Then there was the time that my father spent the day wallpapering the living room. I remember it was green. The next day, Tweety spent his time pecking away at my father's handiwork. Evidently parakeets find fresh wallpaper paste quite delectable. When the day was done, it was a mess. I don't remember my father's reaction, but I do recall my mother getting some green tape and taping over some areas.

On my twelfth birthday I had some friends over, and all was disrupted when Tweety flew out the door as one of my friends came in. Parakeets living inside are confined by ceilings so when they escape they tend to fly very high. We had tall trees on our street. I couldn't see him, but could easily follow his travels by listening to his singing. I climbed on our roof and hung out neighbors' windows during the afternoon, whistling for him to return. Finally, after several hours of such effort, with me sitting on the high-est point of our roof, this small dot appeared coming down from the top of the trees. I extended my index finger and he came in for a landing. After it was over, my mother called the Owego Gazette *and had the exciting story printed.*

All things must end, and Tweety's demise was especially traumatic. One morning when coming down for breakfast I found Tweety sitting on an egg in his (her!) cage. She was so obsessed with being a proper mom that she sat all day on the egg, neglecting her own basic needs. I believe that she then laid another egg and the stress on her became vis-ible. At the vet's urging I removed the eggs from the cage. I don't remember if she laid some further eggs, but soon thereafter she began having convulsions at regular intervals. It was quite a violent end for such a peace loving bird.

Of course I buried Tweety somewhere in the back yard. I hope it was deep enough so that the family cat didn't get the last laugh.

—ALLEN WEITSMAN, personal story

What memories do you have of favorite games or toys or possessions? Recall mem-ories of any items that were special from this time in your life. Did you own a bike? Who taught you to ride?

Remember times when you became completely engrossed in what you were doing. Were there any times you picked up your head and discovered hours had passed, though it felt like only minutes? What were you doing? Did you return to that ex-perience?

Recall where you would go to the movies and any special movies you saw. Imagine you're entering your local movie theater. What did you do? What did others do? Did any movies you saw have an impact on your life? Do you recall any favorite actors or actresses? Did you ever write for a star's photo and autograph? Did you ever see a star in person?

Think back about your musical experiences. Did you play an instrument, or sing? If you took lessons, recall those times. Did you perform before an audience? How good were you? Did your family or friends encourage you musically? Did you ever receive any recognition for your musical ability or performance? Were you ever embarrassed around music? If you were an avid listener, did you attend any concerts? Were there favorite performers or composers?

What memories do you have of favorite TV or radio programs? Recall the programs themselves or events surrounding them. Did you make sure you were home to watch or listen to these programs?

Think back about any hobbies or collections you had. Did you have any collections, such as baseball cards, coins, comic books, bugs, butterflies, dolls, marbles, stamps, or anything else? Any memories of hobbies, like baking, drawing, or horse-backriding? Were you good at them? Did you receive any recognition for them?

Think about each trip you made as a child. Recall what it was like traveling to the destination and back—on a plane, by car, by bus. What did you see when you arrived—people, places, historical things? Were you with anyone? Did you meet interesting people? What did you like or dislike?

Recall your summer vacations. Did you stay home? Doing what? Did you go somewhere? Camp? What was your favorite summer activity? Swimming? Reading? Sleeping?

Recall any special stories or books from childhood. What memories do you have of, or around, reading? What were your favorite stories—read to you or by you as you learned to read? Did you go to the library? If so, recall moments when you were there—the librarians, the readers, the space, the shelves of books. Did you have a favorite reading place there, or at home, or someplace else? Did you find a favorite author and read everything he or she wrote? Did friends or parents or teachers advise and encourage you?

Mrs. Calloway made her own rules about books. You could not take back a book to the Library on the same day you'd taken it out; it made no difference to her that you'd read every word in it and needed another to start. You could take out two books at a time and two only; this applied as long as you were a child and also for the rest of your life, to my mother as severely as to me. So two by two, I read library books as fast as I could go, rushing them home in the basket of my bicycle. From the minute I reached our house, I started to read. Every book I seized on, from Bunny Brown and His Sister Sue at Camp Rest-a-While *to* Twenty Thousand Leagues under the Sea, *stood for the devouring wish to read being instantly granted. I knew this was bliss, knew it at the time. Taste isn't nearly so important; it comes in its own time. I wanted to read* immediately. *The only fear was that of books coming to an end.*

— EUDORA WELTY, *One Writer's Beginnings*

Recall any work experiences you had. Think about what you did—mowing lawns or babysitting or delivering papers. Whom did you work for? What was that person like as a boss? What did you learn? What did you earn? How did you spend the money? Did you enjoy the work? Were you good at it?

Recall any other interests or activities you pursued as a child. What was the activity? Did you do it alone or with others? Why was it important to you?

Notable Events

Though our understanding of the world was limited in childhood, we were still aware that some events, near or far, were noteworthy or important. Some were close enough, like fire and flood, to touch us personally. Others we noted only because our elders paid attention. Later we would come to understand their significance.

FACTS ABOUT NOTABLE EVENTS

❦ Note any historical or noteworthy events you distinctly remember from childhood. These can range from great world events—wars, elections, assassinations—to local occurrences, such as fires, accidents, floods, or other natural disasters.

MEMORIES OF NOTABLE EVENTS

Recall each of the events you noted above. Where were you and what were you doing when it happened or when you heard about it? What made each event memorable—the events themselves or the reactions of people around you?

While the tornado itself was on—while the buckeye trees in our yard were coming apart—Mother had gathered Amy and Molly and held them with her sensibly away from the windows; she urged my father and me to join them. Father had recently re-turned from his river trip and was ensconced tamed in the household again. And here was a pleasant, once-in-a-lifetime tornado, the funnel of which touched down, in an almost delicate point, like a bolt of lightening, on our very street. He and I raced from window to window and watched; we saw the backyard sycamore smash the back-porch roof; we saw the air roaring and blowing full of sideways-flying objects, and saw the leafy buckeye branches out front blow white and upward like skirts.

—ANNIE DILLARD, *An American Childhood*

Other Voices

We don't grow up alone. Others shared our world in childhood. They helped raise us or shared a home with us or played with us or went to school with us or taught us or babysat us or hired us to do chores. The specific connection doesn't matter. What matters is that these people have memories of us, or memories that include us. Their memories, their points of view, can be valuable additions to the story of our lives.

If you want to include other people's memories of you in childhood . . .

1. Make a list of people from your childhood and ask them to share their memories with you, in their own words.
2. Record each memory on a separate sheet of paper. Label each memory "A Memory of Me" and include the memory teller's name, as well as the approximate date and location of the memory.

3. Add these memory sheets to your own memories in your *My Life Story* notebook.

It was the summer of 1957 and my cousins Allen and Carol and I were sitting around the kitchen table at my Aunt Ruth and Uncle Ed's home in Owego, New York. That particular afternoon Allen, in his big brother mode, was probably teasing Carol and me.

Somehow we got onto the topic of the saddest movies we had ever seen. I started retelling the story of Carousel, *which has always tugged at my heart.*

When it came Carol's turn, it is not surprising that the saddest movie she had ever seen was Gallant Bess—*about a military horse. Carol loved horses. The bookshelves in her room were filled with horse figurines and her walls were covered with posters of horses. She could never quite understand why her parents wouldn't let her keep a horse in the garage as they didn't use it for the car.*

Gallant Bess *was a wartime story and the final scenes showed Gallant Bess's owner leaving his beloved horse on the beach as he waded out to the carrier that was to bring him home. At this point in telling of the tale, Carol could no longer contain her sadness and grief at this separation and burst into tears. Allen and I, being the sophisticated elders, burst into laughter. We were transformed into hysterical, giddy teenagers, literally rolling on the floor with tears streaming down our cheeks.*

Hearing the commotion, Aunt Ruth came rushing into the kitchen from the back porch. She surveyed the scene and could only surmise that we had done something to injure Carol. She became enraged. This woman of steady calm who never raised her voice actually yelled at Allen and me and sent us, still laughing hysterically, out of the room.

We never did hear the end of the story of Gallant Bess, and I doubt Carol would have made it through anyway, even if Aunt Ruth hadn't intervened.

—SANDY RUBIN, personal story

THE MEANING OF YOUR CHILDHOOD

The final step in recapturing childhood is to reflect on and record the significance of this stage in your life as a whole. How did childhood help shape the kind of person you became?

As a child, your ability to understand was limited by age and lack of experience. You could see then only through the naïve, inexperienced eyes of a child. Now you can understand that time in a new way—through eyes much more experienced and knowledgeable. Simply knowing what happened afterward gives you a far different and better lens for examining and assessing that time in your life.

Defining Moments

A defining moment in childhood was an event, action, or decision that defined you and shaped your life in the years ahead. You may not have recognized the importance of those moments until you could look back in light of how things worked out afterward.

Consider these: a childhood accident, illness, or physical condition; a change in your family's social or economic status; your own place in your family (for example, being first or last child); something that happened to you in school; or your religious beliefs. Any one of these could serve as a turning point in your life.

When I was about five or six, my father lost his job. And he was totally helpless. He had no recourse. There was no Social Security. There was no pension. And for the next few years it was a real struggle. I mean, he did jobs like loading booze, illicit booze on trucks. He ran summonses for lawyers. He distributed flyers for the Republican Party to earn a buck, or earn a quarter I mean, not a buck. And when he came home and told my mother he'd lost his job, she broke into tears and I felt, "I'm never going to let that happen to me. I'm never going to be at the . . . [mercy] of other people who are going to be able to do that to me. I'm not going to be in a position where I will ever, ever, allow myself to be vulnerable to that helplessness."

—WARREN BENNIS, *Geeks & Geezers*

Values—What Mattered

Values are what's important to us, what matters. What we value can range from high concepts, like truth or beauty, to virtues, like respect or courage, to attributes, like intelligence or savoir faire, to the more tangible and mundane, like athletic ability or beauty or physical strength or being popular. No value is inherently better than another.

Often we don't even recognize consciously the power and presence of values in our lives and minds. But whether we say them out loud, values guide us every day in making dozens of choices, large and small. We use them to decide what to think about, what to worry about, and even how to spend our time.

We'd like to think our values remain constant, but many of them change as we mature. As children we may have valued popularity, for example, but by the time we become adults, we've probably realized that many things in life are more important. So don't judge (and exclude) some of your values in childhood just because they were childish.

Since we rarely talk about values explicitly, they can be difficult to identify and express clearly. Here are some suggestions that may help:

- What was so important to you as a child that you spent time on it, you aspired to it, you expected it of yourself, you admired and sought it out in others?
- What gave you genuine pleasure as a child? What did you truly enjoy? You probably valued those things.
- Who were your heroes and what appealed to you in them? Whom did you aspire to be like?

Look back over your facts and memories of childhood and ask yourself, What significant choices or decisions did I make?—about school, about friends, about what to do, and where to go. Then ask, why or how did I make those choices, especially the tough ones? Was there some consistency in the choices you made?

Think too about the values of the key people in your life: parents, teachers, friends, heroes, other people you admired. Family values were a huge influence for most of us. What did your family value most? Intelligence, humor, knowledge, honesty, courage, toughness, stoicism, musical ability, athletic ability, good grades, education, obedience, religion? Did you share these values? Which were least important? Did you struggle against some of them?

I was a long-legged seven-year-old, but not quite tall enough to remount my horse if I got off to kick some lazy sheep into motion, or to investigate a sick or lame one. Then there would be no getting back on till the next fence, or the rare occasional stump. At first I was not quite secure enough in ego to cope with the space, the silence, and the brooding sky. Occasionally I would find myself crying, half in vexation at my small size and the pigheadedness of sheep, half for the reassurance of a sound. By the family's code it was shameful to weep, and I was supposed to be too grown-up for such babyish behavior. Once the wind carried the sound to my father on the other side of the paddock. By the time we were reunited, I had reached a fence, climbed on my horse, and become secure again by seeing him in the distance. "I thought I heard someone crying," he observed to me as we met. I looked him in the eye. "I didn't," I said. There he let the matter rest.

— JILL KER CONWAY, *The Road from Coorain*

Love

Love here doesn't mean romantic or physical love. It simply refers to deep and special feelings of care and concern and acceptance that can exist between any two people. Parents love children. True friends love each other. Boys or men can love each other. Girls and women can love each other. A boy and girl or a man and woman can love each other without getting involved in romance or attachment. Teachers can love their students and vice versa.

It's important as we recall our lives to remember those who loved us and those we loved, as we have defined the word here. Each of us is wired to need this kind of connection with another person. Not with everyone we meet—only saints can do that—but with some few others. The life of someone unloved and unable to love is the most empty life possible. And the life of much love given and received is in the end the richest of all.

Don't simply list the people who were supposed to love you, or whom you were supposed to love, such as parents or brothers and sisters. List only those special people—it may be only one or two—with whom you felt this special connection at this time in your life, those who cared for you as you were or whom you loved without question or doubt.

Often the person you loved and the person who loved you were the same, but they didn't have to be. The very act of loving, even if it's not returned, can be healing and worthwhile all by itself.

> *I didn't become an overtly affectionate mother, probably because I was revolted by my own mother's intrusive possessiveness, which would alternate with unforeseeable punishments and reprimands. It wasn't she whom I learned to trust, but my nanny, whom I called Anya, and loved dearly. She was young and funny and never laid a guilt trip on you. I can still see her putting on a pair of silk stockings in preparation for going out with her boyfriend, Egon, and I watch her and hope that I, too, will grow up to have long, smooth legs like my Anya. Unlike my mother, she was never suspicious that I meant something other than what I said.*
>
> —Ruth Kluger, "Still Alive"

Learning and Wisdom

Learning concerns more what you learned about life and the life skills you began to develop in childhood than the formal knowledge you acquired. And wisdom goes even beyond that. Wisdom has more to do with knowing how and when to apply what you know. It's judgment, perspective, deep understanding. Your experience of childhood, combined with all you've learned and lived through since, gives you a unique perspective on childhood and how it should be lived.

If no life lessons and wisdom come readily to mind, look over the facts and memories of your childhood and ask yourself whether success or failure taught you anything about life. What about adversity, illness, or an accident? Did teachers, sports, friends, travel, chores, or anything else lead you to insights about how to live?

The goal here is not to conjure up new memories of your childhood. You've probably already touched on all the key people and occasions; indeed, you should have already talked in your memories about such important parts of your life. Your task now is to go beyond simply recalling them. Here you should identify, as best you can, the insights and lessons you learned, and carried forward, from the people, events, and circumstances of childhood.

As you reflect on the lessons of childhood, consider this: not all lessons turned out to be good ones. You could, and many of us did, draw the wrong conclusions from your experience, which later you must unlearn. You perhaps learned to go silent, instead of speaking up when you should, or to flee from pain and discomfort instead of trying to work through them. Did you learn any specific lessons in childhood which you later had to unlearn?

Here's another suggestion, particularly for identifying any wisdom you acquired. What advice would you now give a child, about childhood, that you think could help the youngster grow up to lead a happier, more productive life? Imagine a young person now, someone like you as a child. What would you say to that person as he or she faced the same kinds of challenges and experiences you faced? What do you wish someone else had told you as a child?

Holy Family [School] was at most a mile from our house, but that was quite a distance when I was in kindergarten or first grade, and it seemed a lot longer during those cold Buffalo winters. No matter how bad the weather, we always walked. My parents shared one car, which Dad drove to his jobs, but that wasn't the reason. In those days, at least in our neighborhood, nobody drove their kids to school; it just wasn't done. Our daily walk was twice as long because Holy Family School had no lunch room, so we were all sent home for lunch. None of the mothers we knew worked outside the home, and they all had lunch waiting on the table when we walked in. We ate quickly, because twenty minutes after we came home it was time to return to school.

Four miles of walking a day does not constitute cruel and unusual punishment, but in the early grades it was quite a challenge. It meant that when you were five, six, or seven years old, you had accomplished something real and tangible each morning by the simple act of getting yourself to school. I can't prove it, but I believe these walks made us tougher and better prepared for some of life's hardships. More than once, when facing a problem or a difficult challenge later on, I found strength from telling myself, This is nothing compared to walking to school backward, against the wind, at the age of six in a howling Buffalo snowstorm.

—TIM RUSSERT, *Big Russ and Me*

Summing Up

Here's your opportunity, after all the remembering of facts and events and people of your childhood, to capture that time of your life in a few words. What was it like overall? How did it feel to you? Do you remember it fondly? Or was it a difficult time you struggled to get through? Try to remember a time or moment or occasion that best characterized this time in your life. If there was one, describe it and explain how it seems to you to sum up this time. This is your chance, in a sense, to view your childhood as a whole.

STAGE 2

---

adolescence

Each stage of life—particularly as we pass through it—can feel like the most challenging of all, but in reality adolescence probably merits that distinction more than any other. We enter it as children and leave as young adults—not yet fully mature but light-years beyond our days of childhood.

It was a time our bodies experienced enormous growth, and it only made things worse that growth occurred in spurts, with different body parts growing at different rates. Our feet and hands jumped ahead first, followed by arms and legs—remember when you seemed all clumsy limbs and digits?—with our torsos finally, mercifully, catching up. Girls, soon to be young women, grew first, often leaving the poor boys behind. Then boys' growth picked up and they eventually surged ahead.

More was involved than simply getting bigger, of course. Our bodies *changed*—oh, did they change!—in strange and sometimes embarrassing ways. For adolescence, by definition, began with the onset of puberty. We often weren't sure what to do with those changes. We welcomed them and hated them. Here were milestones everyone remembers. The first efforts at shaving. Going with mother to buy a first bra. A voice that squeaked and cracked, before settling an octave lower. Kotex—the first period. Whispered conversations with closest friends: "Do you know what happened last night?"

Our emotions took roller coaster rides with strange twists and turns and leaps and falls. We began to sense something we'd learn over and over through life: our mind isn't necessarily our friend. For teenage minds could play funny tricks. Some of us believed that the world was fascinated with us and was watching our every move, with particular focus on how we looked and acted. Some of us believed we were unique, with special experiences, insights, and abilities. We were convinced a heroic life stretched before us. We daydreamed of eliminating hunger and poverty from the world, of captaining our team to five Super Bowl victories, of writing plays that surpassed Shakespeare's. Nothing would prevent this destiny from unfolding. Sometimes we even thought we were invincible, that nothing could harm us, no matter what we did, and we did things—leaped into unknown water, drove old rattletraps at one hundred miles an hour—that now send chills through us to remember.

And when we weren't thinking of the glorious, world-saving life we would live, we imagined the rest of the world was watching us—and laughing. At our big feet or big ears or pimples or God knows what. We suffered agonies of shame and embarrassment. We stammered and stuttered and fumbled and died a thousand deaths.

The surging hormones that drove the changes in our bodies also drove sometimes confusing changes in our minds, too. The opposite sex reared its mystifying head and we weren't too sure what to do about any of that, either. We entered adolescence thinking the opposite sex was composed of strange ducks, but by the end of adolescence we were spending an awful lot of time thinking about them. Maybe they weren't so strange, after all, or perhaps they really were strange, but we couldn't do without them.

Slowly, through all the turmoil and confusion, we were becoming our own people. As youngsters we had simply seen ourselves as our parents' children. We more or less adopted their lives and thoughts and feelings as our own. But gradually we began to define ourselves—what we liked, our feelings and beliefs. Some of us simply retained our families' identities wholesale and put off this process until later, but most of us began to sort and review and develop our own sense of who we were. That sense was a long way from complete, but it was beginning to be our own.

A big part of our emerging identity was what Daniel Levinson called our "dream." We were putting together our own definition—still a large part fantasy—of who and what we wanted to be. Maybe we had multiple dreams—to be a school teacher and a veterinarian and a jet pilot and a mother or father. As we advanced through our teen years, we began to convert our dream from fantasy to the beginnings of a real plan. We thought about what we would have to study to qualify for it, or what other steps we would have to pursue.

We were learning more about what it meant to be an adult and what would be expected of us in that looming world of frightening and exhilarating independence. We loved the idea of being on our own and living our own life. Yet the prospect of abandoning the haven of home terrified us. We began working with adults as adults, perhaps at part-time jobs or in high school or college, and slowly learning what it would mean to take responsibility for ourselves. Many of us were taken under the wings of important mentors, adults who took special interest in us and helped us learn how to act and be in the wider world.

We did, many of us, leave home toward the end of this period and go to those halfway institutions, college and the armed services. Some of us passed through both. In them, we weren't quite adults yet or truly on our own, no matter what we may have thought at the time. But they were the start of our journeys as adults.

Remember this tumultuous and giddy and frightening time both from the vantage point of age and experience, when you can place some perspective on it. But do try to recall it as it looked and felt then, when you had no perspective at all.

FACTS AND MEMORIES
FROM YOUR ADOLESCENCE

Here is where you recall adolescence, your teen years, which began with puberty and ended, most likely, in your early twenties. Most of all, capture the memories of that time when *you* began to emerge. That's the great event of this stage: you started to become *you,* sometimes kicking and screaming along the way. You began to decide who *you* were and what *you* believed and what *you* wanted from life. You began to emerge from your childhood family and surroundings. You began to review what you would jettison and what you would take forward from your parents and your life as a child. Perhaps *you* didn't fully emerge until later—and in one sense everyone spends the rest of their lives emerging—but the process began here. Find those moments, those memories, when you began to become *you*.

As you work through the following life segments, a reminder: in each segment, record the facts as directed. Then read and ponder the many questions in the memory section of the segment. See what memories the questions bring to mind. You need not "answer" those memory questions, of course. Their only job is to jog your memory. If a question brings nothing to mind, just go on.

We hope you enjoy bringing your adolescence back to life.

You as an Adolescent

Adolescence is all about developing your own identity and becoming you. So who was the you *at this time in your life?*

FACTS ABOUT YOU AS AN ADOLESCENT

❦ Note your age when your body changes began and you entered adolescence.

❦ Without deep thought or careful recollection, simply list the highlights of your adolescent years—the significant moments, memorable events, or anything that stands out as a key piece of that stage in your life.

❦ Note when adolescence began to end for you. Was it when you entered the service or went away to college or moved out on your own? Note your age then and describe yourself briefly at that time.

MEMORIES OF YOU AS AN ADOLESCENT

Were there moments that marked your entrance into puberty? What was your experience of the rapid growth your body went through at this time? Were you clumsy for a time? Were you ahead of or behind your friends? Did you ever talk to each other about what was happening? Did you ever talk to your parents about these changes?

In my grandmother's house in Brooklyn, in the bedroom in which I slept, there was a painted dresser. One drawer of the dresser held pale blue sanitary napkins, year after year.

These came in handy one year. Visiting, I got my first period—far from my mother, who had remained in Detroit to study for college exams.

I confided in my grandmother. She smacked my face.

I looked to her for a reason. I saw an ironic, apologetic little smile, heard a caught breath that might have been a decimal place's worth of secret amusement or inner regret.

She said: "Now you'll always have rosy cheeks," then went looking for a contraption, elastic and clips.

I knew this slap came out of the past, and she was just doing her duty. I sensed that her investment was less than complete. The smack was not painful, yet burned on my cheek like guilt, like innocence—something she felt was fitting, and I knew was unjust.

Later I stumbled on written words parsing that shtetl *gesture. Thus mother warned daughter, time out of mind, not to compete for the father's attentions; thus mother taught daughter the shame of Eve. . . .*

—ELIZABETH EHRLICH, *Miriam's Kitchen*

What did you see when you looked in the mirror? Who was that person? Did you like him or her? Did you look in the mirror often? What did you want to see there? What were the fads and fashions when you were a teen? Did you follow those trends?

I was entering the period when social acceptance becomes more important to an adolescent girl than almost anything else. Shortly after that is when I had my beautiful braids cut off. Nobody else at school wore braids and they made me feel nerdy. I don't remember who cut them, Mother or a professional, but whoever did it wasn't doing me any favors. The way it was cut, my hair hung to just below my ears as straight and stubborn as a mule's tail, no style, no shape, and my cowlick made my bangs stand up as if they'd been electrocuted. Hair matters just about more than anything when you're that age. . . . I was in every sense just "plain Jane," the cutup—with bad hair.

—JANE FONDA, *My Life So Far*

What did you think others saw when they looked at you? Were there any moments when you felt especially self-conscious about yourself or your looks in particular? What part of your body caused you the most concern? What did you think others first noticed about you? Did you wish you could change your body in some way? Did you try, through dieting or weight training or fashion or some other way?

How did others actually experience *you? What was your personality, how did you act, as a teenager?* How might someone else have described you as a person, not just the way you looked (though that could certainly be part of you). Were you self-conscious or supremely confident, outgoing, friendly, cheerful, quiet, shy, serious? Were you a rebel? Were you different than you had been as a child? Did you wish you could change your personality? Did you try? Was what others saw or experienced of you the real you? Or did you think there was somebody else entirely different inside you who couldn't come out for some reason?

When and where did you feel most like yourself, most happy and content? Some social setting? By yourself? With certain other people? Doing some activity?

Did you believe your life was destined to unfold in a certain way? For example, did you believe you would do something special and unique? Something great and momentous? Or did you feel hopeless about your future? Where did these beliefs come from? Did they make you happy or sad?

What special talents did you think you had? What were your strengths overall? What were your weaknesses? Would others who knew you then have agreed with your self-assessment? Did you ever do anything to distinguish yourself from others, to stand out as *you*?

During the summer between eleventh and twelfth grades, Joe and I and our friend Bob wrote a musical comedy—book, words, and music. The show, of course, had extremely large parts for all three of us. . . .

When school started up again, we asked Father McMahon to read our script, and he didn't flinch; he offered to produce the play on the school stage. . . .

The musical was called Love's the Ticket! *and when we began rehearsals, I suddenly realized I had a solution to the bully problem. It seemed that everybody wanted to be in it: basketball players, football players, even the guys who had wanted to beat me up. Pretty soon, the bullies were up on the stage. And I had them dancing in a chorus line.*

— ALAN ALDA, *Never Have Your Dog Stuffed*

What did you daydream or fantasize about? What were you doing in your fantasies? Who else was there? Did you daydream a lot or only a little?

What did you fear most as an adolescent? Were there instances when this fear changed your life and what you did? Would anything have been different without this fear?

Did you have any goals as a teenager? To go to a certain college? To get a particular job after school? To get a certain car? To be a cheerleader? Were you more focused as an adolescent on achieving success, whatever that meant to you, or avoiding failure?

What was your dream for yourself—the kind of life you would live, the kind of person you would be when you grew up? This is not only a career aspiration—what you would do for work—but also the kind of person you would be, the purpose you would serve, the achievements you might make. Was there someone you hoped to be like? Where did your dream come from? What did you do to pursue it? Did you ever tell anyone about it?

Were you ever treated badly or unfairly, or abused? What effect did that have on you? Were you ever a victim of crime?

Were you ever the object of prejudice or discrimination? What did you do and what came of the incident, if anything?

What was the most trouble you got into as an adolescent? Was it your fault? An accident? Or something you deliberately did? Did you pull any pranks? Was there anything you did that you still wish you could go back and undo?

Did you have a special sanctuary, a haven where you could go and be safe? Think of some times when you went there. What would you do there?

Recall your most intense moments:
- When did you *laugh* or *giggle* uncontrollably?
- Did you ever get *hysterical* about something?
- Did you *embarrass* easily? What was your most embarrassing moment (or moments)?

When I was 17 I went to meet my college boyfriend's parents. We met them for lunch at a local pub. As we ate, the bartender kept peering over his newspaper at me. I knew I was under age, but I wasn't doing anything wrong—just sitting at this booth with my boyfriend and his parents, trying to make a good impression.

A few minutes later the bartender walked up to us and said to me, "I know where I've seen you before. You're one of them there dancers at Gages (a topless bar in my hometown 30 miles away). They had a ruckus there last week. What do you do when that happens?" He stared at me as I stammered, "NO! I've never been to Gages. I don't know what you're talking about." My face went as red as the crimson logo on my sweatshirt. I kept shaking my head, wishing I could crawl under the table. After a moment, with a wink and a smirk, he returned to the bar and didn't come near us again.

Todd's parents only chuckled, thank goodness, and then turned the conversation back to my plans for college in the fall. They never mentioned the incident again. Nor did I.

—SUSAN HUTER, personal story

- What caused you to feel *deeply hurt*?
- When did you feel a strong sense of *love* and *connectedness*?
- Did you ever *lose your temper*? What caused that and what happened?
- When were you the *happiest* in this period?
- Did something *frighten* you uncontrollably?
- What was your *saddest* moment?
- What *disappointed* you the most as an adolescent?
- Did you ever feel an intense sense of *loss* or *grief*?
- Was there anything you *wanted* more than anything else in the world?
- Did you ever *regret* anything you did? What happened and did you act on your regret?
- Were there moments when you felt *proud,* of yourself or someone else?
- What was the most *physical pain* you experienced?
- Did anything make you feel a deep sense of *pleasure*?
- Did anything happen that made you feel *ashamed*?
- Were there any times of *wild abandon* and *joy*?
- What was the most *beautiful sight* you saw as a teenager?
- Did you ever feel *jealous* or *envious*?

When we were girls, my little sister Anne had light shiny hair, fine skin, and guileless eyes. She was a girl whose walk at twelve made men stop to watch her pass, a woman at thirteen who made grown men murderous and teenage boys sweaty with hunger. My mother watched her with the fear of a woman who had been a beautiful girl. I watched her with painful jealousy. Why was she so pretty when I was so plain? When strangers in the grocery store smiled at her and complimented Mama on "that lovely child," I glared and turned away. I wanted to be what my little sister was. I wanted all the things that appeared to be possible for her.

— DOROTHY ALLISON, *Two or Three Things*
I Know for Sure

- What *surprised* you most as an adolescent? Did anything *shock* or *amaze* you? Were you ever *awestruck*?
- Do you have any intense memories around your senses—*sight, sound, smell, taste,* and *touch*?

What was the dumbest, most impulsive thing you did as an adolescent? Do you wish you hadn't done it? What consequences did it have? Did the world find out about it, or did it remain a secret?

Were there any "firsts" that were important to you? First date. First kiss. First love. First car. First gown. First suit or sport jacket or tie. First failure. First sign of physical changes.

Were you ever under high pressure? Recall moments when you felt high stress? What caused it? How did you deal with the pressure?

Did you ever tell a lie? What, why, and what happened?

Did you ever suffer from telling the truth? Did you get in trouble? Did you get someone else in trouble? Did people get mad? What came of the incident?

What rites of passage or other special events occurred in adolescence? Were there parties or birthdays or events, like graduation or confirmation, that you particularly remember? Did you learn to drive? Who taught you? Did you own a car? These could be real rites of passage or just moments that stick in your memory of milestones and changes and turning points.

What health problems or illnesses did you face in adolescence? What effect did they have on your life?

Did you have any physical limitations? Were they temporary or permanent? Did they affect what you were able to do? Did they influence your thoughts and perceptions of yourself?

Were you ever in an accident? What memories do you have of what happened and the aftermath?

Were your parents divorced or always at odds? What effect did this have on you and on your life at this time? Did you ever get caught between them, expected to take sides? What did that do to you?

Were you a stepchild or adopted? How did that special status affect you and your life in general and how you thought about yourself as a teenager? Did it trouble you? Did you feel you were different? Was that good or bad?

When and how did you learn the facts of life? If you hadn't learned the "facts" before, how did you learn them now? Did you and your friends talk about such things? What actual experiences did you have at this time of the facts of life?

Did you encounter life and death? How did you react? Did it involve someone you knew? Someone close to you? How did it affect you?

> *Eventually, we sat down to dinner and choked over our food. . . . The meal seemed surreal. The food on the plate seemed unconnected to the unreal world without my father in it in which I now lived. I was haunted by the consciousness of his body lying close by in the bedroom, which my mother had sternly forbidden me to enter. After we went sleeplessly to bed, we heard a sound never heard before, the sound of my mother weeping hopelessly and inconsolably. It was a terrible and unforgettable sound. To moderate the heat we slept on a screened veranda exposed to any southern breeze which might stir. My brother Barry's bed was next to mine. After listening to this terrible new sound, we both agreed that we wished we were older so that we could go to work and take care of her. We tossed until the sun rose and crept out of bed too shocked to do more than converse in whispers.*
>
> —JILL KER CONWAY, *The Road from Coorain*

Family

For most of us, adolescent life, especially early adolescence, still centered around home and family. But family life was also the key point of comparison as we began to work out our own identities.

If you were adopted, consider the questions and suggestions in regard to your adopted parents and family. Consider them as well for your biological parents if you knew them at this time.

FACTS ABOUT YOUR FAMILY

❧ Note the people who lived in your family household.

❧ Describe your mother during your adolescence: how old was she at this time in your life? What did she do? What life events or milestones (health, work, etc.) occurred in her life at this time?

❧ Describe your father during your adolescence: how old was he? What did he do? What life events or milestones occurred in his life?

❧ Describe your brothers and sisters. How old were they? Where were they (if not in your home), and what life events occurred in each of their lives at this time?

❧ Identify any other family members who lived with you. How old were they? What did they do? Why and when did they live with you? Did anything happen to them during this period in your life?

❧ Name any members of your extended family—aunts, uncles, cousins—who were part of your life in adolescence. Note any milestones that occurred in their lives.

MEMORIES OF YOUR FAMILY

Think of your mother when you were an adolescent:

- *What two or three words would you use to describe her in this period?* What memories do those words evoke? Did she ever make you proud? Did she ever embarrass you? How did she act around your friends? How had she changed from when you were a child? How was her health? Was she noticeably aging? What key moments or incidents or events do you remember from this period?

- *How did you and she get along?* Were you close? Did you ever argue or disagree about anything? Did you ever disagree with her but felt unable to say anything? What did you talk about? Recall any times when you and she did something together? What did she hope for you? Did she ever get involved in your school? What did you learn from her, from what she said or did? Could, did, you confide in her? What secrets did you keep from her?

- *How did she treat you?* What rules did she impose on you at this time? Did you argue or did you simply obey or disobey? Did she ever treat you unfairly? Did she ever help you when you felt lost or in trouble? Did she still see you as a child, or as an emerging adult? What did she want and expect of you? Did she treat you and your brothers and sisters the same?

- *What key events happened in her life at this time and how did she react to them?* Did she ever need help, from you or anyone else? How did she get along with her own family? Was she ever sick? Recall the moments or events when she was happiest, saddest, angriest? Did she ever surprise you?

The next day my mother put vodka in our lunch-box Thermoses.

In the following week, she fed Jell-O to the cats.

She put thumbtacks in my father's shoes.

She bought a used pink Cadillac because the Ford was in the shop. She drove it to the shopping center and then left it there.

She served shoelaces for dinner and said it was spaghetti. When Johnny and I told her it was not spaghetti, it was shoelaces, she said leather is a protein.

She gave my brother's cat, Nemo, away to a girl who lived down the street.

She got in the car and ran down all the neighbors' mailboxes.

She threw eggs at Mrs. Westhouser's front porch because she said she didn't under-stand why she wore her mink to the PTA meetings.

She wrote letters to the Coca-Cola Company, claiming their product made her daughter break out in red spots in the shape of Rhode Island.

She showed up at the PTA meeting wearing nothing but a pair of black lace panties and matching bra, underneath her blue raincoat.

She bit my father in the arm and left two crescent-moon marks.

She took me to the Ford Modeling Agency and demanded they put me on the cover of Glamour *magazine immediately.*

She crashed the Ford into a police car.

My father put my mother into Fairfield Hills Mental Hospital.

— JAMIE CALLAN, "Just Another Movie Star"

- *How did she spend her time?* What do you remember of her work, of what she did around the house, of her hobbies or special interests, of her religious beliefs and practices? What did she love most—music, cooking, literature and the arts, her work, something else? Did she care about politics?

- *How were you and your mother alike, and how were you different, at this time in your life?* What effects did these similarities and differences have in your life?

Think of your father when you were an adolescent:

- *What was his role in your life?* How much contact did you have? Did you talk to him as a child still, or had you become a young grown-up? Did you and your father ever compete—when and in what way? Did he respect you and what you were doing or wanted to do? Did you and he ever discuss religion, politics, sex, authority? What did he expect of you, at home day to day, and in life generally? Was he actively involved and interested in what you were doing? Did your relationship change—get closer or more distant—as you got older? Think of two moments or two events, early and late in your adolescence, which captured the way your relationship with your dad changed. What did you do that you kept secret from your father? What did you learn from him?

- *Did you ever do anything to get his attention?* How *did* you get his attention? By pleasing him? By displeasing him? By agreeing or disagreeing with him? Did you ever need his help or understanding?

- *What was your opinion of your father at this time?* What did he do to merit that opinion? Were there any moments when you began to understand him better? Did something happen to give you greater insight into him? Did he ever surprise you with what he did or didn't do? Did he ever make you proud? Did he ever embarrass you?

- *What rules did your father impose on you?* About going out, about what you could or couldn't do, about chores around the home, about anything? Did you agree with these rules and expectations? Did you argue about them? Did you obey them?

- *How did your father spend his time around the home?* What did he most enjoy doing? Most hate doing? Was he a handyman? What were his hobbies? What talents (e.g., musical) did he possess and use at this time?

- *What was his life like in this period?* How was his work going? Did he enjoy it? How did you know? What key events occurred in his life, of any kind, at this time? Was he ever sick? Was he lucky or unlucky? Did he ever need help? Did you ever need his help or understanding? How did he get along with his family?

- *How were you and your father alike, and how were you different, at this time in your life?* What effects did these similarities and differences have in your life?

Think about your parents' relationship during this time. Did they love each other? Did they argue all the time? Did they show affection and warmth? Did they compete? Recall any moments that revealed how your parents got along.

I remember Dad telling the story of their first kiss. It was a winter night and snow was falling softly. Trees and houses and sidewalks glimmered with a light dusting of snow. Mom and Dad had gone to the movies and Dad was walking her home, and when he reached her house he gathered the courage to embrace her and kiss her good night. He then turned and walked back to the train station. As he approached the station, still feeling the warm glow of that first kiss, he turned back toward her house and noticed something strange—there was not a single footstep in the snow. His feet never touched the ground.

— CAROL FRANCO, personal story

Did they split up during your adolescence? Recall the steps leading to the split, the separation itself, and the aftermath. How did it affect you and your siblings? Was it a relief when they split up? Did you end up living with your mother or father? What was that life like?

Did you live in a single-parent household? Recall that life. How often did you see your other parent? Did you spend time with both? Were there hardships, economic or otherwise?

Recall each of your brothers and sisters when you were an adolescent. What moments captured your relationship, or some part of it, with each? Recall times when you were close. Recall times you fought. What did you fight about? Did you tease each other? What events in your adolescence shaped their lives and how were you involved? Were you jealous of any of them, or they of you? Did you emulate them, if they were older, or did you try to be different? Did they ignore you, help you, look up to you? What key events occurred in their lives, of any kind, at this time? If you were adopted or a stepchild, did that make any difference in your life?

Recall any other household members. What moments or events come to mind around these people that touched you or were important to you?

Remember your grandparents. If your grandparents were part of your life as an adolescent, recall events or moments involving them. What happened in their lives at this time that was important to you?

What was the atmosphere like in your family? Were you eager to grow up and leave or did you dread leaving? Were there family conflicts? Undiscussable topics? What happened at the family dinner table? Who talked, about what? Recall any times at dinner that you loved or hated. Did you play games as a family? Were there any family superstitions?

Were there any family secrets? What was never discussed outside the family, or in the family? How did you find out about family secrets? Did you have any yourself?

Was music important in your home? People singing or playing an instrument? Was there a piano in the house? Was music played often on the radio or phonograph? What kind? Recall any times you as a family went to any musical events or performances? Did your parents have any musical hopes or expectations for you?

My house as I grew up was full of music. Mom was a piano teacher. Dad played, too, and sang in a nice tenor voice. His playing often drove Mom crazy. He only played chords with his left hand—boom-CHICK-boom-CHICK-boom-CHICK, no matter the song. She would stand in the kitchen sighing or looking to heaven or grinding her teeth as he banged that old upright in the living room fifteen feet away. He thought he was pretty good and he knew he had a good voice, and so he usually let it rip.

Piano playing was Dad's chief way to relax. He was superintendent of schools in the small but rapidly growing California town where we lived and he spent all his time in the fifties building new school buildings. I didn't realize it then, but I think his job was fairly stressful. He usually came home every evening and hammered out a few tunes to let off steam before supper. On the nights he had school board meetings he'd come home late, around 10:30 or 11:00, and take it out on the upright. We in bed in our tiny, four-room house got the full repertoire on full volume. MAMMY'S LITTLE CHILLIN, SICK IN BED, TWO WITH THE FEVER AND ONE 'MOS DEAD! . . . BARNEY GOOGLE, WITH THE GOO-GOO-GOOGLEY EYES! . . . CAMP TOWN RACES SING THAT SONG, DOO-DAH, DOO-DAH, CAMP TOWN RACES ALL NIGHT LONG, OH DOO-DAH DAY! I don't think it ever occurred to him not to play and sing any time of day or night, and I don't remember it ever occurred to us to question or protest his doing it.

—KENT LINEBACK, personal story

What memories do you have of food, meals, cooking, and eating in your family? Were there any special meals? What dishes did you love and always remember? Favorite snacks? What was the kitchen like in your home? Was it a special place?

What chores or work were you expected to do in your family? What would happen if you didn't do your chores? Did you get an allowance for doing work around the house?

Recall the holidays in your family. Were these major occasions in your family? Did you return home for such times after you'd left for college or the military or moved out? Were these times different from the same occasions when you were still living at home? Did your family go away on holidays together? Recall any moments or events from such times.

What was the economic and social standing of your family in the community? Did your folks belong to any social, civic, or other groups? Recall any public moments with or involving your family that made you proud, or embarrassed. Did you attend any meetings or functions with family members? Did your folks expect you to join or participate in the same groups?

Other family milestones. Recall any other milestones and life events that happened to key members of your immediate family during your adolescence, such things as illnesses or accidents, births or deaths, divorce, or changes at work. What memories come to mind? Were you present when someone died? How did you and your family express feelings of loss? Did the loss change anything in your family? Did any of these milestones touch your life directly?

When my father was dying in the hospital, there was a desperate last decision to try a blood transfusion. How much was known about compatibility of blood types then, or about the procedure itself, I'm unable to say. All I know is that there was no question in my mother's mind as to who the donor was to be.

I was present when it was done; my two brothers were in school. Both my parents were lying on cots, my father had been brought in on one and my mother lay on the other. Then a tube was simply run from her arm to his.

My father, I believe, was unconscious. My mother was looking at him. I could see her fervent face: there was no doubt as to what she was thinking. This time, she would save his life, as he'd saved hers so long ago, when she was dying of septicemia. What he'd done for her in giving her the champagne, she would be able to do for him now in giving him her own blood.

All at once his face turned dusky red all over. The doctor made a disparaging sound with his lips, the kind a woman knitting makes when she drops a stitch. What the doctor meant by it was that my father had died.

My mother never recovered emotionally. Though she lived for over thirty years more, and suffered other bitter losses, she never stopped blaming herself. She saw this as her failure to save his life.

—EUDORA WELTY, *One Writer's Beginnings*

Recall when you left home. Did you go off to college, or join the military, or move into another residence? Was there a moment of leave-taking? Who was there? What did people say and how did they act? How did you feel about it? Were you homesick? Did your feelings surprise you? What was it like to return home for the first time after leaving? Did home and family feel different? When did you first begin to think of someplace else as your "home"?

Home

For most of your adolescence, your home probably remained the center of your life. But slowly you began cutting the ties and forging an independent life for yourself. If you still lived in the same home as you did in your childhood, simply describe here the ways it was different in your teen years.

FACTS ABOUT YOUR ADOLESCENT HOME

❦ For each place you lived, note the address or location, town or city, and state (and country, if not in the United States).

❦ Describe briefly the physical home or building, the neighborhood, and the town or city—all as they were when you lived there in adolescence.

❧ For each place you lived, note the names of any neighbors you remember, with a brief description of each.

MEMORIES OF YOUR ADOLESCENT HOME

Remember your house or home as it was in your adolescence. Put yourself back into this space. Where did you sleep and keep your things? Walk through the rooms. Imagine coming home from school. Think of weekends or holidays in that place. Room by room, who was there, what was happening?

Remember your yard and the area surrounding your home. What happened there? Did you play there? Did you have a garden? What other people and incidents come to mind?

Put yourself back in the neighborhood during your adolescence. Look at the homes and buildings. Who was there? Let the scenes bring to mind people and incidents. What was the neighborhood like at night? How about early morning, before most people were up?

There was not much grass where I grew up in Brooklyn. We lived in one of three apartment buildings that stood shoulder to shoulder in quiet solidarity against a neighborhood jammed with small houses. Neighbors tended tiny plots of flowers in front of narrow red brick homes. And although East Twelfth Street was overhung with trees whose roots pried up the concrete squares of sidewalk, I reached college with an excellent grasp of photosynthesis but could not tell trees apart. They were just trees. In freshman year, this gap convulsed my roommate. Hiking together that first autumn, she pointed out a blaze of color roaring in the unnatural-to-my-city-girl-ears silence of gray Long Island woods: a magnificent red maple. I stared, amazed. "Trees have names?" *I asked. For all I know, she's dining out on that story to this day.*

— HILLARY GAMEROW, "How I Learned to Cook"

Imagine yourself back in the town or city of your adolescence. You probably roamed more widely through your hometown than you did as a child. Where did you go? What was there? Who would you see? What places did you avoid? Were there places you were still not allowed? Did you go anyplace you weren't supposed to go? What was it like at night, or in the early morning? What happened then? What places and events did you like most? Least?

Did you move as a teenager? Did you want to move? How was your new home different? How did you feel about leaving friends? Was it difficult entering a new school?

Religion or Spirituality

If religion played a role in your adolescence, was it a larger or smaller role than in childhood? Was this an area in which you began to stake out your own identity?

FACTS ABOUT YOUR RELIGIOUS OR SPIRITUAL BELIEFS

❧ Describe briefly the beliefs you held as an adolescent and note whether they came from your family and childhood, or were your own (they could be both, of course).

❧ Describe briefly the religious practices you followed in adolescence—that is, activities associated with your beliefs, like attending services, praying, doing penance, taking on certain roles and responsibilities.

❧ Describe briefly any religious or spiritual experiences you had at this time in your life.

MEMORIES OF YOUR RELIGIOUS OR SPIRITUAL BELIEFS

Recall your beliefs as an adolescent. Recall any moments or events that touched on your beliefs. Did your beliefs change—grow, diminish, change entirely—in adolescence? How and why did that change occur? Did you ever experience doubt?

Mass, Communion, fish on Fridays, the Legion of Decency, were all part of our life. The Holy Days were honored. Belief without question: observation without piety. Once during Lent—it must have been after a scalding sermon condemning our wanton modern pleasures, so few in the thirties (radio programs, a Saturday matinee, an evening of cards)—we knelt together in the living room and attempted the family rosary. My father, playing up his role, intoning the Aves as he'd learned them in the seminary, mother backing him in a whisper, George and me mumbling after. By the time we got up from the floor, stiff with embarrassment, we all knew that charade would never be repeated. But we set out the crèche with solemnity at Christmas and the week before Easter the palms were dutifully carried home from church and would round the finial of the dresser mirror to gather dust.

— MAUREEN HOWARD, *Facts of Life*

Recall each of the practices you identified. What moments or events or other people come to mind from those practices? Did those practices change as you moved through adolescence? Did you continue or undertake any religious training? Recall any moments or events or people around any religious roles you played, such as teaching religion classes, or religious counseling.

Recall ways your beliefs, practices, and daily life were connected. Recall moments when religion and social life intersected. Did you attend social events at your church? Did your beliefs ever influence an important decision or choice you made? Did you do something or not in your daily life—for example, avoid dancing or movies or necking—because of your beliefs? Did your beliefs affect your friendships and other social relationships?

Recall any religious or spiritual experience you had as an adolescent. What brought it on and what happened afterward as a result of it?

What people from the religious side of your life stand out in your memory? Who and what influence did they have on you? Did your experience with them change your religious beliefs, positively or negatively?

How tolerant were you of people with different beliefs? Adolescence can be a time when the world is seen only in black and white and no shades of gray. Was that the case with you? Was your way, your beliefs, right, and opposing views wrong? If so, what events and moments come to mind around that point of view?

High School

High school was most likely an essential part of your adolescence. It was where you took your first steps toward independence and autonomy, a place you could start being you, without having to give up the safe harbor of home and family.

FACTS ABOUT HIGH SCHOOL

❦ List each high school that you attended, its location, and the dates and grades that you were there.

❦ Note how you did in school.

❦ Name your favorite subject. Your least favorite subject.

❦ Name and briefly describe your favorite teachers. Least favorite teachers.

❦ Name your high school friends and memorable classmates.

❦ Name and briefly describe each of the school clubs or groups you belonged to.

❦ Note the sports you played in high school and briefly how you and your teams did.

❦ Name the school social group or clique you were part of, either by choice or reputation.

MEMORIES OF HIGH SCHOOL

Imagine yourself back at each high school you attended. Walk through the front door. Walk down the hallway. Go to your locker. Imagine eating lunch in the cafeteria. Remember the first day of school. The last day. What happened at recess or lunch hour? What people were in those places?

Recall the classes you took and the teachers you had. Imagine yourself back in each of your favorite classes, or with favorite teachers. What did you learn there, or from that teacher? Who sat beside you? Do you remember any specific classes when something funny or sad or unexpected happened? Any memorable tests or projects (papers, whatever)? What classes and teachers did you like least?

Were there any Aha! *moments of learning and revelation in this school?* Were there any moments when you learned something that shifted your view of the world, that made you understand something that you didn't understand at all, that was a revelation, an epiphany?

Recall each of the high school clubs or organizations you belonged to. What role did you play? What individuals—teachers, classmates, anyone—come to mind as you think of each organization?

Remember your high school friends and memorable classmates. Who were your best friends? What memories do you have of each—things you did together or things that happened to you? Recall other classmates who stand out in your memory.

Think of the sports you played in high school. Recall any moments in games or practices that stand out in your memory. Put yourself back in the gym or playing field where you practiced and played. Recall each of your coaches. Were any important to you? Did you achieve any renown for your performance and ability? Did any players particularly impress you?

> *Our team—the Waukegan Township High School Bulldogs Junior Varsity football team of 1952—was so bad that the coach, Ted Damos, had me (of all people!) playing the entire game! I was the center on the offensive team. I snapped the ball for every play of that delightful season. Then when we lost the ball after a fumble, an intercepted pass, a blocked punt, or any other creative way we could come up with to turn the ball over to the other team, coach Damos was so desperate that he had me playing linebacker on the defense! The whole game! I was on the field for every play of every game during that great season and certainly deserve much of the credit for the final results of the games. We did not win a single game. Not only did we not win a single game, we did not score a single point during the entire season. Our best game—our greatest success that fantastic season—was a zero/zero tie.*
>
> —STEPHEN K. BLUMBERG, *A Satisfying Life*

Think about your social life in high school. Recall others in your social group. Where did you hang out? Whom did you dislike? What did you do for fun? How did your social group change as you progressed from freshman to senior years? When did you start to drive? Did that change your social life? Did you have access to a car?

Recall any jobs you held in high school. Review each of your full- or part-time jobs. Recall the place and the work you did and the people you worked with. Who was your boss? What did the organization or group or company you worked for do? What happened in your work—anything funny or memorable or sad?

Think about each of your summer vacations in high school. Recall the place where you spent it and the people you spent it with. If you were there with your family, what happened with and to other family members?

If you went to college, recall the college application process while you were in high school. Was there a specific college you wanted to attend? Did you go there? Recall all the parts of applying—filling out the applications, writing essays, getting recommendations, interviewing, visiting campuses. What highlights, or low moments, come to mind from all that?

College or Other Education

College or other post–high school education, along with the military, could be a stepping-stone out of adolescence and into young adulthood, a time when you began the transition away from home toward a life and world of your own.

FACTS ABOUT COLLEGE OR SCHOOL

❧ Name the colleges or schools you attended—for each, the school name, location, dates attended, what you studied, when you graduated, and with what degree or certificate.

❧ Note how you did in college or school academically. Did you receive any academic awards or distinctions (graduation with honors, Phi Beta Kappa, etc.)?

❧ Note any other recognition or distinctions you received.

❧ Identify your favorite subject. Your least-liked subject.

❧ Identify your favorite professors. Least favorite professors.

❧ Name your friends in school or college.

❧ Note what school clubs or groups you belonged to. Note what each did, when you belonged, and your role in each.

❧ Note what sports you played, when you played, how you did, and how your team did.

MEMORIES OF COLLEGE OR SCHOOL

Imagine yourself back at each school. Walk around the campus. Go through the buildings. Remember the classrooms. Where did you live—in a dorm, in private housing, in a sorority or fraternity? What memories does the place evoke? What happened at various places on campus, or in the surrounding town? What were the highlights of your time there?

Remember the classes you took, the subjects you studied. Think about each of your years in school. Freshman, sophomore, and so on. What classes did you take? Who were the professors? Do any stand out in your memory? Did you ever struggle in a class, or in any other way in school? Can you remember any of the exams you took? Do you remember laboring to complete a paper or project?

Recall each of your friends in school. What memories come to mind around each? Bring to mind any other people connected with the school who were important in your life. Think of other classmates, other than friends, who stood out?

Think of the people or groups you hung out with or spent most of your time with in school. Did those social groups change over your four years? What did you do together? Who else was in these groups? How did other students view you and your group? Were there rivalries? Did you belong to a fraternity or sorority? If so, what events do you remember from that—initiations, etc.? What parties or dances or big weekends do you recall? Where did you usually hang out? Was your social life tied up mostly in the group or groups you belonged to, or did you strike out on your own? Did you stay on campus or get away?

Recall each school club that you belonged to. What did the club do and what was your role in it? Where did you meet? Were there any people you especially remember? If you got together with any other club members now, what memories would you talk about?

Think of each of the sports you played in school. Recall any memorable times in practices. Were there any times you excelled (or not)? Were there moments of triumph? Of bitter defeat? Of embarrassment?

How did your relationship with your family change while you were in school? Did you go home for holidays? Did you still live at home during or after college? What moments do you recall from those continuing contacts with your family? Did day-to-day life with them become more difficult, or easier?

How did you spend your summer vacations? Did you go home? Did you travel? Did you work? Did you have to work?

How would you characterize your time in college or school overall? Was it a good, productive time for you? Were you mature enough to get the most out of college? Think about yourself toward the end of high school, and then think about yourself toward the end of college or school. How were you different—in appearance, in behavior, in attitude, in knowledge, in any other way? What had changed you? What had you outgrown? What had you grown into?

Military

Most who spend time in the military do so in late adolescence. Like college, the military could be a time of transition from youth to young adulthood. If you served in one of the services, recall that experience here.

FACTS ABOUT YOUR MILITARY SERVICE

- Name the branch (Army, Navy, Air Force, etc.) you were in, when you served and where you were stationed, the training you received and work you did, and the rank you attained.

- Describe any combat experience. Note when you fought, where, how long, and any facts you want to record.

- Name the key people—officers, friends, subordinates—who stood out during your time in the service.

❦ List any decorations, awards, or other forms of recognition you received, including what each was for and when you received each.

❦ Note any other facts of your service experience: travel, training, special events, injuries, and so on.

MEMORIES OF YOUR MILITARY SERVICE

Think back over the various places you spent time in your military career. Where were you inducted? Where did you undergo basic training? Advanced or other training? Recall the various locations where you were posted. For each place, put yourself back there in your mind's eye and let the various memories associated with each place rise to the surface.

Recall the specific work you did. What moments or situations come to mind around this work—what was it, where did you do it, what problems did you face, did anything memorable happen? Did you like the work? Did you do it well? Were you ever recognized or reprimanded?

Recall each of the individuals you identified. Who helped you? Whom did you help? Did anything happen to any of these people? Did you stay in touch?

Think about your spouse and children while you were in the military. If you were married, and had children, recall what it was like to spend long periods of time away from them. How did you communicate? Letters? Phone calls? Was their support essential while you were separated? How did you observe special celebrations—birthdays, holidays? Were they able to live nearby? Did the service take a toll on your marriage? Recall times when you were on leave and together.

Were you married to someone in the service? If you lived with him or her, recall that life: where you lived (on base or off), the other spouses, family life around the military, what it was like for your children, and so on.

Think of your birth family while you were in the service. How did your parents and other family members react to your service and your absence? Did you stay in touch? Did you miss them? Recall any times you visited your parents' home while in the military.

Did you join the Army (or Navy or other military branch) and "see the world"? Recall any foreign sights you saw. Did you spend any time in interesting or exotic places?

If you want, recall your experiences in combat. Are there any memories that you want to recall and record? Perhaps there were acts of bravery performed by you or others—what you or they did and what happened. Were you ever injured? What would you want to relate of your experiences? Did you have any close calls? Did you lose any comrades?

After mass Sergeant Benet and I drove to the village market to buy some fresh bread and vegetables. While he did the shopping I leaned back in the passenger seat and closed my eyes. My mood was still churchy, sentimental, liquid. I hadn't slept much the night before, and now, surrounded by friendly indecipherable voices and warmed by the sun, I began to nod off. Then I became aware that the voices had stopped. The silence disturbed me. I sat up and looked around. The crowd had drawn back in a wide circle. They were staring at me. A woman yammered something I couldn't follow and pointed under the jeep. I bent down for a look. There, lying directly below my seat, was a hand grenade. The pin had been pulled. I straightened up and sat there for a while, barely breathing. Then I got out of the jeep and walked over to where everyone else was standing. We were still within the grenade's killing range, especially if it set off the gas tank, but I didn't think of that any more than the others had. I didn't have a thought in my head. We just stood there like a bunch of fools.

Sergeant Benet appeared at the edge of the crowd. "What's going on?" he said.

"There a grenade under the jeep."

He turned and looked. "Oh, man," he said. He dropped the groceries and started pushing people back, his arms outstretched like a riot cop's. . . .

Once the area was cleared Sergeant Benet told a couple of skittish villagers to stand watch until we could send someone to take care of the grenade; then we started walking

back to the battalion. Along the way I found my legs acting funny. My knees wouldn't lock;
I had to lean against a wall. Sergeant Benet put his hand on my arm to steady me. Then
something went slack in my belly and I felt a stream of shit pouring hotly out of me, down
my legs, even into my boots. I put my head against the wall and wept for very shame. . . .

The grenade never did go off on its own. Our ordnance disposal boys covered it with
sandbags and triggered it with a dose of plastique. It was an American grenade, not
some local mad bomber device. The odds of it failing like that were cruelly small—just
about nonexistent, in fact.

That was my first close call.

—TOBIAS WOLFF, *In Pharaoh's Army*

Recall your return to civilian life. Remember the day and place of your separation
from the service and your first weeks and months as a civilian. Were there any
problems of adjustment? Did others, who did not serve, understand what you had
gone through and were experiencing?

Did your career start here? Recall any work, or part of work, you did that was connected with the career you ultimately chose. What happened in that work and
what did it tell you about the career you were considering? When did you discover
what your life's work would be?

Romantic Relationships

What is adolescence without romance? This was the time you probably began
exploring—maybe more in your mind than in reality—the wonderful world of love
and passion and relationships.

FACTS ABOUT ROMANTIC RELATIONSHIPS

❧ Name and describe briefly each boyfriend or girlfriend you had in high school.

❧ Name and describe briefly each girlfriend or boyfriend you had in later adolescence or in college, or while you were in the service.

MEMORIES OF ROMANTIC RELATIONSHIPS

Recall your romantic "firsts." First date. First hand-holding. First kiss. First prom. First making out or necking. Recall, in particular, your first love. This was probably the person you first told, "I love you." Recall that occasion. Were you head over heels in love? How did it affect you? Did you stay in love?

One by one, think back about each high school boy- or girlfriend. Where did you meet? What did you do together? Where did you go on dates? What did you do? What did you particularly like and dislike about him or her? How serious were you? Did you go steady? Did you think or talk of marriage? Recall any tender moments, like a first kiss or your first date, or exchanging rings. Remember, too, the fights and disagreements. Did you ever "cheat" on each other? Recall the circumstances of breaking up (assuming you did). What did you learn about love and relationships in general from this relationship?

Goey and I drove to the pier at the end of the Kennedy compound right near our house, walked out to the very end of it, and stood looking out at the setting sun. I didn't know what to say, so I just stood still. Hoping. Heart racing so loud I was sure he could hear it. Then he put his hands on my shoulders, turned me to him, and looked deeply into my eyes. His look was so long and intense that I felt embarrassed and started to pull away, but he wouldn't let me. He held me firm and then, with his eyes still looking into mine, slowly pulled me into him. My body swooned against him, my knees buckled, and he had to hold me to keep me from falling, which made him laugh while he was kissing me, a laugh of pleasure. When our lips parted I stepped back and had to sit down. Plunk. *Everything was swirling: the sea, the sky. The sky! I will never forget the sky, the way it looked right then. It was a different color from what it had been two minutes before, all covered with a shimmering haze. Hemingway's line "and the earth moved" came to me. This is what he meant! I thought. The earth is moving.*

—JANE FONDA, *My Life So Far*

Recall each of your sweethearts from college or later adolescence. How did you meet? What attracted you to each other? Who pursued whom? What did you do when you were together? How often did you see each other? Remember the good times. And the bad times. Were there any moments of special closeness? Were you ever jealous? Was there a moment when you *knew* this was the person for you (or not)? Did you meet his or her family? What did they think of you and you of them? How long did you go together? How did the relationship end (assuming it did)? What did you learn about love and relationships from this relationship?

Friends and Other Memorable People

You've already recalled many people from high school and college and the service, but perhaps there were others who also played important roles in your adolescence.

FACTS ABOUT FRIENDS AND OTHER MEMORABLE PEOPLE

❦ Name any other good friends you had in adolescence and describe each briefly, when and where you were friends.

❦ Name any other individuals who were important to you at this time—such as people you went to for advice, or who helped or influenced you, or whom you admired and wanted to be like. Note briefly for each how you met, your relationship, and what made this person important in your life.

MEMORIES OF FRIENDS AND OTHER MEMORABLE PEOPLE

Bring to mind your good friends and other people who were important to you. Recall times and circumstances you were together. Remember your first meeting. What created the bond between you? Did any of these friends or other people pass through difficult times and you were able to help them? How did they help you through hard times? Did any of them serve as models for you? Were there any individuals who touched your life briefly but significantly?

In the early '60s when I was 20 and my sister 18, we visited our parents in Sweden for a few weeks one summer and then did some traveling on our way home to the States. Our father was on assignment with Esso and we were on our own at home and abroad. We were naive and unprepared for European travel, encumbered by too much luggage and too little information, but we had a lot of fun. We had so much fun on our last night in West Berlin that my sister carelessly left her purse on a beer hall table while we danced and half of our remaining travel money was gone.

We had just enough money for the bus to our flight to New York, the airport bus to Penn Station, and the train to New Jersey. But that was it. Unfortunately, the airport bus went to Grand Central Station. Ill-prepared to walk the 13 long city blocks in our high-heeled, pointed shoes, suits, and gloves, while carrying heavy luggage (there were no roller bags back then), we gave it a try. But after two blocks, we knew it was futile. I sat down on one of my two huge bags and began to cry while my sister paced back and forth swearing about our stupidity and misfortune. This is still pretty much the way we respond to crisis.

After about five minutes, a man came out of the building we were carrying on in front of. He and his coworkers had been watching us and were curious to know what was going on. I sobbed our story while my sister swore it. The man told us to wait right there and he would be back. In a few minutes he returned in a huge Red Line tour bus, stopped at the curb, loaded all our baggage, and drove us to the front door of Penn Station. Then he took us and our bags to the ticket counter, bought our tickets, and put us on the train to Rahway, New Jersey. Before the train pulled away, he asked us to send him a postcard to let him know we'd arrived home safely.

I have never forgotten that man and his kindness. How he ever kept a straight face while dealing with two emotional, tired, silly, argumentative sisters, I will never know!

—ELSA PENNEWELL, personal story

Sports

Recall any sports you played in adolescence, outside high school and college, or any sports you followed avidly as a fan.

FACTS ABOUT SPORTS

❦ Note any sports you played or pursued that were not part of your high school or college—including what you did, when and where, along with any factual highlights about how you or your team did.

❦ Identify any pro, college, or local teams you followed as a fan. For each team, note when you were a fan, how the team did, and any highlights of this experience, like special games attended and so on.

MEMORIES OF SPORTS

Think of each sport you played.   Were you a solo player or were you on a team? Recall any games or practices that stand out in your mind. Were there any times you excelled in your playing? Were there moments of triumph? Of bitter defeat? Who were the memorable players or coaches?

Think of the teams you followed.   Recall particular moments, of victory or defeat, around each team. Did you attend any games? Which players particularly interested you? Did you ever meet any of them? Did you get their autograph? Did you aspire to play for any of these teams? Did you do anything as a fan, other than watch TV, attend games, or follow your teams in the news?

Causes, Community, and Politics

Adolescence could be a time of passionate beliefs, when you saw the world in stark terms of right and wrong, good and evil. Did you get involved then in any community projects or political campaigns or any causes in general?

FACTS ABOUT CAUSES, COMMUNITY, AND POLITICS

❧ Identify each cause—social, political, or whatever—that you supported and tried to advance in adolescence. Note the purpose, the time of your involvement, the basic facts of what you did, and the reason you supported this cause.

❧ Identify any community work you did as a teenager—what it was, its purpose, when you did it, and your role or involvement.

❧ Identify any ways that you got involved in politics—supporting a specific political candidate or some political cause. Note who or what you supported, when you got involved, and what you did.

MEMORIES OF CAUSES, COMMUNITY, AND POLITICS

Think back about each of the causes you supported. It could have been any cause—civil rights, the environment, some local movement. Did you ever march for or against anything? Think of the occasions or moments, public or private, associated in your memory with each? Who else was involved?

Recall any community work you did. What occasions or memorable people come to mind? What goal were you trying to achieve? Did you succeed?

Recall your involvement with politics. Did you support a candidate or political agenda? Was it a national or statewide candidate? A local candidate? What did you actually do? Were you ever involved in campus politics? Was it a political cause that occupied you? What was the outcome?

Interests and Activities

What filled your time as a teenager, besides school and work and socializing? Adolescence was a time of exploring many new areas of interest. Most were dropped, sooner or later, but some became lifelong pursuits.

FACTS ABOUT YOUR INTERESTS AND ACTIVITIES

❦ List your favorite books and movies from this period in your life.

❦ Note any favorite actors, artists, personalities, and so on.

❦ Identify any radio or television programs you enjoyed.

❦ Identify any pets that were part of your life as an adolescent.

❦ List any hobbies or games you pursued.

❦ If music was important in your life, note briefly what music you enjoyed or performed.

❦ Note any honors or distinctions you earned, when you earned them, and from whom.

❦ Note if you and others made up your own organization, such as a private club.

❦ Note any trips you took as an adolescent. Record where you went, with whom, when, why, and what you saw.

MEMORIES OF YOUR INTERESTS AND ACTIVITIES

What memories come back when you think of favorite books, radio, or TV programs, movies, or performers? What were your favorites? Were any events or performances truly memorable? Did a book or movie change your life somehow? Think of where you went to the movies.

It is still there, the Pastime Theater, only now it's called the Bristol Cinema and is divided into two narrow screening rooms. . . .

My parents said it was really Joanie's aunt who ran the Pastime, that the man who owned it couldn't have managed without her. She sold the tickets and, trotting across the tiny lobby, sold the candy, and on Saturday afternoons walked the aisles after the curtain went up, flashing a light on whoever was tossing spitballs or whistling through their fingers or squabbling with the kids in the next row. I was a regular at the Saturday matinee, bouncing on the cracked leather seats, gumming up my teeth with jujubes and dodging the flashlight, drunk on the darkness and the big screen and the pervasive salt/grease smell of Spanish peanuts. I loved the serial, the cartoon, the newsreel, the Fitzgerald travelogue, the Peter Smith specialty, the feature, and whatever served as dessert—the Three Stooges usually. . . .

— MARY CANTWELL, *Manhattan Memoir*

Think back about each hobby. Recall any moments that brought you pleasure. Were others involved too? How did you first develop an interest in this hobby? How serious were you?

Remember the games you played, either alone or with others. When and where did you play these games? How important were they to you? Were others involved? Were there any moments that stand out in your memory?

Think of each pet that was part of your life. What did you do with them? Did you have a special relationship? What happened to them?

What memories do you have around music? What music was popular when you were a teen? Any memorable performances? What pieces of music mattered most to you? Who were your favorite performers? Did you go to live concerts? Did you like to dance? If you played an instrument or sang, what performances stand out? Did you hope to make something of music in your life as you grew older?

Think of each club or organization you belonged to as an adolescent. Were any groups important in your life? What events or occasions come to mind around each? Did you play a role in any of them?

Remember the trips you took. Recall traveling to your destination and back. What did you see and do? Did something memorable happen? Did you meet anyone special? Did you have any travel-related problems—flight problems, delays, accidents, problems with language, and so on?

Notable Events

As a teenager, you probably began to pay more attention to the world around you. What events in that world, near and far, highlighted and marked your adolescence?

FACTS ABOUT NOTABLE EVENTS

❦ Identify any historical or newsworthy events that occurred during your adolescence. These can be anything from great world events, such as wars, elections, and assassinations, to something more local, like a fire or flood or bank robbery.

MEMORIES OF NOTABLE EVENTS

Think of each event you identified. How did it touch you or others important to you? Were you or anyone else hurt? Did you lose any friends or family members? If it was a great national or world event, how did you learn about it? Where were you and what were you doing when you first heard about it? What was your first reaction?

Other Voices

Is there anyone you still know or could contact who knew you as an adolescent? Ask them to supply memories of you from that time in your life. What were you like? What events or occasions involving you do these people remember? What role did you play in their lives? You may be surprised by what they say. Their memories can be an important part of your story.

If you want to include other people's memories of you in adolescence . . .

1. Make a list of people from your adolescence and ask them to share their memories with you, in their own words.
2. Record each memory on a separate sheet of paper. Label each memory "A Memory of Me" and include the memory teller's name, as well as the approximate date and location of the memory.
3. Add these memory sheets to your own memories in your *My Life Story* notebook.

THE MEANING OF YOUR ADOLESCENCE

Now that you've recorded the facts and memories of your adolescence, it's time to step back and think about the significance of this period in your life. What role did it play in creating the person you became and are now? It was a crucial period, because in it you laid the foundation for your own sense of who you were, and you formed some idea of what you wanted to be and do in your life. These two notions—who you were and what you wanted to be—would play themselves out in your life for many years to come.

Defining Moments

A defining moment or turning point might be as real but intangible as the sudden recognition of a talent you possessed, or of some activity that you truly loved. Appearing, for example, in a school play might have revealed to you the deep satisfaction from performing before a group of people. Perhaps it was taking a course in a new subject that somehow opened your eyes. Or meeting a person who was different from anyone else you'd ever met. Or falling in love, or falling in love and being hurt.

Don't forget to consider such things as an accident, illness, or physical condition; a change in your family's social or economic status; something that happened to you in school; your religious beliefs or experiences; a near accident. Difficult moments, hardship, times of stress and pressure and testing can also reveal and shape who you are.

> *Now and then Father put the drafting tools aside and took me with him on trips to factories where he was supervising the setting up of his presses. One day, in the plant in Dunellen, New Jersey, where for many years his rotary presses were built, I saw a foundry for the first time. I remember climbing with him to a sooty balcony and looking down into the mysterious depths below. "Wait," Father said, and then in a rush the blackness was broken by a sudden magic of flowing metal and flying sparks. I can hardly describe my joy. To me at that age, a foundry represented the beginning and end of all beauty. Later when I became a photographer, with that instinctive desire that photographers have to show their world to others, this memory was so vivid and so alive that it shaped the whole course of my career.*
>
> —MARGARET BOURKE-WHITE,
> *Portrait of Myself*

Values—What Mattered

Values are what matters to us. Love. Winning. Success. Nature and natural things. By definition, we feel strongly about our values, even if we've never stated them explicitly, and we probably tend to seek out friends and acquaintances who share them with us. We use them to make decisions every day. Values are what give our lives a sense of meaning and significance.

Values are also driven by our stage in life. As adolescents, for example, we often valued freedom, independence, autonomy, being different and distinct. We often saw the world in black and white, because in struggling to find our own identities we couldn't abide shades of gray. Our values then were sometimes in conflict, as we experimented with different identities and tested values and outlooks different from those we grew up with.

The following questions might help you understand what truly mattered to you as an adolescent:

- *Look at the major choices you made* as an adolescent, such as picking a boy- or girlfriend, the college you attended, the organizations you chose to join. How did you make those choices? Choices usually contain the most clues about our real values.

- *In adolescence, some real clues about values can also be found in how we chose to be different from parents and other authority figures.* What were these disagreements? What did you want, versus what your parents (or any other authority figure) wanted? In what ways did you decide to be like your parents and family or to be different? Did your values shift—say, away from your parents' to something more your own? At the end of adolescence, how were you different from your parents?

- *Look at times of high emotion.* Times of loss, for example. Or sorrow and regret. Or deep satisfaction and pleasure. There was often a link between those emotions and your values.

- *How did you tend to spend your time as an adolescent, especially when you had a choice?* Did you seek out people to be with, or did you prefer to read or do something solitary?

- *What did you aspire to in your life beyond adolescence?* What about that goal attracted you? What need would attaining that goal satisfy?

Sometimes there's a difference between what we *say* our values are and what they really are. Sometimes we live under pressure to possess certain values—for example, if our parents happen to be religious and we finally decide we don't share their beliefs. Record here your real values, not the values you were supposed to maintain.

I had wanted to escape from my class prison; and I did. . . .

Living among those very poor people, my sense of values changed curiously. I was used to hard self-respecting New England, insensibly dominated by the fundamental duty of paying one's debts, after which, if one had a fairly safe bank balance, the luxury of charity might be enjoyed. I found, half a mile away, a different psychological make-up. The patience of the poor! Their amiability, crowded as they were into those mean tenements! Their extraordinary hospitality! I thought how carefully we planned our guests for our one dainty guest-room. . . . Here, with matter-of-fact readiness, in time of need, one more child, a derelict friend out of work, any neighbor in distress, would be added to the cramped quarters. . . . Untidiness, of course. Smells, hitherto unknown. What did it matter?

—VIDA DUTTON SCUDDER, *On Journey*

Love

In the end, the richness of life depends heavily on the love we receive and give. So it's important as we recall our lives to take note of those who loved us and those we loved.

Some of us struggle to call our feelings "love." Men, especially young men less secure in themselves and their gender, or men of an older generation who were raised to pay little attention to feelings, may find this notion of love discomfiting. Many men feel comfortable with such feelings, and with expressing them, only in highly masculine situations of aggression and competition, like war and sports. Such settings seem to make these feelings acceptable. But in fact such feelings can and do exist in a variety of settings—in all settings of life, in fact—and it's a loss to deny them, or refuse to remember them, where they actually existed.

The people you identified in childhood were probably those closest to you, your parents or brothers or sisters or someone else in your family. Here in adolescence, however, as our worlds expanded and we tried to define who we were, the connections we made with individuals outside that small world became more important. It might have been a teacher who mentored you in some special way, or a friend. Perhaps at the time you never even thought of your connection with this person as "love," but it was, in the sense we've defined it here.

Learning and Wisdom

Adolescence was a particularly rich time for learning because our lives changed and broadened so dramatically in these few, often tumultuous years. Our universe expanded in just a short time from home and school to the whole wide world. That kind of extraordinary change was bound to produce confusion and conclusions—often tentative—about what we wanted from life and how we wanted to live our lives.

It may help to scan the facts and memories of your life in this time and ask yourself: what did I learn from this experience or event or outcome? What did I know, what wisdom did I have when I was twenty, twenty-one, twenty-two that I didn't have when I was ten years old?

Another way to think about learning and wisdom in adolescence is this: What advice would you give an adolescent today that might help this teen survive an often difficult period and grow up to lead a happier, more productive life? What does that young person need to know or understand about this time of life? What would you say to your child or grandchild about adolescence? What do you wish someone had told you when you were an adolescent? What insight and wisdom would have helped you? What would you tell yourself if you could travel back in time and talk to yourself when you were a teenager?

Finally late that spring I saw an amoeba. The week before, I had gathered puddle water from Frick Park; it had been festering in a jar in the basement. This June night after dinner I figured I had waited long enough. In the basement at my microscope table I spread a scummy drop of Frick Park puddle water on a slide, peeked in, and lo, there was the famous amoeba. He was as blobby and grainy as his picture; I would have known him anywhere.

Before I had watched him at all, I ran upstairs. My parents were still at the table, drinking coffee. They, too, could see the famous amoeba. I told them, bursting, that he was all set up, that they should hurry before his water dried. It was the chance of a lifetime.

Father had stretched out his long legs and was tilting back in his chair. Mother sat with her knees crossed, in blue slacks, smoking a Chesterfield. The dessert dishes were still on the table. My sisters were nowhere in evidence. It was a warm evening; the big dining-room windows gave onto blooming rhododendrons.

Mother regarded me warmly. She gave me to understand that she was glad I had found what I had been looking for, but that she and Father were happy to sit with their coffee, and would not be coming down.

She did not say, but I understood at once, that they had their pursuits (coffee) and I had mine. She did not say, but I began to understand then, that you do what you do out of your private passion for the thing itself.

— ANNIE DILLARD, *An American Childhood*

Summing Up

Here you have the opportunity to capture your adolescence in a few words. As we said before, it's your chance to describe the forest and not just the trees—what that period of life was like for you, what you did in it, what kind of person you were, how it felt to you. Was it a happy time? A troubled time? What was it like overall? What should someone who's just read the story of your childhood think of that time in your life?

STAGE 3

---

young adult

The twenties for many of us was a time of exhilarating beginnings and exciting possibilities. Life, our own life as a finally free and independent person, stretched before us.

This —rather than childhood or adolescence—felt like the real beginning of life, and we set out in search of our place in the world. Our minds and bodies were operating at their peak. We thought we could do anything.

As we moved out of our parents' home, or graduated from college, or emerged from the armed forces and began life on our own, most of us faced two great life tasks. Find the work that would engage us through the rest of our time. And find someone with whom we could create our own homes and families. To do this, many of us loosened the family, ethnic, and religious ties of our youth and set out to create our own worlds.

In the middle years of the twentieth century, the proper sequence of steps was clear. Finish your schooling, settle your obligation to Uncle Sam (if you were male), find a life partner, get married, have children, and settle into running a household (for most women) or pursue a career (for most men, often with the same company for life). It all seemed natural at the time, and only in comparison with the fluidity of life in a person's twenties today does it seem as rigid as, in fact, it was.

Only rarely, of course, did it ever work out quite as neatly as it was supposed to. Some of us found a mate in short order, but not a career. Perhaps we tried two or three or more different jobs before settling (happily or not) on one line of work. Or we quickly found work to our liking but relationships came and went. Finding the right mate was often not easy. Sometimes nothing fell into place and our twenties felt like a big series of experiments. That wasn't unusual. Creating a life that would last decades took a lot of work and many false starts.

Sometimes external events played major roles in setting the course of our lives. Indeed, the mid-twentieth century was fraught with such great world-changing occurrences: the Depression, when jobs, let alone careers, were hard to come by; World War II, when virtually everyone's life was diverted to the war effort; the Cold War, the Korean conflict, and the war in Vietnam, not to mention lesser or local shocks, all of which altered the course of our lives in direct and indirect ways.

In the sixties and seventies, that sequence of life steps—school, marriage, family, career—was already growing less rigid. With the social revolution of that period, marriage and sex got disconnected. For many of us, though certainly not all of us, it was no longer necessary to marry in order to have a physical relationship. Plus, with birth control (the Pill), the link between sex and pregnancy was broken. It became possible and permissible (for many) to explore more relationships than would have been possible before.

Perhaps the most daunting task of our twenties was to manage the tension between two conflicting pressures. One was the need to make career and partnership choices. The other was the natural desire to experiment before making any lifelong commitments. Did we know enough at twenty-three or twenty-five to choose a life partner and start raising children, or to settle on a thirty- or forty-year career? In hindsight, some of us would say no. But when we were coming of age, in the mid-twentieth century, a twentysomething woman or man was still expected to settle down and get serious. Perhaps men were given a little more time to sow their oats (whatever that meant), but a thirty-year-old man without his own family or a definite occupation was considered somehow odd. A thirty-year-old unmarried woman was, sadly, felt to be on her way to lonely spinsterdom. Even a married couple without children at thirty was thought to be unusual as well, assuming they were capable of having children. If they weren't, they were pitied.

If we did commit to marriage and family, we had to cope with the sea changes wrought in our lives by the arrival of children. No one could fully anticipate the differences that would make. Our lives no longer belonged to us alone. With the joy of creating life came constraint and responsibility as well, sometimes sooner and more than we expected.

And if that weren't enough, we faced in marriage, even without children, the difficult task of learning to create and maintain an intimate relationship with another person. We struggled, especially at this still young age, with the fear and vulnerability of opening ourselves to someone else.

Yet another source of tension, as if this time of life needed more, was our dream—that image of ourselves as adults we developed as children and adolescents—what we would do, how the world would view us, what we would accomplish. For many of us the most exciting aspect of our twenties was the ability it brought to pursue our dream in reality, to make it come true. For some of us, creating a family and choosing a career were part and parcel of it. For others, however, the dream was more unorthodox. It may have involved a choice—becoming an actor or baseball announcer or dancer, for example—for which there was no career path or clearly marked guideposts and way stations. Sometimes we remained true to our dream. Sometimes we modified it to be more realistic. Sometimes we dropped it because it didn't fit the paradigm of family and traditional career, and we felt we had to make a choice. This stage was when we got serious about the dream or set it aside, perhaps forever, or perhaps, we hoped, to be picked up sometime later.

For all its uncertainties and tensions, the twenties was a time of beginnings and high hopes for most of us, the start of bringing our dreams to life, a time of experimentation and ultimately a time when we felt an urgent need to make important choices and commitments. Most of us entered this time free spirits and left it embedded in a new life of our own.

Here you begin your journey back to the time of young adulthood when you sought to build a life of your own, separate from your birth family and the life structures of childhood and adolescence. This period began at twenty or not long after and probably lasted until roughly thirty, when you put in place the basic structure for an autonomous adult life built around your own home and a chosen field of work.

Was this young adult stage a time for you of experimentation, transition, and searching for the independent life you wanted as an adult? Perhaps you settled early into your own family and work, so that by thirty or even earlier the fundamental pieces of your life were in place.

Whatever form this stage took, get down now the facts and memories of your twenties. Record the facts as directed in each of the various life segments. Then, in each segment, review the memory questions to see what moments and occasions any of them bring to mind.

You as a Young Adult

You became a young adult when you took your first steps to establish a life of your own, separate from the home and family where you grew up. Who was this emerging young adult?

FACTS ABOUT YOU AS A YOUNG ADULT

❦ Note when you entered young adulthood. What was the event or change that, in your mind, signaled your entry into this stage? How old were you when this happened?

❦ Without great thought or reminiscence, identify the highlights and most memorable events when you think of this period in your life.

❦ Note when you began to question your life, or some key part of it, as a young adult and to think about changing it in some important way. Perhaps you began to feel a need to settle down or get serious or even grow up. Note when this occurred and what was driving these feelings.

MEMORIES OF YOU AS A YOUNG ADULT

When you looked in a mirror at this time, what did you see? Recall what you looked like then. Did you like that person you saw in the mirror? What pleased or displeased you? What did you think others saw when they looked at you? Did they see what you saw? If there was a difference, why was that? How important was your appearance? If clothing was important to you, recall how you dressed. What effect did you try to achieve with the way you dressed? Did your clothing taste change over this period? What were the clothing fads and fashions of the time, and how did you follow them?

How did you generally act or behave? Were you shy or outgoing? Did you usually defer to others, or were you outspoken and opinionated? Recall times and occasions when you were most like yourself. Did you ever surprise yourself by the way you acted, by doing something unusual and unexpected? What did others say about you then? What was your reputation? Was it accurate? How would a good but candid friend have described you as a person at this time?

What kind of person were you becoming? Were you a dreamer or a realist? Were you more focused on achieving success or avoiding failure? Were you a risk taker or not? What risks did you take or avoid? What happened and what were the consequences? What were your real strengths and weaknesses? How did you discover them? What talents did you have or were you developing? What did you *think* your talents were? How did you exercise those talents? Did you wish you had talents you didn't have? What were they? Why did you want them? Who did have them? Did you prefer solitary activities, like individual sports or hobbies, or did you tend toward group activities, like team sports or group socializing?

Were you happy with yourself at this time in your life? Think of ways you worked on changing or improving yourself during this period. Did you do bodybuilding? Did you diet? Remember the New Year's resolutions you typically made. Did you read self-improvement books? About what? What was wrong with what you were, and what did you want to become?

What did you think about most? When your mind wandered as a young adult, try to remember where it tended to go. Sex? Action or romance stories with you as the hero? Worries of some kind? Dreams of future success and acclaim, or failure and disgrace? Why was that mental destination, the place your mind tended to go, important to you?

What was your dream? Try to remember, not the garden variety dreams you had, but *the* dream you had for yourself and your future. What kind of life did you hope for yourself in all its parts—work, family, society? Did you still carry the same dream for your life that you developed as a child and adolescent? Did it change? Did you give it up at this time? Why? Did you continue to pursue it? Did it become more realistic? What were you doing in your life to achieve it, whatever it was?

Did you have any specific goals for yourself and your life? These may have been related to your dream, or perhaps they were simply things you wanted to accomplish for whatever reason. What were they? What did you do to work toward them? What did you hope to accomplish by the age of thirty?

Did you have a sense of fate, a sense that your life would unfold in a certain way? Perhaps it was a feeling that persisted from childhood and adolescence. Perhaps you simply lived from day to day. Did you live without any real thought for the future? Or, were you focused on the future—finishing your education or training, starting a family, and so on? Did you believe your future was something you could shape? Or was it something that would happen to you?

Remember when you first truly began to take responsibility for yourself. When did you begin to decide for yourself where you lived and your living conditions? When did you assume responsibility for supporting yourself? When did you truly become independent emotionally, financially, materially? Do any moments or occasions or discussions or arguments come to mind around this transition?

What did you do as a young adult that you now recall with anxiety or embarrassment? What were the bravest or dumbest or most frightening things you did? Do you laugh now at these experiences, or do you wish you could undo them? Why did you do them? What happened because you did them?

Were there any important rites of passage, rituals, or special occasions in this period of your life? Think back about any moments, like graduations or being released from the Army, that were special for you or those close to you. What memories do they bring to mind? Were there any moments not generally considered important that nonetheless were to you significant times in that they signaled a change or turning point in your life?

Recall how you felt about authority and people in authority at this time. Did you usually do everything that you were told? Or did you resist automatically? Did you tend to struggle against anyone in authority? Did you resist actively, or passive-aggressively? What happened when you did this?

What key decisions did you make as a young adult? What choices did you make that shaped you and your life and set your course? Were they good decisions, and, if not, how did you try to change or undo them? Recall any times you felt caught between two opposing needs or goals. Did others sometimes want you to do things you didn't feel ready to do, or want to do? Did you ever face a difficult choice and not know how to decide? What did you do?

What was your daily routine like in your twenties? When did you get up, when and where did you eat, what people did you typically see? What were your afternoons like? Your evenings? Were any parts of your routine important rituals? If your routine changed through the period, think back over each routine.

How did you tend to spend your free time? Alone? With others? Recall the times that were your own. Which were memorable for some reason? What happened? Did you have a haven or sanctuary? Recall some times and occasions when you went there. Did anyone else know about it?

Recall your most intense moments and events as a young adult. Remember what happened in each case to cause your feelings.

- Did you have any moments of *joy and happiness*?
- What happened to make you truly *angry,* and what did you do? Recall any times you lost your temper and your anger got away from you.

- Did you ever feel a sense of *regret* or *sorrow*? Did you ever express your regret or ask for forgiveness?

I always wanted to tell my dad how much it meant to me that he stuck around when I was little. It was the Depression. Mom kicked him out. Other people's fathers disappeared when they couldn't support their families. They hit the road.

Not my dad. Even though Mom wouldn't let him visit, he'd wait for me till school was out and then walk me home. It was our little secret. Then, when I was sixteen, I got married. My husband was transferred out west and I hardly ever saw Dad after that. I was busy raising my own family. I did see him one Christmas when we went home, but so much was going on. You know how it is with holidays.

There was one moment I'll never forget. We were in the car together, going to pick up some groceries, stopped at a red light. I opened my mouth to say how I felt about him. He was looking right at me. But all of a sudden, I felt so shy, and then the light changed. The moment was gone. Dad died the following spring. I never got another chance.

— Mildred Potter, in *What's Worth Knowing*

- Recall some times when you felt particularly *uncertain, insecure,* or *unsure of yourself.*
- Were you ever filled with a sense of *love and closeness*?
- Did you ever feel *betrayed*?
- When did you feel truly *jealous or envious*?
- Did you ever *grieve* or feel a real *sense of loss*? Why? How did you cope?
- What was the most intense *physical pain* you felt?
- Did you ever *laugh* uncontrollably?
- Did you ever feel intense *stress or pressure*? How did you handle it?
- Were you ever deeply *disillusioned*?
- What was your greatest *disappointment*?
- Were your *feelings* ever hurt?
- Were you ever deeply *misunderstood*?
- When were you most *frustrated*?

- Did you experience any intense moments around any of your senses: *sight, sound, smell, taste,* or *touch?*
- What *surprised* you most as a young adult? Did anything *shock* or *amaze* you? Were you ever *awestruck?*

What possessions mattered most to you at this time? Bring to mind the things that you owned. A car? A piece of jewelry? Sporting equipment? Clothing? Heirlooms? Books, or even one particular book? It could be anything, including something seemingly small and trivial.

How much self-confidence did you have at this time in your life? Were you sure of your skills and abilities? Or did you have a sense in some parts of your life that you were faking it and that any day you'd be discovered for what you really were? How and where did you exhibit this self-confidence, or lack of it? What were its origins? How did it change your life and what you did?

My insecurity had something to do with both my mother and Phil. My mother seemed to undermine so much of what I did, subtly belittling my choices and my activities in light of her greater, more important ones. My very eccentric relations with her were exemplified in an incident of these years. I would often call on her when she was in bed or resting. We would endlessly discuss her activities and speeches, interspersed with occasional contributions from me about the children. One day I decided very deliberately that I would bring up my project to get children out of Junior Village, a large shelter in the District, and into foster homes. It took some courageous determination, but I started to say she might be interested in some work I was doing. As I went on, she cut me off decisively, saying, "Oh, darling, I gave up on the District years ago." So ended my abortive effort to talk with her about something that mattered to me.

— KATHARINE GRAHAM, *Personal History*

Were you ever the victim of discrimination in this period? Recall any times you were treated differently and unfairly because of your race or religion or some other aspect of who you were?

Were there times that being a young adult woman caused you to be treated differently and unfairly? Recall any times that being female made a difference as you entered the adult world—in your work, in your social or religious life, or in any other way. Did you have to fight harder in some ways because you were female? Recall times when you struggled to develop and maintain your own identity, your own separate sense of who you were and how you were different. Were there times when you struggled to express yourself?

Did you suffer in some way during this time in your life? Did you face hardship? Recall times when you had to endure great suffering for more than a short time. An extreme example might be imprisonment and terrible abuse, as victims of wars have had to endure.

Recall any health issues you faced as a young adult. Illnesses? Injuries? Diseases? Physical problems? Accidents? Did you experience, temporarily or permanently, any physical limitations?

When John and I decided to marry, I began dreaming about the son who would have his father's merry eyes and mischievous humor. That child, and his sister, a less determinate figure, but real nonetheless, lived so profoundly in my imagination that it took a long time for it to sink in that I would not give birth to them. . . .

I had severe endometriosis, so severe that I needed surgery to correct the pressure building up on other internal organs. My pain wasn't normal, never had been. It was caused by the wrenching around of bladder and bowel each month, as my body struggled to function appropriately. There was a chance I could manage to get pregnant and not miscarry, but it was slight.

All those in such a situation believe they will be special, part of the positive statistics, and the specialists who work to help them can't function without conveying to each case that the chances are good. I never took in how stacked the odds were against the birth of that son and daughter. My hopes still rose with each new chance, only to plummet grievously. It became cruelly hard for me to congratulate my friends at the arrival of another sunny infant. Sometimes the sales woman in the children's shop would be astonished by my brimming eyes and shaking voice as I purchased each new blue- or pink-bound gift, and wrote the card. It was a deeper grief than any I had yet had to bear, and there was no assuaging it.

— JILL KER CONWAY, *True North*

What experiences of life and death did you have at this time? Did you lose anyone close to you? Was someone very ill or in an accident? Did you come near death yourself? What happened and how did it affect you?

Was it difficult to let go of adolescence? Try to remember any parts of your childhood or adolescence that lingered in some way into young adulthood. Did it include people you spent time with? Or, the way you spent your time? The things that interested you? Was it difficult to let any of this go? Was there someone in your life, such as your mother or father, who resisted letting go of you? Did you resist letting go of dependence, of having someone else take care of you in some way?

Romantic Relationships

Romance—whether the search for fun or the search for a mate—sits front and center of life as a young adult. For many people at this time of life, there is almost nothing more important.

FACTS ABOUT YOUR ROMANTIC RELATIONSHIPS

❦ Name each of the people with whom you were romantically involved.

❦ For each person, note who he or she was, his or her age, and where, when, and how long you were involved.

MEMORIES OF YOUR ROMANTIC RELATIONSHIPS

One at a time, imagine yourself back with the people you identified above and reflect on the following:

- *Where and how did you meet? When you think about this person, where are you and what is he or she doing? When did you know this was a special relationship? Did the other person share your feelings? When did you first make your feelings known to each other? Were you lovestruck?*

Bea Brown was a violist and orchestra conductor I had met on the boat coming home from Europe. Bea knew I wanted to learn more about music, and I was hoping she would invite me to her apartment again. Weeks later she did, this time for dinner and then to the opera, where Bea was playing in the pit.

The clarinetist was invited, too, and this time we talked. There were twelve of us around the table, and I was thrilled to see that I could make her laugh. But what brought us together was the rum cake. Bea had made a cake for dessert and put it on top of the refrigerator to cool. It was an ancient Philco refrigerator with a sloping top—so old that it shook from the grinding of its moving parts. Slowly, during dinner, the rum cake jiggled its way to the edge of the sloping top and finally took a dive to the floor. When the guests heard the cake splat, there was laughter, but I couldn't let it rest at that. I reached for my fork and headed for the kitchen. The only other person who picked up her fork was the clarinetist. We sat down and ate rum cake off the linoleum with a flirtatious show of appetite. Was ever woman in this way wooed. . . ?

Her name was Arlene.

I was in love.

—ALAN ALDA, *Never Have Your Dog Stuffed*

- *What did you especially like about him or her?* What did you dislike? Did you ever consider marrying? Did you have any differences? Over what? How did you fight? How did you make up?
- *Recall the most romantic moments.* What were they like? What other moments or events or occasions do you most remember from this relationship? Did you have a song, or poem, or place that meant something special to you both? When did the relationship end (if it did)? What caused it to end? Did you have any regrets? Did you get hurt?

Were their any obstacles or challenges in the way of your romance? Did your parents disapprove? Did you live in different cities, or parts of the country? Was there a rival for his or her affection?

What did you want from a relationship at this time in your life? Were you mostly looking for a good time? Or was your goal to get serious and find a mate? Did you ever go with anyone whose goal was different from yours? Did your goals change over the course of this period? Did your notion of what love was change? If so, what caused the change?

What important firsts occurred here in this part of your life? Your first time being head over heels in love, your first time sleeping with someone, your first breakup, and so on?

Try to remember your best dates and your worst dates. What happened? Were they blind dates? Did you have any dates that you told stories about afterward? Do you think the other person ever told stories about you afterward?

Getting Married (or Entering a Committed Relationship)

This is the period, your twenties, when you probably got married. If it was, consider the following questions and suggestions.

FACTS ABOUT GETTING MARRIED

❦ Name and describe briefly your new spouse (or partner)—age, appearance, work, interests, etc.

❦ Note where and when you got married. In a few words, describe the ceremony, who attended, where you went on your honeymoon, and any other factual highlights from that day, the ceremony itself, and the preparations for it.

MEMORIES OF GETTING MARRIED

How and when did you and your mate decide to get married? Was it love at first sight? Or did a friendship develop into love? Was there a formal proposal? Did you (the future groom) ask your future in-laws for permission to marry? Was there an engagement ring or some other symbol of intent? Did you live together before getting married? How long was your engagement?

Recall your wedding and all the preparations leading up to it. Who did what? Was it fairly straightforward or complicated? Did you struggle with the expectations of parents or parents-in-law? What was the location and building where you were married? Who was in the wedding party? Who officiated? Was there anything unusual in your wedding vows? What parents and relatives were there? Recall that day and walk through it in your mind. What moments stand out? Who else was there? What did they do? What was the highlight? Did anything go wrong, or threaten to go wrong? Where was the reception? What happened there? How did the two families—the bride's and the groom's—get along? Where did you go on your honeymoon? Recall any highlights of that trip.

Recall your early days of married life. What changes, discoveries, surprises, happy and less-than-happy moments occurred in your first year or two together? Was it a time of significant adjustment? What was a typical weekday like for you as a new couple? A typical weekend? What did you do together? What did you do apart? What happened to the romance between you? What did you disagree about?

What were the best times together? The worst times? Were there tough moments? What was the first real challenge of any kind that you faced together?

How did you get along with your in-laws? Where and how did you meet? What
were they like? What did they do? Where did they live? Did you see them often?
What did you do together? How did your spouse and your family meet and how
did they get along? Did you or your spouse ever struggle with in-law relationships?
What happened?

> *I sat at the table in the warm kitchen and waited for Linda's father to come in. I was
> here on the traditional "meet the parents" visit. Linda's and my relationship had gotten
> serious enough—I was a junior in college and she was finishing nursing school—that
> it was time to declare ourselves to her family. It was an obligatory moment in their tra-
> ditional Polish Catholic culture. Linda and I had arrived an hour earlier and I'd al-
> ready met her sweet mother and shy younger sister.*
>
> *Now I waited, more than a little nervous. Suddenly the door opened, I jumped up,
> and a stocky, dark-haired, dark-skinned man walked in. Ignoring me entirely, he put a
> newspaper on the radiator and left. Some kind of older paper boy, I thought. But in a
> moment he was back. Again he ignored me and said a few brusque words to Linda's
> mother. I stood waiting silently. He left the room but returned in a moment carrying
> something. He approached me, said, "I'm Joe, Linda's father," and shook my hand.*
>
> *With his left hand he put a bottle of Seagram's Seven and two shot glasses on the
> table. From the fridge he took out two Buds and put them on the table too, with two
> beer glasses. We sat down. Without a word he poured my first boilermaker. It was the
> start of a beautiful relationship.*
>
> —KENT LINEBACK, personal story

Marriage or Partnership

*Choosing a good partner, adjusting to married life, and continuing the process of
growing into adulthood can be complicated. If you got married in your twenties,
how did it work for you?*

FACTS ABOUT YOUR MARRIAGE OR PARTNERSHIP

❦ Note any turning points or memorable moments in the life of your spouse or partner during this period in your life.

❦ Note any highlights or turning points in your relationship at this time.

MEMORIES OF YOUR MARRIAGE OR PARTNERSHIP

What was life like together? After the early days of marriage, what kind of relationship did the two of you settle into? What was the glue that kept you together? Were you able to talk comfortably about your relationship? Or was there tension? How did you settle arguments or disagreements? What was your economic status? How did it affect the relationship? What did you typically talk about—at dinner, for example? What were the ways you took care of each other? Did you become good friends (if you weren't already)?

It seems to me that we were just sort of typical young married people at the time. We went to movies, out to eat probably once a week, spent some time with Muriel and Allen and their family, did a few things with the fraternity—including chaperoning some functions!—and occasionally visited with other young married couples we met. One time we invited one of my fraternity brothers, Marshall Wolf, over for a dinner Wendy had lovingly prepared. Her dry chicken tasted like sawdust. Cauliflower is a cultivated plant whose inflorescence forms a compact, whitish head. The cauliflower Wendy prepared that evening was so hard that it could hardly be cut! The taffy apples Wendy made for dessert stuck to the little plates each one was on so that as we held the stick to eat the apple the plate was attached like a hat on top of the apple. We have never again seen Marshall since that evening.

—STEPHEN K. BLUMBERG, *A Satisfying Life*

What roles did you each fall into (breadwinner, homemaker, other)? What daily rituals did you develop? Did the early roles and responsibilities stay the same, or change? How did work and marriage coexist?

Did you share basically the same dream for your lives? Did one of you have to put his or her dream on hold? If your two dreams were at odds in some way, how did you reconcile the differences?

Was the relationship ever under stress? Depression, alcoholism, chronic illness, infidelity? How did the two of you deal with adversity? Were there any sudden changes in fortune—a job loss, an accident, a stroke of luck, a promotion—that changed your lives? What happened and how was it resolved?

What were the pleasures of the relationship? What about the relationship made you happy or gave you the sense of completion? Recall moments of particular closeness. How did you show affection? Did you have nicknames or special endearments? How did you mark special moments or anniversaries or birthdays?

Did you share friends? Did you like each other's friends? What did you do together socially?

What hobbies or interests did you share? How did you each spend spare or leisure time? Did you play sports together? Travel together? Where, to do what? What did you do on holidays, vacations, or special occasions?

Was religion important in your relationship? Was it a source of closeness or of contention?

What habits and patterns and practices did you each bring from your parents' relationships? Were you aware at the time that you were bringing them into your relationship?

Did you agree about having children? Was this issue important in your relationship? How did you settle any differences? Were you as a couple unable to conceive? What extraordinary efforts did you make to have children—medical tests, morning temperature-taking, special medical procedures, whatever? Did you consider adopting?

Children and Family Life

If you started a family in your twenties, look over the following suggestions and questions. When children arrived, were you surprised at the impact they had on your life as a young adult? Were you ready?

FACTS ABOUT YOUR CHILDREN AND LIFE AS A FAMILY

❦ For each child, note the child's name, birth date, sex, place of birth, and any other noteworthy circumstances of the birth.

❦ For each child, note too any significant milestones or highlights or turning points in his or her life during this period.

❦ Note any other people living with you in your family (or you with them), who they were and why you all were living together, and anything noteworthy that occurred in their lives during this period.

MEMORIES OF YOUR CHILDREN AND LIFE AS A FAMILY

Recall how you and your spouse decided on the timing of your children. Or did it simply happen? Recall any moments around these issues—discussions, disagreements, whatever. Were there any miscarriages or other medical problems associated with an unsuccessful pregnancy? How did you and your spouse deal with this experience?

Recall how your lives changed when children arrived. Were you prepared for the changes? What did you have to give up? Did you struggle personally with the changes? Did your roles change when children came—who was supposed to do what? How did you settle any disagreements?

Think of each of your children born to you as a young adult.

- *Pregnancy.* What moments come to mind around the conception of this child (where, when, any special efforts)? What was your reaction to the news of pregnancy? What was your spouse's reaction? How did you deliver the news? What happened during the pregnancy—any funny or surprising or sad or memorable moments? Were you hoping for a boy or girl? What names did you pick and why? Did you think about nicknames at that time?

> *"A boy," I cried. Leaned over, doubled over. I wept as if they had just told me, "You have black lung." But the news was "a boy." A snapshot of the evidence. The doctor wrote "penis" on the sonogram. Said I could embarrass him in years to come. Put it in the album. But I was crushed.*
>
> *My dream of pink girls. My dream of girlhood. My dream of femininity, prissiness, lace dolls, crayons and purple drapes and flowers was gone. The childhood I had never had.*
>
> —ERIN CRESSIDA WILSON,
> "Milk Dress: A Nursing Song"

- *Birth.* Recall the events around the actual birth of this child. What preparations did you make for the arrival of this child? When did labor begin? How did you get to the hospital? Did everything happen as expected? Were there any dicey moments? How did you (the mother) feel right after delivery? Where were you (the father)? Any memories around mother and child coming home?
- *Infancy.* Recall the room or space where this child slept. What kind of baby was he or she? What did you worry about? Did someone visit to help with the newborn? How did that work out?
- *What milestones do you remember from his or her earliest life?* Rolling over, first word, first smile, first steps, and so on? Any health problems or accidents?
- *What kind of personality did he or she develop?* Whom did this child take after? Look like? When did his or her personality first reveal itself and what was it? Happy? Quiet? Introvert? Extrovert? How was this child different

from his or her brothers and sisters? Recall times when it was clear this child took after you or your spouse or some other relative. What was he or she especially good at—what talents began to reveal themselves even as he or she was a child? What did you do to encourage those talents?

- *When did this child go to school and what changes did that bring in his or her life and in yours?* What dreams, hopes, and expectations did you have for this child? Did you send this child to a private school? Did you get involved in this child's schooling? Did you attend PTA meetings? What did this child do outside school—music, sports, dance lessons?
- *What other adults were important in this child's life?* A teacher, an uncle, a neighbor, a nanny, a camp counselor?
- *Was this child adopted or a stepchild?* Recall any events, episodes, or moments in this child's life that were tied to being adopted or a stepchild. Remember any other issues that arose from the fact that this child was not your biological child.

What was your relationship with this child? Were you a relaxed parent or a nervous one? What rules did you impose? What was the biggest disagreement you had with this child? Did you ever punish this child? For what? Did you ever praise this child? For what? Did you and your spouse treat this child differently? What did you learn, if anything, from this child, or from caring for him or her? What was hardest for you about this child? What was good and happiest for you? What would you do differently?

Recall how each set of grandparents reacted to the arrival of grandchildren. What did they do? Did they help? Did they seem happy? Did children change your relationship with them? Did they visit? What did they think about the way you and your spouse were raising your children? Did they try to offer advice? What was it like when you visited their homes? Were they nervous or happy to have children in their homes? Remember what ongoing roles they played in the upbringing of your children. Recall what your children thought of their grandparents and how they acted with and around them.

What was daily life like in your family? What was the atmosphere in the home? Recall the daily routine—what was everyone doing in the morning as they prepared for the day? What happened typically in the evening? What times did you normally spend with your children? Recall family mealtimes. Remember a good day, a frustrating day, and an ordinary day.

> What's for dinner?
>
> *This question gets asked in millions of homes, and answered in millions of ways. Roast beef and potatoes. Pizza. Pasta putanesca. Soy burgers, miso soup. Whatever you want. I don't know yet. Same as yesterday. Let's go out.*
>
> *To which children respond in many ways. "I'm not hungry . . . Not polenta! . . . Can I have cereal instead?" So it is in my house. Once I cooked a veal stew, brought it to the table, and lifted the cover of the dish with a flourish.*
>
> *"Voila!" I crowed.*
>
> *"I hate Voila," wailed a three-year-old boy.*
>
> —ELIZABETH EHRLICH, *Miriam's Kitchen*

How did you spend holidays, vacations, and special times? Did you develop any family traditions at, say, the holidays, like Christmas or Thanksgiving? Were there certain places you always went, or certain people who came to your home? How did you celebrate birthdays?

How did your family life compare with family life when you were growing up? Think back when your parents were young adults, or you were the age of your children here. How would you compare your family life with the family life you experienced growing up with your parents? Were the similarities and differences based on conscious choices you made? What did you want to carry forward? What did you want to avoid?

What had you expected parenthood to be like and what was the reality of it? What were some of the pressures you felt? Had you been raised to believe that having children was an important part of your identity and your manhood or woman-hood? What adjustments did you have to make?

Did you have occasion to tell a child the facts of life? How did that occasion arise? Did the child ask questions? Did you simply decide it was time to explain things? What did you say? How did the child react?

Single parenthood. Did the burden of raising your children fall on you alone at this time in your life? Recall those moments and that life. What memorable times come to mind? How did you become a single parent? If you divorced, did you get any help from your ex-spouse or partner? Did you try to compensate in any way for the lack of a parental partner? How did that work?

I am a single mother. I am beginning to understand what that means. We are a unique tribe of the hardy and desperate. We pillage packages of saltines from cafeterias, never knowing how tired we will be later and whether we will have energy to prepare a meal. We peel food out of our children's hair at night, alone, when they have finally fallen asleep. We fall asleep beside them fully clothed, abandoning the formalities of pajamas and cribs.

—ELIZABETH COHEN,
The House on Beartown Road

Home

Now is the time of life when your notion of home began to change. Home used to be where you grew up and your parents still lived. But you most likely moved on from that place as a young adult. This could be a truly transient time of life, so spend some time revisiting the places you lived.

FACTS OF YOUR HOME

🌑 List the address (or location), town or city, and state (and country, if not the United States) of each place you lived as a young adult.

🌑 Provide a brief description of each, and the years you lived there.

For each place you lived:

- *Recall the house or building.* Imagine yourself back in it. Walk through it, space by space, room by room. What happened in each of those places? Did you have a basement? An attic? A patio? Who was there with you?
- *Recall the yard around the house or building.* Imagine yourself walking around the outside of the house or building. What was there? What moments and events come to mind?
- *Recall the neighborhood.* What were your neighbors like? What buildings and stores and businesses were there? Were there landmarks, or favorite haunts? What happened there? Who else was there?
- *Recall the town or city.* If this was where you grew up, how was it different for you as a young adult? Where did you go? Who was with you? Was there a rich side? A poor side? Which was yours?
- *Recall your move to this place.* Remember your preparations and reasons for it, the move itself, and what was involved in settling into a new place.

Which residence did you first think of as your own home? Why did you choose that community? What about that place made it feel like your home? Was it that you lived there with your spouse and children? Was it the gathering place for friends and family? What moments or events made you feel connected to it?

If you did set up your first home, recall the process of doing that. How did you find it? Did you own or rent? Was financing your first home a challenge? What were its good points and its faults? How did you fix it up? Did you ever remodel your home? How did you like being responsible for your own home?

Divorce/Splitting Up

Perhaps you discovered in your twenties that the relationship you'd entered wasn't a good one, or perhaps your partner decided that on his or her own. If you divorced or left a committed relationship as a young adult, think back about that experience.

FACTS ABOUT YOUR DIVORCE

❦ Note the date and place of your divorce.

❦ Note any memorable *factual* highlights of the split-up itself, the steps leading up to it, and the immediate aftermath.

❦ Describe briefly what happened with any children you had.

MEMORIES OF YOUR DIVORCE

What caused the breakup? What were the underlying causes? What was the immediate cause—that is, what events actually precipitated the split? Was the divorce by mutual agreement? Or was it driven by you or your spouse?

I think we must have just finished lunch; I know we were sitting at the table in the small winter-garden of a porch at Durham Cottage and that it was daylight. It came like a small bolt from the blue, like a drop of water, I almost thought my ears had deceived me: "I don't love you any more." I must have looked as stricken as I felt, for she [Vivien Leigh] went on: "There's no one else or anything like that; I mean, I still love you but in a different way, sort of, well, like a brother." She actually used those words. I felt as if I had been told that I had been condemned to death. The central force of my life, my heart in fact, as if by the world's most skillful surgeon, had been removed. It left me agasp but not gasping; it was as if I had been rendered forever still inside, like a fish in a refrigerator. It had always been inconceivable that this great, this glorious passion could ever not exist, like a crowned head after the execution.

— LAURENCE OLIVIER, *Confessions of an Actor*

Recall the divorce process itself. Negotiating the divorce and navigating the various issues that arose during this process could be difficult. Was there contention over children and their custody? Property or alimony? Or was your divorce relatively amicable? How did your family react?

How did your children handle your breakup? How did their lives change? What did you or your spouse do to relieve the effects on them? Did either of you expect the children to take sides?

How did you find life as a divorced parent? If you had children, did they stay with you, primarily, or with your spouse? How often did you, or your spouse, see them? How did that arrangement work out?

How did you adjust to single life? Was it a shock? Did you move to new quarters? What do you remember most vividly about adjusting to this new life? What was the most difficult time? Was your family there for you? Did friends feel they had to choose between you and your spouse? Did you start going out again? Did you do all right financially—either from receiving alimony, for example, or after having to pay alimony? Were you relieved or sad to be single again?

Was there someone else? Did you hope to find someone else? Did you leave your marriage for a new partner? Or did you hope to find another partner soon? Did you question whether to get involved again? If you wanted a partner, what did you do to pursue that goal?

Birth Family

Even as you began to establish your own life as a young adult, with your own home and family, your original family probably remained part of your life.

FACTS ABOUT YOUR BIRTH FAMILY

❦ Note the ages of your father, mother, brothers and sisters, grandparents, and close extended family members at the beginning of this period.

❦ Note briefly anything memorable or significant that occurred in each of their lives during this time.

MEMORIES of your birth family

Reflect on your parents' lives during this period. Think of any milestones or turning points you identified in their lives.

- *What was your mother and father's relationship at this time?* Were they still happily married? Or did they get divorced or struggle in their marriage?
- *How did their lives change in this period?* They were probably in their forties and fifties and still in their prime. What were their lives like? What work were they doing? How was their health? Were you ever worried about them?
- *What was your relationship with them?* Were you still living at home? How involved were you in their lives? How involved did you want to be? Did you see them often? Were you close? Did you ever express your feelings to either of them? What happened? How did they, or each individually, view you (and your spouse and children in general, if you had your own family now)? Was your relationship changing? Recall any special moments or occasions in your relationship with them.

Reflect on each of your brothers and sisters during this time in your life.

- *What was your relationship with this brother or sister?* Were you close or was there tension between you? Had your relationship matured, or did it remain as it always had? On what occasions did you get together? What happened at those times? What did you talk about? Did you share interests? How much contact did you have?
- *How did this brother or sister deal with any problems your parents were having?* Did you and your siblings agree on how to handle their problems, and did this affect your relationship?
- *Think of the milestones you identified in the life of each sibling.* Did any of the life events affect your relationship with this sibling? How was their health? Did you lose a brother or sister during this period?

"Come home!" I cried when Sean died. "Please come home!" I would be driving my car, and the terror of his absence would come over me. . . .

Before returning to New York, I had the dream I'd hoped I would never have. I was at a picnic with lots of people. It seemed as if everyone I knew was there—my entire family and all my friends. I had the feeling that no one was missing. . . .

Though Sean looked fifteen in the dream, Kelley was only two or three. My mother was helping her float. "Can you let her go yet? Can she float?" I kept asking. Sean came back. "Can I play?" he asked, but before we dealt him in he was gone again, and a little later I saw him in the pool, swimming laps by himself.

The day went on with all kinds of activities, but we kept playing cards, people getting in the game and going out, and suddenly I realized that I hadn't seen Sean in a while. I put down my cards and went looking for him. I looked by the tennis courts and the playground. I looked among the people playing volleyball. I went to the pool and got in. I thought I saw him swimming near me, under water, the flash of his body going by, but when I swam to him, it turned out to be someone else. I got out of the pool and searched the picnic grounds, but I couldn't find him. Finally, I asked a friend whether she had seen him. As I spoke, I wondered why I was asking her. She was a friend from New York who had never known him. "Sean?" She smiled, and her face lit up. "He was here," she said, "but he left early."

"He was here, but he left early," I said to my mother, telling her the dream the next day. It was such a simple statement. "He was here, but he left early." I started crying as I told her, though it wasn't really sadness that made me cry. A flood of relief flowed through me, a long-awaited ending. I had a strong sense that I wouldn't be seeing him in my dreams again—or that if I saw him, it would not be soon—but instead of feeling sad, I felt strangely peaceful. In the dream, we had a happy time together, and then he was gone. Still, I was crying. He left before the rest of us. He never came back to say goodbye.

— KATHLEEN FINNERAN, *The Tender Land*

Recall any special family events that occurred in this time. Reunions? Major birthdays? Parties? Celebrations? Illnesses? Emergencies?

Recall how family members got along with each other at this time. Were family
members close? Did you share major events of your lives? Or was there discord or
disagreement or tension between any family members? Over what? How did it get
resolved (if it got resolved)?

Did any family members experience some form of hardship at this time? Were
there illnesses or financial problems or problems of some other kind that made
life particularly hard for any family members? Was this shared with family members or kept quiet? What did other family members do to help?

Think about your grandparents at this time. Were they still alive and part of your
life? What was happening to them during this period? Did you have any special
times with them? Were you involved in each other's lives?

*After college I went to work in Japan. I was young, single, excited about learning a new
culture, but sorry to be so far away from family. The distance caused me to miss many
family events—both happy and sad. One sad occasion I missed was my grandmother's
funeral. She had passed away suddenly. I didn't know about it until I tried to call her
from a public phone booth in Japan while waiting for a train. My sister from California answered the phone. I said, "I didn't know you'd planned a trip to Connecticut."
She didn't know what to say. My grandfather got on the phone and told me the news. I
was shocked, sad, and alone.*

*One year later, my family was planning a reunion at my grandfather's home for the
unveiling of my grandmother's gravestone. I knew I wanted to be there. However, I decided to keep my plans a secret from everyone except my aunt and my grandfather. My
grandfather was especially excited about this secret! He asked my uncle to make an extra reservation at the family dinner planned the evening of the graveside gathering. He
was bringing a woman. This caused quite a stir in our family. Imagine Grandpa's bringing a date to dinner the same evening his wife's gravestone is unveiled!*

The evening before the event, my family gathered at my grandfather's house. It was about 8 p.m. when I rang the doorbell. For some reason, my three sisters all came to the door. When they saw me standing there, they were speechless. My mom walked out of the bathroom to see who was there and instantly burst into tears. My grandfather stood there beaming. His "date" had been a well-kept secret and turned a sad occasion into a joyous reunion.

—DEBORAH OGAWA, personal story

Religion or Spirituality

As you became a young adult and began making your own choices, did religion remain or become an important part of your life? Or was this a time of drifting away, permanently or temporarily, from the beliefs and practices you grew up with? Perhaps your beliefs shifted from formal religion to something spiritual and less dogmatic.

FACTS ABOUT YOUR RELIGIOUS OR SPIRITUAL BELIEFS

❧ Name or describe the religious or spiritual beliefs that remained or became important to you as a young adult. Did your beliefs change during this period?

❧ Note any religious or spiritual practices that you regularly observed such as going to church, observing holy days, regular prayer, meditation, yoga, proselytizing.

❧ Describe briefly any religious experiences you had during this period.

MEMORIES OF YOUR RELIGIOUS OR SPIRITUAL BELIEFS

Reflect on your beliefs at this time. Recall any memories related to those beliefs, and other people who shared them (or didn't). Did these beliefs give you comfort in difficult times? Did you ever talk about them?

Did you retain the beliefs of your childhood? What religious (or spiritual) rituals or practices or traditions did you practice in your family? Going to church? Daily prayers? Religious teaching and discussion? Was any of this based on how you were raised? Did you add any new practices of your own? If you dropped the religious legacy of your upbringing, was it a clear-cut decision? When and where did it occur? Or did it just happen? Did you ever talk to your parents about it? What was their reaction? How did it change your relationships with any other people?

If you married at this time, did you and your spouse share beliefs? What moments or experiences together do you recall around these beliefs and the practices based on them? Did you carry any religious practices into your home? Did one of you convert? If you and your spouse did not share the same beliefs, how did those differences play out in your relationship?

What memories do you have around any religious experiences? Where did each experience occur? What brought it on? Did it change your life? How? What happened afterward?

Were there any times your beliefs and practices shaped your daily life? What did you do or not do or do differently because of your beliefs? What was the outcome?

Education

Did you attend school of any kind through your twenties? Perhaps you went to college a little later than your peers, or you went to graduate or trade/professional school.

FACTS ABOUT YOUR EDUCATION

🌢 For each school or program you attended, note: the name, location, and a brief description of the school or program; the years you attended; the program or courses you took (e.g., MBA program, or evening classes in social work); your goals or intentions; how you did; and any degree or certificate you received at the end.

MEMORIES OF YOUR EDUCATION

Imagine yourself back on campus or in that school. In your mind, return to this place and walk through it, whether it was one building or an entire campus. What does that place bring to mind—events and moments and people? If you attended college as a young adult, you were there a little later than most of your classmates. What difference did that make in your college experience?

Recall your purpose or goal in being there. Why did you choose this school? What was your field of study? Where did that goal come from? What was driving you to achieve it? What did you do to achieve those ends? Who else was involved? What decisions did you make or change while you were in this place?

Recall the various classes you took and the teachers who taught you. Put yourself in each of those classrooms. Who was teaching? What fellow students were there? What was your favorite class? Favorite teacher? What happened in that class, or with that person? Did you have any mentors in school—teachers, for example, who took a special interest in you and your learning and who helped and guided you in some special way? Who was your least favorite teacher? Did any classes or teachers change your mind about what you wanted to do? How did you do in your classes and overall? Any awards or recognition? Did you ever get in trouble?

Remember your friends and classmates, one by one. What attracted you to them? What would you do together? What happened with or to them?

Recall your social life that was centered around school. What social group did you belong to? What did you have in common? What did you do together? What other activities were you involved in? Any highlights of that time?

Recall the school clubs and groups you belonged to. Why did you join this club or group? What events or occasions stand out in your memory of this group?

Did you play any sports at this school? Recall the sports, the games or tournaments, and how you or your team did. Who else was involved with you? Were any games memorable? Where did you practice and play? Do any teammates stand out in your memory?

Recall your graduation. Who was there? What happened? Did you go through some sort of ceremony? Was there a celebration? How did you feel?

Did you work while going to school? What did you do? Where? Who were your coworkers? Your boss? Was the work interesting? Did anything noteworthy happen there? Was it difficult to balance work and school?

Recall your summer vacations. Think about each summer vacation and how you spent it. Where did you go, with whom, and what did you do?

Work and Career

Young adulthood, just out of college or the service, was the time when you probably had your first serious job, with real responsibility, and you embarked on the journey known as a career. Perhaps you found your life work right away. Perhaps you had a number of false starts.

FACTS ABOUT YOUR WORK AND CAREER

For each job you held in this period:

❦ List the jobs you held as a young adult: the organization you worked for, your title, and when you worked there.

❦ For each job, note what you did, and any factual highlights of that work.

MEMORIES OF YOUR WORK AND CAREER

Recall your first real job. What was it? How and why did you get it? How much did you earn? What did you learn from it about yourself and about working? What did you like about it, and what did you dislike?

If your career started here in young adulthood, recall how that happened. What was the job that really launched your career? Did you move from job to job for a time, before settling into some line of work? Recall some of those moments of hope and disappointment. What were you looking for? If you did settle on a career at this stage of your life, did you consciously think about it and make a real choice? Or did you just seem to gravitate to the line of work you ultimately pursued—did your career discover *you?* What were the stepping-stones along the way? Were there any people who were important to the choices you made?

Think about each job you held.

- *How you found and landed that job.* Was it the job you'd aspired to find or was it an entry-level position where you'd need to work your way up? Was it with the company you hoped to work for? Did you have any difficulty finding the job?
- *The place where you worked.* Recall the location, the building, where you sat or did your work, any tools or equipment you used, and so on. Imagine yourself back in that place; remember what happened there.
- *The organization/business.* Think back about the kind of company it was. What did it do? How was it to work for?
- *The other people you worked with.* What were they like? What did they do? How did you work with them? Did all of you get along or not? Did you get together apart from work?
- *Your boss.* Picture your boss in your mind's eye. What was he or she like? Did you consider him or her a good, competent boss? What did you learn from working for this boss? How were you treated? What did he or she think of you and your work?

Now we come to my editor, Allene Talmey, Allene who was as short and firmly packed as a Boston bull and had a Boston bull's bright brown eyes. . . .

On my first day at Vogue, *she dumped on my desk a pile of research, all of it in French, which was to help me in my first assignment. . . . No one, certainly not she, had ever asked me if I read French. . . .*

I lasted for about nine months, or maybe it was seven, until the winter morning when I wrote a deep caption about an actress. It was a monument to adjectives, strong verbs, and the rule of three, and Allene liked it. She even smiled. Still, there was something wrong—she didn't say what—with the last sentence. I slid the paper off her desk, stood up, and did what I should have done a long time before. I said, "I quit."

"You can't do that," Allene barked, then, terrier to the last, added, "I don't care if you spend the rest of the week in the infirmary, but no one just walks out of here."

"I do," I replied, and left her office.

Pausing only to pick up the stone from Prince Edward Island that I was using as a paperweight and the cellophane bag of dried apricots with which I was trying to beef up my blood, I ran for the elevator and home. There I did what I always did when I had lost my temper. I cried.

— MARY CANTWELL, *Manhattan Memoir*

- *Mentors.* Try to remember if anyone, your boss or someone else, mentored you—took you under his or her wing and advised and helped you with your work, helped you learn and get ahead.
- *Your work.* Recall a typical workday. What were the work hours? What was the most difficult part? The easiest? The part you found most satisfying? Hated most? Which of your skills did you bring to this work? What special projects or events did you work on? Did you deal with customers or other outsiders?
- *Were you a boss?* Did you manage others? What was that experience like? What conclusions did you draw about leading people? What training did you get in managing people—either on the job or in training courses at or away from work? Did your boss help you be a better boss yourself? Did you encounter employee problems? What were they? How did you handle them? Did you ever have to fire anyone?
- *Training you received or specific skills you learned on the job.* What training programs or seminars did you attend and what skills and knowledge did you acquire?
- *Promotions/recognition.* Recall any promotions or recognition you received for your work. What did you do? What made it good or special? Who else was involved? Did you advance in the job? Was it something you wanted, or did it just come your way?

- *Best times—worst times.* Recall the best (and worst) decisions you made at work. Recall some good work times and some rocky times, for example, when you weren't getting along with your boss, your coworkers, or your subordinates. Were you ever in trouble or reprimanded or fired? How did it affect you or change you?
- *Travel for work.* If you traveled as part of this work, think back about the trips you took. What was a typical trip like? Do any specific trips stand out in your memory? Whom did you see? What did you do? Did you have any personal time for seeing the sights or doing something on your own? Did anything unusual or exciting happen on these trips?

Recall the way you felt about work in your twenties. Was it important to you? Was it part of who you were, your identity, the way you thought about yourself? Or was it simply the way to pay the rent or mortgage so you could do what you really wanted to do. If so, what was that? Recall moments or incidents that made these feelings clear.

Did you start your own business as a young adult? If so, recall what it did, where it was located, and who else was there. What prompted you to start a business? How big was it? How many people were employed? Imagine yourself back in that place—walk through it. What scenes and moments and occasions come to mind? What memories in general stand out from this experience? Did the business grow and prosper? If you sold it or closed it down, why—what happened? What other people were involved?

If you are a woman, recall what it was like to be a young woman in the work world. Did you do the work you wanted to do, or did you feel your choices were limited? If you held a position usually held by men, what was that like? How did you do? Were you paid appropriately? Were you ever harassed in some way? Did you have any issues with subordinates? Think of each organization where you worked and how each organization treated women.

Recall any instances when you felt discriminated against. Was it because of your race or ethnic/cultural background or religion or gender or some other aspect of what you were? What happened? Who was involved? What did you do? What came of it?

How many prejudices am I going to get hit with in my life, I wondered . . . talk about being on the bottom of the heap. Black. And not just black but a dark-skinned *black. And not just a dark-skinned black but a dark-skinned black* woman. *And not just a dark-skinned black woman but a dark-skinned black* American *woman. It did seem like a very large eight-ball for just one person to be behind.*

As of graduation day, however, I had something to weigh in with on the other side of the scales. I was now Yvonne Thornton, M.D. Was it going to be enough?

The wave of change making things easier for blacks had inched up through the high schools, colleges, and medical schools by the 1970s, but it had not necessarily influenced minds and hearts at the postgraduate level, as I discovered when I applied for an OB/GYN residency at Mount Sinai Hospital in New York.

"What are you doing here?" the interviewer demanded when I walked into his office. "We don't accept black people. You wouldn't fit in with our other residents."

"Thank you for telling me," I replied, without knowing whether I meant to be sarcastic or not; my mouth was functioning but my head was blank with shock. "If that's the case, why did you schedule me for an interview?"

"Obviously we didn't know you were black."

—YVONNE THORNTON,
The Ditchdigger's Daughters

Recall any times when you felt that the requirements of work conflicted with your sense of ethics or morals. Were you ever expected to do something that seemed to you unfair or dishonest? How did you resolve this dilemma?

Military

Perhaps you served in the military in your twenties, maybe after attending college. If so, recall here the facts and memories of that experience. If you chose the military as a career, you should use both the questions below and those under "Work and Career" to evoke memories of this time.

FACTS ABOUT YOUR MILITARY SERVICE

❦ Name the branch (Army, Navy, Air Force, etc.) you were in, when you served and where you were stationed, the training you received and work you did, and the rank you attained.

❦ Name the people—officers, friends, subordinates—who stood out in your time in the service.

❦ Describe any combat experiences you had. Note when you fought, where, how long, and any facts you want to record about the experience.

❦ List any decorations, awards, or recognition you received during your service years. For what, and when?

MEMORIES OF YOUR MILITARY SERVICE

Think back over the various places you spent time in your military career. Did you enlist or were you drafted? Where did you undergo basic training? Advanced or other training? Recall the various locations where you were posted. For each place, put yourself back there in your mind's eye and let the various memories associated with each place rise to the surface.

Recall the specific work you did. What moments or situations come to mind around this work—what it was, where you did it, problems you faced, anything memorable that happened? Who did you do this work with? Did you like the work? Did you do it well? Were you ever recognized or reprimanded for your work?

Bring to mind each step of your military experience and remember the key people along the way. What moments or events come to mind around these experiences and people? Did anyone make a difference in your life, or you in theirs during this period?

Think about your spouse and any children while you were in the military. If you were married at the time, and had children, recall what it was like to leave them and spend long periods of time away from them. Was it difficult to be apart? Did it take a toll on your marriage? Was their support essential during your postings away? How did you observe special celebrations such as birthdays and holidays? How did you communicate? What were the times like when you were on leave and together?

Think of your birth family while you were in the service. How did your parents and family members react to your service and your absence? Did you stay in touch? Did you miss them? Recall any times you visited your parents' home while in the military.

Were you married to someone in the service? If you lived with him or her, recall that life: where you lived (on-base or off), the other couples, family life around the military, what it was like for your children, and so on.

Did you join the Army (or Navy or other military branch) and "see the world"? Recall any foreign countries you saw or places you visited. What did you see? What happened there?

If you want, recall your experiences in combat. Perhaps there were acts of bravery performed by you or others. Were you ever injured? Did you have any close calls? What would you want to tell others of your experiences? Did you lose any close comrades?

Recall your return to civilian life. Remember the day and place of your separation from the service. Recall your first weeks and months as a civilian. Were there any problems or issues of adjustment? Did any of them continue beyond those first weeks and months? Did others, who did not serve, understand what you had gone through and were experiencing?

I'm coming home! It's official as of this morning. . . .

Yeah, I'm looking forward to seeing you again, but I'm in no hurry to see the expressions on your faces when you see me. I want to see you try to hide the shock on your faces. You might even ask me for proof I'm your son. Don't feel bad. I see it in my own face every day. I have spent 12 months over here. The longest 30 years of my life . . .

I can't hear as well out of my left ear anymore. The 105 is no slingshot. Something about the big cells of the ear crushing the small cells of the ear further, and, further in until it makes a blockage. I hear what you're saying all right. It just takes time to get to where I can understand it, so, be a little patient, okay?

You know, it's almost funny, we see a guy in a wheel chair, a guy on crutches, one arm, hooks for hands, and, we break our backs trying to help him. But, what about the wounds you can't see? The phantoms, the nightmares, the ghosts in your head? I am going to tell you now. You'll need a lot of patience with me. Patience, and, understanding. We all will. See you soon. See you soon. See you soon.

—AL PUNTASECCA, in *Behind the Lines*

Friends and Other Memorable People

Who were the people, other than family, who meant most to you or had the greatest impact on your life as a young adult? Did anyone take you under his or her wing?

FACTS ABOUT FRIENDS AND OTHER MEMORABLE PEOPLE

❦ Identify those people from your young adulthood whom you considered good friends. Describe each briefly, and note how you knew each one.

❦ Identify anyone you would consider your mentor at this time. Did someone take you under his or her wing and give you special help or guidance? Note where this relationship occurred and when.

❦ Note any individuals who served as a model for you at this time. Was there someone you admired in some way and whose example you tried to follow?

❦ Identify anyone else who stands out in your memory. Note where and when you knew them and why they remain memorable.

❦ Describe briefly the circle of people (or circles, if there was more than one or they changed over time) with whom you tended to socialize as a young adult, what held you together, and how you spent time together.

MEMORIES OF FRIENDS AND OTHER MEMORABLE PEOPLE

Recall your friends, one by one:

- *Think of moments and occasions and events that you spent together.* How did you meet? What was the bond between you? What good times did you experience? If you were together often, recall what you usually did.
- *What interests did you share?* Sports, music, children, work, shopping, some other activity?
- *Did you help each other through tough times?* Recall those times and how you made a difference in each other's lives.
- *Did you ever have a disagreement or falling out?* What happened? Why did it happen? What came of it—was it resolved?

Were any of these friendships with someone of the opposite sex? Did either of you ever want the relationship to go beyond friendship? What attracted you to each other, and what kept the friendship only a friendship?

Did a good friend undergo great suffering or die? Were you involved? If a friend died, how did you cope and grieve this loss?

Recall the people who mentored you. Recall your interactions with each of these people and how they helped you. Think of specific instances when you sought or received help and advice from them.

Recall each of the people who somehow served as a model for you. Remember the times and places when you consciously copied the behavior or words or manner of that person. Remember, too, where you observed this model and what he or she was doing that you thought was worth emulating.

Recall any other individuals who stand out from this time. Bring to mind the times and places you were with (or you observed) each of these people. What effect did they have on your life?

> "I used to baby-sit for Lois, who lived in a neighboring band within our tribe. Once a week I'd go the few miles to her community and take care of Lois's little ones. But after about two months, I started to wonder, 'What could Lois possibly be doing every Tuesday night? There's not much to do around here in these villages.' So one evening after Lois left to go to the meeting lodge, I packed up the children and went over to the lodge to find out what she was doing. We looked through a window into the lodge and saw a big circle of chairs, all neatly in place, with Lois sitting in a chair all by herself. The chairs in the circle were empty.
>
> "I was really curious, you know, so when Lois came home that evening, I asked her, 'Lois, what are you doing every Tuesday night?' And she said, 'I thought I told you weeks ago, I've been holding AA [Alcoholics Anonymous] meetings.' So I asked her back, 'What do you mean you're holding meetings? I went over there tonight with the children and looked through the window. We watched you sitting there in that circle of chairs, all alone.'
>
> "Lois got quiet—'I wasn't alone,' she said. 'I was there with the spirits and the ancestors; and one day, our people will come.'"
>
> Lois never gave up. "Every week Lois set up those chairs neatly in a circle, and for two hours, she just sat there. . . . No one came to those meetings for a long time, and even after three years, there were only a few people in the room. But ten years later, the room was filled with people. The community began turning around. People began ridding themselves of alcohol."
>
> —MAGGIE BROOKE, in *Leadership on the Line*

Did you have a wider social circle, apart from your close friends? What brought you together? What did you do together? Recall some of the specific activities and events you enjoyed together. What memories are linked to those places? Are there things you still talk about? If you met any of these people today what memories would you share?

Did marriage change your social life? If you got married, record how your social life changed. Did you continue to maintain an active relationship with friends? Did you find new groups of friends? If your friends got married, how did that change the nature and activities of the social group?

Sports

You were most likely at your physical peak in your twenties, and so you may have continued to play sports actively. Of course, no one's too old or too young to be a fan.

FACTS ABOUT SPORTS YOU PLAYED OR FOLLOWED

❧ List any team sports you played as a young adult, and note for each: the team you played on, the position you played, where your team played (city league, etc.), your team's win-loss record, and any awards or championships your team won.

❧ If your sport was individual—whether completely solitary, like marathon running or fly-fishing, or individual but social, like golf or singles tennis—note the sport, where and how you pursued it, any competitions you entered and how you did, and any other noteworthy facts about it.

❧ Note any sports you played casually but regularly, like tennis, hiking, and golf. Note where and how and how often you pursued it.

❧ If you were a serious sports fan, list the pro, college, or local teams you followed, and note how they did during this period, as well as any factual highlights about them (or about individual players) that seemed important to you.

MEMORIES OF SPORTS YOU PLAYED OR FOLLOWED

Think of each of the sports you actively pursued. For each sport, recall any memorable games or practices or other events. How much time did you devote to sports? What moments gave you genuine satisfaction? Which gave you deep disappointment? Who were the best players? Were you ever injured?

Recall each of the teams you followed as a fan. What appealed to you about that team? Who were your heroes? Did you ever attend games? Do you remember any memorable games? Did friends share your zeal for this team? What did you do together related to following this team? Were you attracted to just one team? Or did you love a particular sport in general, like football or ice skating, and did you follow it and all its teams and participants in general?

Causes, Community, and Politics

For many, this time of young adulthood was full of passion and idealism. What occupied your time and interest? How did you fulfill your need to help others, or work toward a cause greater than yourself?

FACTS ABOUT CAUSES, COMMUNITY, AND POLITICS

❦ Describe each of the causes—social, political, or whatever—that you supported and tried to advance as a young adult, its purpose, the time of your involvement, and the basic facts of what you did. It might have been a political campaign (say, for Eugene McCarthy or Ronald Reagan), or a protest movement (for example, against the Vietnam War), or a social cause (say, the civil rights movement).

❦ Describe any community work you did—what it was, its purpose, when you did it, and your role and degree of involvement.

❦ Describe how you got involved with politics—getting yourself or someone else elected to office, or supporting a political cause or agenda. Note who or what you supported, its purpose, when you did it, and your role or involvement.

MEMORIES OF CAUSES, COMMUNITY, AND POLITICS

Bring to mind each of the causes or movements that absorbed you at this time in your life. Recall what you did to support each cause. What were the most memorable moments? What did you accomplish? Who else was involved?

Recall each community work project you did. What occasions or memorable people come to mind that are linked to each? What goal were you and the others trying to achieve? Did you succeed?

Recall your involvement with politics. Did you help a candidate campaign? A national or statewide candidate? A local candidate? Did you participate yourself in politics? Did you run for office? Was it a political cause that occupied you?

Interests and Activities

What causes, interests, or hobbies occupied your time as a young adult? Perhaps you continued interests from your adolescence, or perhaps you took up something new.

FACTS ABOUT INTERESTS AND ACTIVITIES

❦ Name the clubs or organizations or other mutual-interest groups you belonged to and when. Note the purpose and your personal involvement with each.

❦ Note the games (such as poker) you played seriously, and when, where, and with whom.

❦ Recall the books or movies from this time that stand out in your memory.

❦ Name your favorite radio or television programs.

❦ Name and briefly describe any pets you or your family kept, or any other animals you were involved with.

❦ List any hobbies you pursued at this time.

❦ Describe any involvement you had with the arts, active or passive—music, theater, literature, dance, and so on. Describe briefly what you did, when, and where.

❦ Identify any honors or distinctions you earned as a young adult. Note what you received, from whom, and for what.

❦ Name and describe any organizations you and others created yourselves—such as a private club or an advocacy group or something else.

❦ Note any trips you took as a young adult—where you went, when, with whom, and what of interest you saw.

MEMORIES OF INTERESTS AND ACTIVITIES

Recall the pets and other animals in your life at this time. What moments or occasions do you remember? Recall moments of pleasure, and moments of worry or sadness with each.

Remember the hobbies you pursued seriously. Photography? Woodworking? Birdwatching? Stamp collecting? Gourmet cooking? Wine tasting? Recall the specific actions or training you took to pursue your interests. What special moments or occasions did each provide? Who else, if anyone, shared these interests?

Reflect on any games you enjoyed playing at this time. Did you play cards, like bridge? What highlights do you recall—special losses or victories, for example? Remember the people you regularly played or played with.

Recall anything you read at this time (fictions, nonfiction, or other) that somehow, directly or indirectly, made a difference in your life. If reading was important to you, what did you read that was especially memorable? Did you have a favorite book or author? What kind of reading did you prefer—history, science fiction, romance, biography?

Remember your involvement with the arts. Were you a performer or part of the audience? Did you enjoy singing or dancing? Recall the special moments of music or theater or poetry or dance or any other form of art you experienced. Remember the performers you enjoyed. Recall any other memorable players.

Recall the radio or television programs you especially enjoyed. Did you prefer music or talk shows? Did you ever watch the soaps? How were they a part of your life? Who else enjoyed them with you?

Recall any movies from this time that especially touched you. Remember any actors, female and male, or directors whom you particularly enjoyed.

Remember the special-interest clubs or other organizations (such as Rotary or the Junior Chamber of Commerce) that played an important role in your life. Recall where each group met, the other people there, memorable meetings, or special events. What role did you play? Did you ever receive any special recognition?

Recall each of the personal trips you took at this time. Recall who, if anyone, accompanied you: friends, parents, spouse, or a travel group. In your mind, go back over each trip, travel to and from your destination, and remember the sights you saw and other memorable events and scenes. Did you bring back souvenirs? Did you have any adventures? Did you meet anyone special? What stories did you return with and tell your friends?

I had one big problem left to solve: a painless way to get rid of unwanted admirers. . . . The average Brazilian man is convinced that he's the greatest lover in the universe, and will carry on giving you the opportunity to try him out for as long as you let him talk. I have never been seriously harassed in Brazil, and know of no other woman who had been (groping, Italian-style, is almost unheard of), but I was getting into some very complicated situations, simply because I couldn't find any tactful means of persuading someone so persistent to go away. One day, I tried a quote from the previous evening's soap opera: "I need to be alone!," delivered as dramatically as possible. "Ah!," came the response, verbatim. "Sometimes it's good to be alone." Pushing my luck, I repeated the next line, which went something like: "Yes, there are many things I must consider. In solitude." I could hardly believe it when my new friend told me where to find him if I got tired of thinking, and left.

By the miraculous intervention of television drama, I'd hit on one of the few reasons allowable, in a sociable Latin society, for rejecting company. It wasn't ideal: it meant finishing conversations as soon as they'd started, when I wanted the practice. But it saved me from having to get up and leave places before I was ready, from shouting matches in the middle of the night, and from the near-fatal insult of telling a macho male you don't actually fancy him. I must have gained one hell of a reputation as a deep thinker around Rio de Janeiro.

— CHERRY AUSTIN, in *Women Travel*

Notable Events

This last century hardly lacked for momentous events that shaped the lives of millions of people. Did some of them—such as the Depression, World War II, Korea, Vietnam, the Cold War, Desert Storm—touch you or those around you when you were young adults? What about local events, like floods and fires? Remember any of those events that occurred when you were in your twenties.

FACTS ABOUT NOTABLE EVENTS

❦ Briefly describe any historical or newsworthy events you distinctly remember from the time you were a young adult. Note when and where they occurred and how they touched your life or the lives of those around you.

✤ Describe in the same way any local events that occurred near you that somehow touched your life.

MEMORIES of notable events

Think about each of the notable or historical events you identified. Recall how and when you first learned about them. Remember how they affected your life and the lives of others around you. Were you somehow personally involved in these great events?

It was 6:01 a.m., February 9th, 1971. I thought we were at war, with bombs exploding over the city of Los Angeles. It was an earthquake, magnitude 6.6.

I had arrived the night before to visit my sister Toby and her family in the San Fernando Valley, one mile from the epicenter as it turned out. I'm not sure exactly what woke me—my bed sliding from one end of the room to the other, rumbling from deep within the San Gabriel Mountains, or kitchen plates crashing to the floor. Whatever it was, I was terrified. I could hear my sister cry out from the living room, where she was nursing her newborn, "Bill, an earthquake! Bill, an earthquake!" Only when a bedside lamp fell on his head did her husband, Bill, a sound sleeper, wake up.

The earthquake lasted a full minute—a lifetime. We huddled together under a doorway awaiting the aftershock, which came quickly and was nearly as powerful as the original. We were frozen, not sure what to do. There we stayed, all day, hoping the door frames would protect us if the house collapsed. We left our spots only to use the bathroom or eat whatever hadn't spilled out of the refrigerator.

It was the longest day, and most terrifying night, I can recall. Tremors continued to shake the small wood-frame house, and our nerves. We later learned that it was California's third worst earthquake in terms of lives lost (sixty-five) and property damage ($.5 billion).

My visit was to last a week, but I left the next day for San Diego and didn't have the courage to return to Los Angeles for many years. My sister resumed life as if nothing had happened.

—CAROL FRANCO, personal story

Think back about any significant local events you identified. Recall the details of what happened and how your life changed.

Other Voices

Are you still in touch with anyone who knew you as a young adult? Capture here their memories of you. If you want, track down others who were important to you at this time in your life.

If you want to include other people's memories of you as a young adult . . .

1. Make a list of people from your time as a young adult and ask them to share their memories with you, in their own words.
2. Record each memory on a separate sheet of paper. Label each memory "A Memory of Me" and include the memory teller's name, as well as the approximate date and location of the memory.
3. Add these memory sheets to your own memories in your *My Life Story* notebook.

> *I grabbed my sleeping bag, emblazoned with colorful cartoon characters (I don't re-member which ones) and designed only for sleeping indoors, and announced I was run-ning away. After some time, as I was lying confused and angry under the flittering stars, a few hundred feet from the house, my father came up and settled in next to me. "Are you ready to come home?"*
>
> —ERIC LINEBACK, personal story

Every stage of our lives is rich with meaning, if we know how to look for it. But the young adult stage was particularly rich for many of us. Why? Because most of us began to make big choices here of jobs and careers and life partners. Those choices then drove further choices: where and how to live, whether and where to pursue more schooling, whether and when to have children.

Since we reveal ourselves in our choices and how we make them, there is much that happened in this stage to illuminate who we were and what we wanted at that time of our lives. What makes these choices especially noteworthy is that we had to make such big decisions with so little knowledge or life experience. We were still so young! Did you feel this pressure to choose before you felt ready, or were you comfortable with the decisions you had to make?

Here's your opportunity to step back from the details of this time, the individual facts and discrete memories, and think about your young adult years as a whole.

Defining Moments

Think of yourself at the beginning of this stage, in your early twenties, and then think of yourself at the end of the stage, around thirty or shortly after. How did you change from twenty to thirty? How did you and your life become different in that interval? Once you've thought of the few basic ways you'd changed, then ask yourself, where and how did those changes occur? The answer is the defining moments you're seeking here.

Another approach: the choices you made, such as choosing a life partner or a career, can obviously be defining moments as well. Think back over your various choices and decide if any of them were real defining moments in your life. Dilemmas you faced offer clues—times when you didn't know which way to turn or what choice to make. Resolving those puzzles can also be defining moments.

I entered every class in existence and was working every hour of the day and often in the evening; and yet, for some strange reason, I had not discovered the one class that was to mean so much to me.

This discovery came about quite casually. I had noticed from time to time very untidy-looking students going in and out of a room on the basement floor; I hadn't an idea what the white stuff was that covered their aprons nor what the work was that they were doing—plaster and clay meant nothing to me then. One day, seeing all these strange-looking students go out and leave the door open after them, I crept in to see what on earth could have been going on in that room. It was a bare room with high windows, much like all the others; but what caught my attention at once was that the floor and tables and walls were covered with plaster casts. Another drawing class, I thought; but there were no easels or quantities of paper and pencils about. It must be some form of art that I had not heard about. I approached an object covered with a damp cloth. I gingerly raised the cloth and found a wet clay bust in the process of formation. I next found a mound of soft clay. I picked up a handful, rolled it between my fingers and suddenly felt an almost overwhelming delight course through me. The feel of that clay in my hand was entirely different from anything I had ever experienced before. Just the mere sensual part of it, the touch, seemed to fire me with something tremendously stimulating.

—JANET SCUDDER, *Modeling My Life*

Values—What Mattered

Think of the two or three or four big life decisions you made as a young adult. Take each one and recall whatever choices you had for each decision, and then try to recall how you made the choice you did. That "how" almost certainly reflected your values.

All of us try to find meaning by connecting with something—a set of beliefs, an institution, a profession—that reflects something bigger and more important than ourselves, something that will outlive us. Were such things important to you in your twenties?

Think of yourself at the end of your twenties—call to mind where you were then and what you were doing at work and home—and compare what was important to you at that time with what had been important when you were, say, eighteen or nineteen. Did you want the same things, spend your time in the same ways? Surely not, and the differences reflected many changes, not least changes in what was important to you.

Consider this as well: young adulthood is typically a time when we're deeply concerned with taking on roles. How important was it to you to be or become what you'd been taught was a "man" or "woman," for example? Perhaps you spent time and effort convincing your family that you were no longer "the kid." If you had children, was it important to be a "good parent"? In your marriage or serious relationships, did you try to play roles, such as the "strong man" or "supportive woman"? Most of us, to some extent in this stage, tried hard to take on such roles and prove ourselves worthy of them. They were part of what we expected of ourselves, a piece of our life dream.

For some of us, this period was a time of searching and we spent much of it feeling lost or, at least, at loose ends. We perhaps fought conventional notions of what we should hold most important. Perhaps we fought being defined ourselves. We were rebels. Those attitudes were values too, or perhaps "anti-values" would be a better term. They were values that might be described as "not this" or "not that." But they were values nonetheless and can be described here.

"Look at your mom and me," Daddy said. "We were young kids. Yeah, we liked each other, but it's working together, it's sacrificing together, it's doing the same things, caring for each other when one's sick, doin' something you maybe don't want to do—when you've done all that, then you can start talkin' about love."

I felt lucky that Mommy and Daddy had talked like that to us when we were kids because when I was twenty-one and got in the situation of having to make choices, their words came back to me. I listened to other women saying, "Oh, look at that hunk. Look at those buns." I watched them fall head over heels for somebody who was cute and flashy, which is what the culture says you're supposed to want. And then I'd look at Shearwood. He was no Rudolph Valentino. What he was, was my best friend. Our love affair, if such it was, wasn't exciting, wasn't romantic. But when I looked five years, ten years down the road, as Daddy had always taught us to do—"Size up the situation first. Try to see to the end of it. If it looks okay to the end of it, take that path. But if there's any problem with it, don't even bother wasting your time"—I looked, and as far as I looked, there was Shearwood: intelligent, gentle, generous, caring. Yes, he was the man for me.

—YVONNE THORNTON,
The Ditchdigger's Daughters

Love

Young adulthood is certainly a time of romantic love. So let us emphasize again that when we say "love," we mean it in the broader sense of "charity" that Paul (in the King James Bible) used in one of the most famous New Testament passages: "And now abide faith, hope, charity, these three; but the greatest of these is charity." Love can encompass romantic love but really refers to deep and special feelings of care and concern and acceptance between any two people. We stress it here, and in every stage, because love is one of the most important ingredients of life.

Take note here of all those people in this stage who loved you and by whom you felt loved in the sense of St. Paul's "charity." In one sense we strive to have "charity for all," as Abraham Lincoln said, but here your goal is to identify those few people from whom and for whom you felt a bond of special care and concern. Don't be confused or concerned if at the time you never thought of the bond as one of "love."

Learning and Wisdom

A good way to approach this part is to review the facts and memories you recorded of your young adult life and ask this question of each fact and memory: What did I learn from this? What did I think it taught me? The goal is not to create a long list but to identify the one or two, five at most, great lessons you learned.

For example, you might have learned: My long illness taught me I don't ultimately control my life. Or: I found out from that yearlong project that I'm a better marathoner than I am a sprinter. I'm better when I work long and steady on something than when I try to dash through it quickly.

How did you succeed or fail as a young adult, and what did success or failure teach you about life? What about adversity, illness, or accident? Did teachers, sports, friends, travel, chores, or anything else lead you to insights about how to live? Who taught you something of special value—either something they told you or something evident in their actions, or both?

What learning or wisdom you had gained from your childhood and adolescence did you consciously give up—unlearn, if you will? What did you keep?

What advice would you give a young adult that you think could help him or her make the right choices and do the right things in this stage of life? What would make this period happier and more productive? Think of a child or grandchild, or a nephew or niece, or even a young friend, who now faces the great challenges and tasks of this time of life. What could you tell them that might help?

Knowing what you know now, what advice would you have given to yourself as a young adult? Remember yourself then at some key moment or occasion—when you were hurt or happy or embarrassed, for example. If you now as a fully mature adult could enter that scene and say something to that person, impart some wisdom that might have helped you then, what would you say?

It was a caramel-colored, hard-sided suitcase with snapping locks, a leather handle, and the motto OSHKOSH on an oval brass plate. Inside it had golden-brown satin linings, two soft secret pockets, and satin tie ribbons. It was a small suitcase, neat and clean-looking, and it was Dad's little suitcase, one of the few belonging so specifically named and claimed in the communal life of my childhood.

I loved that suitcase. I knew, or perhaps imagined, that my father had bought it to move to Detroit in 1948. It fit the image I had of him as a young man, before my mother married him, and, I imagined, roped him into frustrating, limiting, domesticity—slim and spare, ascetic and refined, classy but not showy. It represented travel, change, risk. One day, I, too, would pack up and leave.

That was fantasy. What was real was the family, the house, and the basement. The basement, filled with belongings, made leaving unlikely. Our family's history was down there, its mysteries were down there. What was down there, in fact, was often revealed in someone's bored moment just looking. Once a thousand dollars in silver certificates, stored in an unmarked envelope, casually turned up in a shopping bag.

I wanted to live in the basement. Not in the clutter of the main "rec" room, paneled in knotty pine and upholstered in green vinyl by the landlord, who had lived in the house when new—but in a small room in the rear of the basement. This the landlord had fixed up as a bedroom for two young sons, before moving his family on to grander quarters. There were built-in bunks of knotty pine, and shiplike closets and drawers. But my father was resistant to clear out what was called "Dad's little room," resistant too, I believed, to losing physical—was it control?—over a growing child away from the family. My mother feared that the basement was cold.

In one closet was a plaid mackinaw jacket that would fit my father but that I had never seen him wear. Years later I found a photograph of him in the jacket on a New York street. One bunk was filled with drafting paper, seven-foot-long rolls of smooth white stock, heavy buff paper, and brown stock, stencils and drawing implements, drafting machines and tool boxes. These were his working tools as he went about the job shops of automotive Detroit, and here they rested during months of unemployment, for his trade was seasonal.

The second bunk held the family's luggage. A large navy pasteboard valise with a gray lining, a heavy vinyl garment bag, something with my grandmother's Queen Elizabeth ship decals on it—I did know there was a wider world out there—and that little brown suitcase. I would open it, smell it, carry it, hide a postcard in it. I wanted my whole life to be as classic, as neat, as golden brown and satin smooth as that suitcase. I wanted to live in it.

When I started taking trips in high school, I took Dad's suitcase. It went with me as a teenager, to New York to visit my aunt, and to Cleveland to visit a girl met in summer camp. I took it to college, and to my first apartments. In my twenties, I stored scarves and jewelry within. I displayed it. On a bentwood chair it became an end table.

Then I got married and it sat under the bed for five years, holding nothing but my wedding veil and a pair of lace gloves. With the next move I became ruthless. I had begun to worry about becoming a hoarder, a prisoner of things. The basement of my childhood rose to haunt me after dark.

I began throwing out. Gone: an iridescent Mexican shawl brought back to Canada in the 1950s, smelling slightly of mildew. Gone: a stained and frayed apron handsewn by a great-aunt. Gone: my high school yearbook, a file of college papers, a stack of real wooden cigar boxes. And I put it out too, in front of the service elevator, the little tan suitcase, now with a broken lock, a dent in its side, a torn lining. Time to streamline, to go spare and classy. What the suitcase represented, I thought.

Several moves later, installed in a house with not only a basement but also an attic, my daughter turned five. For three weeks I turned the house upside down, inside out, looking for it, the perfect little suitcase for doll clothes, with all that history beside. Finally it hit me. I remember. I had lost it, wasted it, while filled with blind passion of destroying the past and moving on. Until that day, and I sat down limply, sick at the pit of my stomach, in my own basement empty and bare.

—ELIZABETH EHRLICH, *Miriam's Kitchen*

Summing Up

Here is an opportunity to apply the wisdom of years and hindsight and sum up your young adult stage. How would you characterize it in a few words? What role did this period play in your life? Was it a time of life-shaping choices? Was it a time of searching and wandering and experimenting? What kind of person were you and what kind of person did you become by the end of it? What should someone who's just read the story of your young adult years think of this time in your life?

Capture in the words you write not only a summary of what you did or accomplished (or not) at this time, but try to summarize too how this period *felt*. Do you look back on it fondly? Do you wish you could do it over?

STAGE 4

---

adult

If the word searching *best captures the essence of life as a young adult, then the word that best captures the essence of this next stage of life is probably* striving.

Many of us struggled through our twenties, a time of some uncertainty—much for some, less for others—as we let go the habits and thoughts of feckless youth and sought somehow to establish ourselves as full-fledged adults. Perhaps we experimented with jobs and relationships far longer than others thought we should; perhaps we experimented almost not at all, choosing a career virtually in college and marrying soon after graduation. Even for those early deciders, the twenties still were likely to feel uncertain and provisional. Our marriages may have needed work and adjustment before they settled into place, or the work we chose may have proved to be unhappy and require change or adaptation. Whatever the case, we finally completed our experiments and made the necessary commitments—to a life partner and to a career—and then were ready for the next great challenges.

Having thus declared our place in the adult world, we began to strive toward "making it," whatever form that would take in the world we'd chosen. For most of us, it meant raising happy, well-adjusted children who were ultimately able to succeed on their own in the world, and achieving some success in the line of work we'd chosen.

To accomplish these dual aims, we rose every morning, strapped on our harness (so to speak), and labored faithfully to pull our duties, responsibilities, and goals a few more feet up the steep hill. For this was a time dominated by a sense of ascending some great peak. Many of us could even identify the exact nature of the "peak." It was a promotion to a certain level in one's company, or the achievement of tenure and full professorship on some faculty, or the graduation of children from high school and their admittance to some prestigious college. Even those of us who'd chosen an unconventional life probably sought *something* in this period, some goal, some milestone that had great significance to us, and perhaps only to us.

Whatever this goal, it signified far more than some simple accomplishment. It meant instead the realization of our life dream, what has been called the "hopes of youth" for what we would be and achieve as adults. It was the aspiration and self-image we had developed that gave our lives meaning and purpose. Achieving our life dream, whatever it was, would determine the success or failure of our very lives themselves. Its achievement would justify our very existence. And achieving that dream at this period often came down to that specific goal. If we could achieve that goal, and thus our life dream, our lives thereafter would be wonderful, we thought, for we would have not only "made it" but we would also have proven our right to be alive, fulfilled our purpose for living. If we failed to achieve it, the rest of our lives would be . . . well, problematic, a failure, something too frightening to contemplate. At least that's the way it often felt to us in this stage of life.

We were driven by the conviction, the fear, that this was the time when we had to achieve whatever we were going to achieve. Later would be too late. For later we would be past our prime. Age and its unsettling physical signs did not yet play a role in our lives—the thirties were still *young*, after all—but we knew *age* was now just over the horizon. In our thirties we believed that forty was the end of vital youth. We could still remember our days as youngsters when anyone over forty seemed old. Now nothing but a few years separated us from that unknown and frightening territory. We struggled with a sense that there wasn't much time left to do what we wanted, to live life as we wanted, to grasp what we wanted.

So life in our thirties was an exciting time when we strove mightily, full of a sense of purpose, but it was a time of high stress as well, for most of us. We had high hopes and expectations for the future, but success was far from assured. For many of us, life felt like a game in which only a few could succeed and most would fail. In many cases, that was literally true. As we rose in organizations—whether business, nonprofit, or governmental—the number of positions available decreased. If we set our sights high, it meant we could only succeed if many others faltered. The natural competitiveness of youth turned into a driven search for promotion and recognition. Many of us found ourselves uncomfortable in that world, but there was little we could do to change it without dropping out and choosing some form of alternative life. That was something many of us considered, more or less seriously, at one time or another, but usually did nothing about. We suspected the alternative life was far from all it was cracked up to be.

The challenges for women in this stage could be particularly acute, especially for those increasing numbers who sought to raise families *and* pursue a career. The need to struggle daily against the perceptions and prejudices arrayed against women in the workplace could be exhausting and emotionally draining. To raise children simultaneously would take everything a woman had and more. For women who had put aside careers, or from the beginning had chosen the role of homemaker, this was a time to begin contemplating life beyond children, with all the questions and uncertainties that raised.

With all the striving and stress, and the need to put our heads down and work hard day after day after day, we were so busy we had little time for ourselves, to spend on activities and pleasures that nourished us. To find quiet time when we could decompress in some way was a daily challenge that most of us lost. Life seemed to be one long raft trip through white water rapids. Perhaps this was why we tended in this period *not* to question things—Why are we doing this? Do I really want that stupid life dream I'm pursuing? Do my children really have to excel at everything? We just plowed ahead.

There were genuine pleasures too. For all the stress and pressure, there were days we went home feeling like we'd done something good. We were growing in our professions and work; we were becoming expert in something, and doing good work was always a source of deep satisfaction. Watching the progress of children into the world, and their growing mastery of knowledge and life, could offer profound gratification. If we had chosen a partner and work wisely, or luckily, we were blessed.

FACTS AND MEMORIES FROM YOUR ADULT STAGE

Now recall and record the facts and memories of the adult stage as you lived it—roughly your thirties. For most, this period began with putting in place the basic pieces of life—work, your own home, and perhaps a family. It was then a time of striving to bring those pieces to fruition—getting ahead in one's line of work or career, raising children, making a place in adult society.

For many, perhaps you, it retained some elements of experimentation: a first attempt at marriage failed and you had to start again the search for a life partner; or a career proved ultimately unsatisfying and you had to transition somehow to a new line of work.

Get down here the facts and memories of that period. As always, record the facts as requested in each life segment and then see what memories come to mind when you ponder the many questions in each memory section.

You as an Adult

As an adult, you were the real you, the person you really were. No more growing up. No more experimenting. No more trying on different facets of personality. At least that's the way it's supposed to work. So what kind of person had you become as you entered your thirties?

FACTS ABOUT YOU AS AN ADULT

❦ Note when, in your mind, this stage of your life began. Perhaps you simply decided to get serious, or you committed to a career or a relationship, or you had children. This was when you truly settled down, which could occur years after getting married or even having children. Note how old you were when this occurred.

❦ Without great thought or reflection, simply list the major life events, the milestones, the big moments that occurred to you in this period.

❦ Note when you began to question the life, or some part of it, that you'd been living through your thirties and into your forties. Perhaps, instead of questioning, you simply began to feel some sense of unease or slight unhappiness. Perhaps you suddenly realized you were aging, that you had limited time. Perhaps some event (being passed over for promotion; children not getting into the college of your choice) started this questioning. Perhaps you just woke up one day and there it was. Perhaps all the above. However it happened, it was the beginning of the end of this stage. How old were you then?

MEMORIES OF YOU AS AN ADULT

What happened to your life dream? Did you pursue and achieve the life dream you'd carried into this period from your youth? Did you have a life dream–related goal at this time, something you wanted that would indicate you had achieved the dream or were on track? Did your life dream change in some way? Had it become more realistic? Had you given it up?

Whether related to a life dream or not, what specific goals did you want to accomplish in your thirties? What did you hope to accomplish by the age of forty or thereabouts? Was there some goal, maybe never explicitly stated, that you were working toward? A promotion? A certain kind of recognition? Writing a book? Getting your children into good jobs or prestigious colleges?

What, if anything—fear, fate, lack of knowledge, etc.—held you back? Bad luck? A lack of training or skills or knowledge? Some decision or choice you'd made earlier? Resources? Responsibilities? Other people? Did fear prevent you from doing something? What would you have done if you hadn't been afraid? What did you fear? Failure? Ridicule? Appearing weak or soft? Appearing tough and unfeeling? Economic ruin? Did you feel you'd been born into a part of society or a set of circumstances that you couldn't overcome and that set the course of your life?

How did I finally get comfortable with the immensity of motherhood? How did I put my fears to rest? I didn't. But one day I was talking to a fellow thirty-year-old, a friend who was terrified of marriage. She said it was the word forever *that got her; she just didn't see how two people could make a life with something that big, that final hanging over them. I explained to her that once you are married, the idea of marriage doesn't sit in the middle of the room like an elephant while you live your life. Eternity doesn't peer out at you from your morning coffee or down at you from the ceiling as you and your husband laugh your heads off at* The Graduate *for the tenth time; it doesn't poke its head around the corner as you fight. Later, it occurred to me that the same must be true for motherhood. It must be like any other kind of love, figured out minute to minute, achieved in acts and dailiness. And, like any other kind of love, it requires a leap of faith.*

— MARISA DE LOS SANTOS, "Wide Awake"

What dilemmas or difficult decisions did you have to make at this time in your life? Was your life fully settled and committed now? Or were there times you felt torn between two wonderful or awful alternatives? For example, did you ever have to choose between two jobs? Did you forego getting married or having children for some other goal? Did you ever find yourself caught between people's expectations?

What risks did you take? Recall the big decisions you made as an adult in your thirties and think about the risks you were taking in each. How did each turn out? What was the biggest risk you took at this time? Did having a family and responsibility for others change your outlook? What decisions or choices did you make that reflected this greater or lesser willingness to take risks? What risks did you avoid?

Did you consider yourself a success or failure at the age of forty? What did you achieve in this stage that you think was noteworthy? Your life dream? Other goals? Did you achieve something that turned out to be a significant accomplishment only in hindsight?

What were your strengths and weaknesses at this time? In what area of life did you consider yourself highly proficient? How did you develop this mastery? Think of times when you demonstrated it. How did others react? What were you not good at? Think of times those weaknesses made themselves apparent.

Who were you now? Did you have or develop a clear and distinct sense of yourself and your unique identity? Did you find your own voice, so to speak? How was this identity different from your sense of yourself in your twenties or earlier? Think of times when your identity revealed or asserted itself.

> *I am convinced that I have been a lesbian all my life. Having said that, I have to admit that I was blissfully unaware of this until about the age of twelve, when I developed my first major crush, and—like the leopard—knew I couldn't change my spots.*
>
> *It was not for want of trying. . . . I finally did find a really nice guy. We got married. It was a disastrous choice on my part—I had everything a nice girl could want, but it just didn't work. . . .*
>
> *Leaving my marriage was an enormous relief but brought with it all the attendant trials of coming out to friends, family and at work. Family was more difficult than the others I suppose, but I was luckier than some and it really wasn't that bad. In some ways it was made easier by my mother's persistent confusion about lesbianism and vegetarianism. By some quirk of fate I had decided to be a vegetarian at more or less the same time as I "became" a lesbian, and my mother could never distinguish between the two. "I never realized that all those tennis stars were vegetarian too," she would announce; or very confidentially to someone offering me a plate of smoked salmon, "No, my daughter's a lesbian you know—she doesn't eat fish." This became so funny that it went some way to removing the sting of her disapproval and dislike of the turn I had taken.*
>
> —SUKEY FIELD, in *Reinvented Lives*

Did you try to change yourself in any way? Did anyone ever tell you that you needed to change in some way? Did you diet? Did you make New Year's resolutions? Read self-help books? Attend self-improvement programs? What was wrong with what you were, and what did you want to become? Who or what was that person you were striving to be?

Recall what a typical day was like for you in your thirties. (If your daily routines changed through this period, think of each one separately.) When did you get up? What did you have for breakfast? Did you exercise? What was your morning typically like? Your afternoons? Where would you go? How would you get there? What was a typical evening? What about a typical weekend?

What had the power to engross you totally as an adult? What at this time in your life had the power to capture your attention completely and keep you captivated for hours? Recall those moments—what were you doing?

What tended to occupy your mind? What did you most worry about? When you daydreamed, where did your mind go? Did you have any recurring dreams at night? Did they reflect anything about your awake life?

What were your most intense emotional moments and events as an adult?

- Can you recall a time or times when you *laughed* and *laughed* and *laughed*?

As we grow up, our lives become so cluttered. We become shackled with responsibility, and bogged down with work and kids and the daily rituals and problems of our everyday lives. We forget how to play. . . .

I remember one day, not so long ago, when I pulled my car up to a stoplight in Los Angeles, on Wilshire and Twenty-sixth Street, right near where I lived. I was by myself and an Elton John song I love, "I'm Still Standing," came on the radio. I began to move my body to the music, bouncing up and down in my seat, singing at the top of my voice. But this wasn't enough.

"The hell with it!" I cried, and, opening my car door, I jumped out, stood in the street and really let myself go. I started to really dance with abandon. I didn't care what I looked like. I was feeling the rhythm, feeling the joy, and I went with it. The man in the car behind me started to laugh. Before I knew it, he jumped out of his car and he started dancing, too. The two of us strutted our stuff and shook and wriggled and danced until the stoplight suddenly changed. Then we dashed back into our cars, laughing, and went our separate ways.

—GOLDIE HAWN, *A Lotus Grows in the Mud*

- Were there any moments when you felt or exhibited your own *drive* and *ambition*?
- Did you ever feel *guilty*—about what you should have done or about choices you made?
- What brought you *joy* and *happiness*?
- Recall moments of *stress* and *pressure*. How did you handle them?
- What provided the strongest *sense of accomplishment*?
- What *disappointed* you the most? What had you wanted and hoped for at this time that did not happen or was not given to you?
- Remember moments of *love* and *closeness*.
- What *frightened* you?
- What times were the most *romantic* and *passionate*?
- When were you most *embarrassed* or *ashamed*?
- Did something ever absolutely *delight* you?
- How about moments of *extreme anger* or *losing your temper*?
- Did anything ever make you *jealous* or *envious*?
- When did you feel a *real connection* with another person?
- What moments of *grief* or *loss* did you experience?
- What moments did you experience of deep *emotional pain* and *hurt*?
- How about moments of real *physical pain*?
- When did you experience *deep regret*?
- Did you ever feel deeply *misunderstood*?
- What *surprised, shocked,* or *amazed* you?
- Did something ever *frustrate* you?
- What were your most intense experiences around your senses: *sight, sound, smell, taste,* and *touch*?

How did you usually spend free time? Did you have any time for yourself? Were any of these times memorable for some reason? Was there a place or a time of day that was your own? Did you have a haven or sanctuary where you could go to be renewed and refreshed?

I've been scheming to reclaim the smallest corner of myself. I steal time. I sneak away from work and go to movies in the middle of the day. I see sci-fi thrillers and stupid comedies. I see scary movies. They remove me from my life, if only for a few hours. . . .

And I wake up before dawn, before Ava and Daddy, and go outside and run through the cemetery. I leave Samo inside, whining at the door. I want to be alone. I want to hear my feet thud and splash with no doggy echo. I want to be a person without baggage, if only for a few minutes. If only in a cemetery in the rain.

—Elizabeth Cohen,
The House on Beartown Road

How did you come across to other people? How would a candid friend who knew you well have described your personality? How did you come across to strangers? What kind of reputation did you have? Did any aspect of your personality change in this period?

How did you dress and present yourself? Was your appearance important? Was it different from earlier years? What effect were you trying to achieve? What was the purpose of caring about your appearance? What were the clothing fads and fashions of the time and how did you follow them (or not)?

Were any possessions particularly important to you? Why were they valuable? What did they mean to you? How did you get them?

Did you ever have to struggle against hardship? Were you touched—by war, famine, epidemics, great social movements, financial setbacks, and the like? How did you come through? Recall moments and events that capture that experience.

What was your experience as an adult woman? How did you find your gender made a difference as you worked to establish your place in the adult world—in your work, in your social or religious life, or in any other way? Did you have to fight harder for recognition and achievement and to be heard? If you were a homemaker, what did you like most about this role? What did you like least? Did you feel society valued this role enough? In general, was it difficult to have your own voice, to express yourself, to be heard and valued as a person?

Were you ever discriminated against as an adult? What about you led to the discrimination? Who discriminated against you? How did you feel? What did you do in response?

How was your health and physical well-being as an adult? Did you suffer any health problems, physical or mental? Were they acute (serious but they went away) or chronic (you had to live with them, at least for a while)? Were you in any accidents? Did you experience, temporarily or permanently, any physical limitations? When were you under the greatest health or physical strain?

Did anything from your past still occupy you? Were issues of your earlier life—childhood, adolescence, young adulthood—resolved? Or did you still have to settle—if only in your own mind—anything that felt unresolved?

What did NOT happen that was significant? What did *not* happen that you wished had, for yourself or someone close to you? For example, not getting a promotion or assignment you wanted. Or, your child not achieving something you felt would have been desirable.

What encounters did you have with life and death as an adult? Did a friend, family member, or someone else close to you die? How did it affect you or those close to you? Was the loss traumatic for you?

Steven and I drove in silence in Larry's white Tahoe to the Mt. Wilson trail. We had decided to take the same hike that Larry was on when he died. The warmth of his voice and smile were fresh in our memories, but we needed to place our feet in the exact path that his had last traveled only two days earlier.

We parked near the trailhead and noticed a sign-in book. One page was turned up at the corner. It contained my brother's recognizable signature. Just the L before Williams. The artistic flow of humps resolved itself only at the last moment. The other names were followed by start and completion times for their hikes. Larry's had neither a beginning nor an end.

We walked the narrow path in single file. It was sandy with a steady upward slope. Dry dirt gathered in our nostrils and throats. As we gained height, we got a panoramic view of Los Angeles. *I thought about my last conversation with Larry, only a couple weeks before, when he told me he knew as a child he could never take over our father's business. He felt compelled to make his way in the wider world. And he did—he was an amazing artist, photographer, and director.*

The trail eventually turned back on itself so the city was no longer visible. Succulents and wildflowers hugged the mountain. The ledge dropped off to a deep crevasse and there were no guardrails. A nearby stream muted other sounds except the heaviness of our footsteps and the occasional piercing birdcall.

Steven had spoken with the hiker who found Larry, so he knew exactly what spot to look for. "This is it," he said. Someone had tucked a bouquet of white and yellow wildflowers there.

I leaned against the rocky ledge that probably held Larry's slumped body when the heart attack stopped him. Across the canyon brown protrusions of land met in a V-shape, forming a perfect heart. There weren't many trees, but one with a broad canopy reached directly overhead. I listened to water flowing. It comforted me to know that his last moments were infused with these impressions. It was spectacularly beautiful, gentle, and calm. Not far from the city, he'd found a pathway to paradise.

—MARJORIE WILLIAMS, personal story

Children and Family Life

Perhaps your family life was well established and your children far along as you lived through your thirties. Perhaps you were just starting a family. Either way, if you had children, remember what that was like in these adult years.

FACTS ABOUT YOUR CHILDREN AND FAMILY LIFE

❧ For each child born in this period, record the child's name, sex, birthplace and date, and age at the end of this stage.

🍁 Note any highlights or milestones in his or her life, such as health problems, injuries or accidents, or any other facts that seem to you to mark the progress of growing up.

🍁 For any of your children born before this stage (including adopted children and stepchildren), note any milestones or highlights in their lives during this period.

🍁 Name any people living with you, besides spouse and children. Describe very briefly who they were, their ages, why they were living with you, and any milestones in their lives.

MEMORIES of your children and family life

For each of your children born in this period:

- *How did you and your spouse decide to have this child?* Did the pregnancy simply happen, or was it a conscious choice? Recall any occasions or moments around making that choice.
- *Did you lose this child?* What happened? How did you and your spouse and family deal with this terrible loss?
- *Did anything memorable happen during pregnancy?* What moments come to mind around the conception of this child (where, when, any special efforts)? What happened during the pregnancy—any funny or surprising or sad or memorable moments? Were you hoping for a boy or a girl? What names did you pick and why? Were there any medical problems?

One day when I was about five months pregnant, I thought I felt the baby move. This was what I'd been waiting for, the moment all my patients spoke about reverently. Slowly, I lay down on the couch in our apartment, barely breathing so as not to confuse any other natural occurrence with the baby's movement. Sure enough, I felt it! It wasn't a kick as I had expected and as my patients and the textbooks described it. It was more like holding a fluttering butterfly in my cupped hands. It was an ecstatic experience. I felt life. I felt my baby.

—Yvonne Thornton,
The Ditchdigger's Daughters

- *Recall the events around the actual birth of this child.* When did labor begin? How did you get to the hospital? Did everything happen as expected? Were there any dicey moments?
- *Recall the early life of this child.* Did someone visit to help with the newborn? What kind of baby was he or she? Did he or she adapt to a schedule quickly, or slowly and reluctantly? What did you worry about? Think about the milestones you identified from this child's earliest life—rolling over, first word, first smile, first step, and so on? When did his or her personality first reveal itself and what was it? Happy? Quiet? Introvert? Extrovert? Whom did this child look like? Act like? Any health problems or injuries? How easy or hard was this period for you and your spouse? Were you tired most of the time? Was your life shaped by the child, or did he or she eventually adapt well to your life and schedule?

One spring evening in 2003 I was with a group of musicians at The Abbey, the home of Severin Browne, where he and his brother Jackson (yes, that Jackson Browne) had grown up. It was a landmark, nearly mystical. One of the first structures built in the area, the Abbey was fashioned after an old mission complete with a chapel—and a dungeon. You would expect to find magic there. I found caterpillars.

I always feel a little guilty taking an evening away from the kids, then aged 1 and 6. So when I spotted those two fuzzy black critters crawling around the courtyard, I decided to bring them home—sort of a consolation prize. The two caterpillars were dubbed Flutterby and Wing and they lived a lavish life over the next couple of weeks in their bug cage, complete with habitat and food supplied daily.

When we were about to leave for vacation, my husband convinced our older daughter, Anika, to let them go free. She was reluctant until he said Flutterby (hers) would show his appreciation for her good care by returning to see her when he turned into a butterfly. Anika waited for weeks. Sure enough, she saw a grey-white butterfly (Wing) and a black and brown butterfly (Flutterby) wherever she went. One day she spotted Flutterby heading into our back yard and went running to greet him. It must have been her grateful caterpillar; he actually landed on her outstretched hand.

Some places are just magical. But no place more than the mind of a child.

— STACY YOUNG, *personal story*

- *What were this child's younger years like during this period of your life?* What kind of personality did he or she eventually develop? Recall ways it revealed itself. Whom did he or she take after? What was the daily routine for this child? What was he or she especially good at—what talents began to show themselves even in childhood? What did you do to encourage those talents?

- *How was your life different because of this child?* What did you do with this child? Read? Play? Do you recall special moments with this child? What rules did you impose? Were you a relaxed parent, or a nervous one? Recall moments that revealed your relationship with this child. What did you learn, if anything, from this child, or from caring for him or her? What was hardest for you about this child? What was most rewarding for you?

- *When did he or she go to school and what changes did that bring in this child's life and in yours?* What dreams, hopes, and expectations did you have for this child? How was this child different from his or her brothers and sisters? Did you get involved in this child's schooling?

- *What was the biggest challenge you had with this child during his or her early years?* Did you and your spouse disagree in any way about how to raise this child? Did you ever punish this child? For what? Did you ever praise this child? For what?

- *What other adults were important in this child's life*—a teacher, an uncle, a neighbor, a nanny?

Think about other children born before this period in your life:

- *Look at the milestones you identified for this child.* What memories do they arouse? Were there any other highlights you remember—birthdays, trips together, times together, troubles together?

- *Recall the good times with this child. Recall the difficult times.* Were there times you got along especially well? Were there times when the child had difficulty with you? Or when you were having trouble with each other?

- *What talents and abilities did this child begin to demonstrate?* Music? Writing? Sports? How did he or she develop them? Did you help?

- *What did you worry most about in regard to this child?* Health? School? Social skills? Some physical feature or disability? Some other form of handicap? Were there any medical emergencies?

- *What did you expect of this child?* Did this child ever make you proud? Ever embarrass you? What happened?
- *If this child entered the teen years at this time, did you find those years difficult?* What was difficult? Do you remember any specific moments?

As a parent, you hope that your child has a good self image at all stages and that you can contribute to that confidence. I remember my mother pointing out my poor complexion, a hair style she thought unbecoming, and other legitimate shortcomings of my appearance that I was aware of and felt worse about when she spoke of them. My goal as a parent was to never do that to my children.

When my son was in the fifth grade and his sweat glands fully operational, I bought him a tube of stick deodorant and explained to him that it was time to use it since his body was growing up and changing. He thanked me and took it to his room. About a week later when I was putting clean laundry in his dresser drawer, I noticed the deodorant stick and that it hadn't been used. Later that day I asked him about it and reminded him that the odor his glands were now producing was unpleasant to others. He thought for a minute before saying, "But I really like the smell!" I didn't argue with him and let it go. He had a strong sense of himself at that young age and was comfortable with his stink. I didn't want to mess with that.

—KARIN BARTOW, personal story

- *Did this child ever question your authority?* What happened? How did you feel about that?
- *Recall times this child came to you for help.* For what? What did you do?
- *How was this child like you? Different from you?* Think of yourself at that age and compare the two of you, child to child.
- *Do you recall any times or occasions involving this child's friends?* Did his or her friends come home with your child? What did they do together? Did you like the friends? Or did you wish your child would choose different friends?
- *If this child attended school, how did he or she do?* What happened at school that you remember?

- *If your child was adopted think about any times that issues arose around the fact this child was adopted.* How did it affect the child? When did you tell the child about his or her background? Did the child seek to find his or her biological parents? Was this difficult for you? For the child?

- *If you were a stepparent how did you and this child get along?* Was it difficult at first for this child to accept you? Did you form a good relationship?

What about the grandparents? What kind of relationship did your children have with their grandparents? Did your parents see much of your children? Did they help raise them? Did they seem happy in their roles as grandparents? Did having children change your relationship with them? Did they visit? What did they think about the way you and your spouse were raising your children? Did they try to offer advice?

What was daily life in your family like? Recall a typical day in your home. What were people doing in the morning as they prepared for the day? What happened typically in the evening? What times did you normally spend with your spouse? With your children? Recall a good day, a frustrating day, and an ordinary day. What was the atmosphere in the home? What was dinner like?

Zeb and Jake argued, before a single light had been turned on, about who got to use the bathroom first when they woke up; I had to tell Jacob four times to comb his hair; I had to tell Zeb three times to clear the breakfast dishes; the sink was full of pots and pans from the dinner party last night. . . .

I yelled. I shouted. I threw my hands up in the air, ranted about obeying your father; ranted about the fire ants out there on the grass where we park our old VW Bug, those ants just waiting for bare feet and the opportunity to bite; ranted about never listening to me; ranted about and about and about.

I yelled the first ten minutes of the fifteen-minute drive to the studio. . . .

But when we parked in front of the studio, Zeb already with his door open, ready to climb out; I reached to him, put my arm around his neck, pulled him to me. I hugged him, said, "I'm sorry I yelled. I shouldn't have done that."

"That's okay" he said into my shoulder.

"Can we go to Wendy's for lunch?" Jacob said from the backseat, sensing this window of opportunity, his father contrite. . . .

There are days like today. Days with no story, really, other than the misstep, the idiot words and gestures, the sincere belief for a moment, however blind, that all this yelling might actually do some good, when the world and Velcro sandals seem somehow malevolently aligned against you. Then the right word, the right gesture. The lunch at Wendy's, atonement after confession.

No story, really, other than that of being a father.

— BRET LOTT, *Fathers, Sons & Brothers*

If both you and your spouse worked, did that affect your relationship with any of your children? What were the pluses and minuses of having both parents work? Do you think that you missed anything because of working? Did the child miss something?

What family rituals and routines did you follow? These might be family dinner or daily prayer, reading before bed at night, ritual meals (like pot roast every Sunday). Were they liked or endured by your children? Were they the same rituals and traditions your family had followed when you were growing up?

How did you and your family spend major holidays, vacations, and special occasions? Christmas? Thanksgiving? Spring breaks? Summer vacation? Were there certain places you always went, or certain people who came to your home?

Did you face any hardships as a family? Were there any tough times, when you and your family struggled for some reason? Ill health? Misfortune? Job loss? How did your family face them? Did the hardships pull you apart or bring you together?

Recall telling children the facts of life. What happened? How did you feel? How did the child respond?

When my two older kids were about 10 and 11, I decided it was the right time for me to tell them where babies come from. We went into the basement so that my younger daughter wouldn't hear. I sat them down and began my explanation. When I was finished, they looked at each other and then at me, and exclaimed: "You did that three times?!"

— SONJA BENSON, personal story

Single parenthood. Did the responsibility of raising your children fall on you alone at this time in your life? What memorable times come to mind? How did you become a single parent? If you divorced, did you get any help from your ex-spouse or partner? Did you try to compensate in any way for the absence of a parental partner?

Marriage/Partnership

What was married life like in your thirties? Were you and your spouse focused on family and work? What different roles did the two of you play—homemaker and breadwinner, two breadwinners?

FACTS ABOUT YOUR MARRIAGE OR PARTNERSHIP

❦ Note your spouse's/partner's age at the beginning and end of this period.

❦ In a few words, factually describe his or her life in this period—work, interests, etc. Note any highlights or significant moments for your spouse or partner that occurred. What happened, when, and where?

MEMORIES OF YOUR MARRIAGE OR PARTNERSHIP

When were you happiest in the relationship? When did the relationship feel like it was working well and you were both getting from it what you needed? What would pull you together? What was the glue between you? Recall happy moments together.

We never thought we'd be here, in a playground on a Saturday night. We're not twenty anymore, and we can't quit our jobs or sleep all day. (Or all night, for that matter.) You can't fish whenever you want, and my New Yorkers *pile up on the bedside table, waiting to be read.*

The businessman in the window seat sees a harried mother, but in your eyes, I'm still a crazy novelist; a girl with big dreams and Timberland boots. And that means a lot to me, as we move into our middle age. I know you're a sunburned grad student who sleeps in a sleeping bag unrolled on a mattress, no matter how fine our cotton sheets.

This feels like a confusing time to me: we're changing from being someone's children to someone's mom and dad. From making pronouncements to making real decisions. I'm glad you're along with me for this ride.

Remember our small backyard with two bushy trees in Texas? I had lived in Greece, and one night as we sat outside under the moon, I told you that I missed Greek tavernas. They have little lights hanging above the tables, I told you, and I loved that. We talked about where we'd go in the world and what we'd do.

A few weeks later, when I returned home after a weekend away, you led me outside by the hand. You had cut away the low branches of the trees, and strung lights. You had put a table and two chairs under the lights. It was a magical place, my taverna in Texas.

Your mind, your zaniness, your kindness—you fill me with wonder.

—AMANDA EYRE WARD,
"To All the Men I've Loved Before"

How did the relationship change, for better or worse, over the course of this stage? What happened to the romantic side of your relationship? Did you ever talk about your relationship? Did you both agree on what you wanted from the relationship? What did you wish you had more of? What did you typically talk about—at dinner, for example? Did your personalities match or conflict? Did you complement or compete with each other in any way? What ways did you find to meet your own individual needs? What habits of each were endearing, and maddening? Did you become good friends (if you weren't already)? How would each of you have completed the sentence, You always . . . ?

What routines and interests did you share? How did you each spend spare or leisure time, together or apart? What was a typical day for the two of you like then—weekday and weekend or holiday? What roles did you each fall into (breadwinner, homemaker, other)? What did you do together socially? What hobbies or interests did you share? Did you do anything together in the community?

What goals and aspirations did you share? Did you two have basically the same life dreams? If your two life dreams were at odds in some way, how did you reconcile the differences?

If you both worked, how did you sort through the issues and conflicts that raised? How did work and marriage coexist? Comfortably? Was there any tension rising from the conflicting demands of your two jobs? Did you both work because you had to, or because it was important for the identity and independence of each of you?

How did you face challenges in your relationship? What were the hardest times in your marriage? Did differences in background, upbringing, education, or interests affect your relationship? How did you deal with such things as job loss, an accident, illness, a stroke of luck, a promotion and move, a child's illness or death? Did you draw together? How did such things change you individually and as a couple?

While the circumstances of our life on our return to Rome were now idyllic, there were dark patches caused by the return of John's bouts of deep depression. I thought of his temperament as having the qualities of a medieval stained-glass window, rich in its range of colors, complex in texture, mediating great beauty. But just as the colors of a stained-glass window vanish when the sun disappears behind a cloud, so John's beautiful personality could be suddenly, temporarily, extinguished, replaced by swift-moving moods of anger, suspicion, and despair. In time I came to see these moods as following a rigid calendar—Christmas, spring, midsummer—sometimes announced by a period of elation, always marked by a change in facial expression which was striking. John's deep brown eyes normally sparkled with laughter, and his face was mobile in its quick ebb and flow of expression. But when darkness descended, his right eye drooped, his expression became mask-like, and the sparkle left his eyes. It was as though a stranger had replaced my sensitive and loving husband, someone possessed by demons of rage, tormented by suspicion. The man I knew of heroic courage would be overwhelmed by fear and despair, silent, without energy or hope.

When these moods descended I kept remembering that they would pass, and when I encountered outbursts of anger or exasperation, that it was the mood, not the man, speaking. With the immaturity of the young, I expected that the strength of our love for each other, and our happiness, would eventually vanquish them. Influenced by the therapeutic attitudes of the day, I expected that this suffering could be "cured" or "made better." In time, I was to come to a chastened recognition that there was nothing I could do to help avert what was to be a chronic condition. That I could be a companion but never a cure, to someone I loved so much, was to be the discovery that marked my real growing up.

—JILL KER CONWAY, *True North*

Was the relationship ever in danger? Did you somehow seek to save or renew the relationship during this period? Did you as a couple ever seek outside help, such as from a marriage counselor? What held your relationship together? What forces worked to pull you apart? What got you through whatever troubles you faced?

Were you or your spouse previously married? How did a previous marriage and your or your spouse's experience in it affect this relationship? Did you or your spouse have any contact, or a continuing relationship, with the ex-spouse?

Were you ever abused or mistreated in any way by your spouse or partner? If you can, recall what happened. What did you do as a result?

How did each of you get along with your in-laws (and they with you)? Did you see much of your families? Recall good times together. Were the relationships close or contentious? Did you and your spouse ever disagree about in-law issues?

Home

By your thirties, especially if you had a spouse and family, home was where you and they lived. Think now of that place, or those places, and see what memories arise.

FACTS ABOUT YOUR HOME

❦ List the address, town or city, and state (and country, if not the United States) of each place you (and your family, if you had one) lived in this stage.

MEMORIES OF YOUR HOME

Recall each house or building where you lived. Recall the physical structure where you lived as an adult. Who was there with you? If it was the same home as in earlier stages, try to remember it from this time in your life. Enter it in your imagination, as though, for example, coming home from work, and walk through it, space by space, room by room. What smells and sounds seemed to be part of the house? What highlights, memorable moments, of your life occurred in this place in this period?

Back in 1974, Carol and I were in Washington, D.C., and planning to move to Cambridge, Massachusetts. I had friends there and would often tell Carol about them—the work we did together, the fun we had, what they were like, and how good it would be to reconnect with all of them.

I often spoke about my friend, Randy. He was a very good carpenter, and someone I was looking forward to seeing again and getting to know better. He was tall, red-

haired and red-bearded, and very good-looking. We had fallen out of touch for the past year or so, but I was always able to keep track of him and others through my friend Todd. Randy was working here and there, doing this or that.

When Carol and I finally settled in Cambridge, I asked Todd for Randy's phone number. We wanted to invite him to our apartment for dinner. Date and time were set, and Carol was cooking up a storm, Coquille St. Jacques, I believe. We were renting a cute little apartment above Todd's house. The entrance was on the floor below, and then up the stairs to our kitchen.

Right on time, there came a knock at the door. "Come on up," I called out, and started down the stairs to meet Randy, only to find myself greeting a person by the name of Randy whom I had never seen before. Neither of us skipped a beat. We had a great meal and a delightful evening, chatting about mutual friends, construction, music, and the meaning of life. Randy and I went on to become close friends and work partners for many years and never once brought up the fact that we had never crossed paths before our dinner.

—ZACK GOULD, personal story

Think back to the yard outside each house or building. Imagine yourself as an adult walking around the outside of the house or building. Again, what moments and events come to mind from that space?

Take a walk through each neighborhood. Put yourself back there. Were you friendly with the neighbors? What buildings and stores and businesses do you recall? What happened there? Who was there?

Imagine yourself back in each town or city. What kind of place was this? What were the major businesses of the town or city? Did you know any of the community leaders? What did you do there? Where did you usually go? With whom? Did you feel connected to this place? What happened to make you feel that way?

What were the seasons like in each place? The heat of summer, the changes and chill of fall, the cold of winter, the new life of spring—or whatever the seasonal rhythms were in that place. Does the memory of seasons bring any moments to mind?

Romantic Relationships

Perhaps your thirties found you still uncommitted, or perhaps you were divorced or widowed. Romance probably remained a part of your life. Was it harder or easier to find partners at this age—still young but no longer youthful—when most friends were probably married?

FACTS ABOUT YOUR ROMANTIC RELATIONSHIPS

❦ List the names of each person with whom you were romantically involved.

❦ Describe each of these people very briefly—age, appearance, work, interests, background, etc.

MEMORIES OF YOUR ROMANTIC RELATIONSHIPS

Imagine each of these people in front of you now, one at a time.

- *Where did you meet?* Where are you and this other person? What is he or she doing in your image? How did the first date, or time together, happen? Where did you go?
- *Recall highlights of your relationship.* When did you know this was a special relationship? Did the other person share your feelings? When did you first make your feelings known to each other? Recall your most romantic moments. What did you especially like about him or her? What did you dislike? Did you ever consider marrying? Did you have any disagreements? Over what?
- *How and why did each relationship end?* Was there a blowup, or did it just peter out? Do you have any regrets—that it ended, or that it ended the way it did?

What were you looking for from these relationships? Were you mostly looking for a good time? Or was your goal to get serious and find a mate? Did you ever go with anyone whose goal was different from yours? If so, what happened because of those differences? Did your goals change over the course of this period—from seeking a good time to seeking a serious relationship?

Try to recall your best dates and worst dates. Were there any memorable dates, like a blind date, that you'll never forget for some reason? Did your friends or family try to set you up? How did that work out?

Did you use any matchmaking services? How did that work out? Recall the process by which you were matched up with someone else? Recall the people you met this way. Do you have a favorite story you like to tell?

Were you ever divorced and single again? Was the single life, after being married, different from the single life before marriage? Did it change how you sought out romantic partners, or what you looked for in a life partner? Did it change how you acted with the other person?

Getting Married (or Entering a Committed Relationship)

If you waited until your thirties to get married, or perhaps you remarried at this time, recall what that was like.

FACTS ABOUT GETTING MARRIED

🌿 Name and describe briefly your new spouse (or partner)—age, appearance, work, background, interests, etc.

🌿 Note where and when you got married. Briefly describe the ceremony and those who were there, the honeymoon, and any other factual highlights of that day.

MEMORIES OF GETTING MARRIED

Think back about your courtship. How and when did you meet? What was your early relationship like? When did you both know marriage might be in the cards? How and when did you both actually decide to get married? Was there a formal proposal? Did you live together before getting married? How long was your engagement? If this was a remarriage, was this courtship different from your previous one? How and why?

Imagine yourself back on your wedding day. Recall the preparations for the wedding and the location and building where you were married. Remember who was in the wedding party. Who officiated? What parents and relatives were there? Walk through that day in your mind. What were the highlights? Did anything go wrong, or threaten to go wrong? Where was the reception? How did the two families—the bride's and the groom's—get along? Recall any highlights of your honeymoon.

What about your new in-laws? Recall first meeting your in-laws. How did you get along with them? Did you see them often? How did your spouse and your family get along? Did these relationships grow or change over time during this period?

> *When we married, I wore my husband's mother's wedding dress, remade to fit me, and at the end of the ceremony my father-in-law stood to read the Quaker marriage certificate, the first, after my husband and me, to announce that I was now a member of his family. Neither my mother-in-law nor my husband begrudges me the kind of crush I have on my father-in-law—benign, daughterly, reverent. Probably they know what I don't, that he is the only person who could put back together what my own father broke.*
>
> — KATHRYN HARRISON, "Keeping Vigil"

Recall the early days of marriage. What was a typical day like for you as a newly married couple? What did you do together? What did you do apart? What changes, discoveries, surprises occurred in the first year or so of your marriage? Was it a time of significant adjustment? What was the first real challenge that you faced together?

If you were married before how did that experience change this marriage? Did it change what you expected and wanted from it, for example? Did it change the kind of person you wanted for a partner?

Divorce/Splitting Up

If you divorced or left a committed relationship in your thirties, look through the following suggestions and questions.

FACTS ABOUT YOUR DIVORCE

❦ Note the date and place of your divorce.

❦ Note any factual highlights of the split itself, the steps leading up to it and the immediate aftermath.

❦ Note what happened with any children.

MEMORIES OF YOUR DIVORCE

What caused the breakup? What were the underlying causes of the split? What was the immediate cause? Was the divorce by mutual agreement? What were your feelings and fears?

In the end there was a September night when I sat, legs crossed under me, in the big blue wing chair in the dining room and cried until it seemed my intestines would spill from my mouth, afraid to put my bare feet to the floor, afraid the chill would be irreversible. My husband stayed upstairs. He would not leave until I gave him permission.

How can you hear this? I could never stand to let you cry like this, I thought, and huddled in the wing chair until morning.

When I went upstairs, B. said, "You're killing me," and I, finally guilty of the murder I was always afraid I would commit, said, "Then I guess you'd better leave."

— MARY CANTWELL, *Manhattan Memoir*

Recall the divorce process itself. Was it difficult and contentious or relatively amicable? Who was there to help you through it? Friends? Family?

What about children? How did you find life as a divorced parent? Did your children stay with you, primarily, or with your spouse? How did the children handle the divorce and the new arrangement? How did you try to help them?

How did you adjust to single life? Was a return to single life a shock? Did you move to new quarters? What do you remember most vividly about adjusting to this new life? Did you start going out again? Did you do all right financially? Were you relieved or sad to be single again? Did you have any regrets?

Was there someone else? Did you hope to find someone else? Did you leave your marriage for a new partner? Or did you hope to find another partner soon? Did you question whether to get involved again? If you wanted a partner, what did you do to pursue that goal?

Birth Family

In this stage, as a thirtysomething taking your place in the adult world, your relationships with parents and siblings probably took on new character as you and they grew older. You were no longer "the child." In this stage, the baton gradually began to pass from your parents' generation to yours.

FACTS ABOUT YOUR BIRTH FAMILY

❧ Note the names of those who remained in your birth family at the beginning of this period—parents, brothers and sisters, grandparents. Note the age of each at this time.

❧ Note anything factual and significant, with the year of occurrence, that happened in their lives during this period—death, illness, accidents, great accomplishments, marriage/divorce, and so on.

MEMORIES OF YOUR BIRTH FAMILY

What was your parents' relationship and life together at this time? Were they still working? Was their relationship different or the same as always? What were their lives like?

What was your relationship with them? Were you close? Was your relationship with them different compared, say, with ten years earlier? Were you still involved in their lives, and/or they in yours? Did issues come up that had been long dormant? Did you ever express your feelings to each other?

If your parents were divorced. What effect did that have on their relationships with you and your family, and with each other on family occasions?

Recall the events surrounding the milestones and turning points in their lives. Think particularly of the ways those moments and events touched and changed your life. Did your parents suffer any hardships at this time? Did either of them decline physically or mentally? Did either die?

When doctors have bad news to report, they take you into a little room with Holiday Inn lobby furniture. You sit down and they sit down and everyone's knees are bunched together and there is a will on the face of the teller and the listener, both hoping the little room is big enough to contain everything that might happen there. Dr. D'Amico is a graceful reed of a man, a surgeon with pianist fingers and a mellifluous voice and very poor eye contact.

It was lung cancer, he said, and I nodded as if I already knew. "Does he know?" I asked. I'm not sure why this was so important to me right then. Of all the things I needed to ask, why that? I suppose I thought the news itself might kill him. "Who will tell him?" I wanted to know. I certainly couldn't, but I hated the idea of a stranger telling him when he was alone. I would tell him. I could do that, at least. Ann would have done that. "He knows. They always know," said the doctor. "I don't know how, but they're never surprised."

I went to the recovery room and he knew, just as Dr. D'Amico said he would. He looked so old and tired just then, his eyes gluey from the anesthesia. I knew he knew because when he saw me he gave me the tight smile, an apologetic smile like the one he used when talking about my mother after they got divorced. That tight, sad-eyed smile. And I saw something else in that smile, too, the purity of parenthood. I realized he was thinking of me, that he was worried about me, sorry for me that he had cancer. That was the most heartbreaking of all.

—LOUISE JARVIS FLYNN,
"Plus One, Plus Two, Plus Three"

Think about each of your brothers and sisters during this stage in your life. Where was this person and what was he or she doing? Think of the life events you identified for him or her. Were there any difficulties or hardships? How were you involved, or how did these events touch you? What was your contact with this sibling now? Did you see each other on holidays or special times? How often did you talk and what did you talk about? Were you close? Were you comfortable together? Were there any issues between you? Had your relationship with this brother or sister changed now that you both were adults? Did you ever agree or disagree about your parents and what was happening in their lives?

Remember your grandparents. Were your grandparents still part of your life? They were probably becoming elderly. How were they coping with old age? Did you worry about them? Recall times when you saw them.

Bring your extended family to mind. What moments do you recall? What were the highlights of their lives during your adult years? What do you remember best about them? What did you do together? Was there anything that remained unspoken or mysterious about their lives?

When I was 10 or 11, I remember seeing a card my Aunt Esther received from a Louis in Cleveland.

When I was in my 20's, she had something for me in her apartment and started calling to ask when I was going to pick it up. It almost seemed as if she was nagging me to get it, which was very uncharacteristic of her. I finally decided to stop by to retrieve it even though she wasn't home (I had the key to her apartment). I had brought along a batch of magazines to give to her, and as I placed them on her dining room table and picked up my stuff, I noticed a man's jacket hanging on the back of one of the chairs, a vase with roses on the table, and an airline ticket to Cleveland. I "freaked," grabbed the magazines, put back my things, and left.

It had to have been Louis. He had to be one of the young men in so many of the photos of my aunt with her friends in rowboats, picnicking, or playing ball that were dated 1923, 1924, etc., that filled her albums.

When I saw her a few days later, I asked about the limp roses in the vase on her table. She said she had bought them from a vendor on the corner. Why did I let her keep the secret? Why didn't I just come out and ask her?

Years later, when she was in her 80's, I asked her to identify the people in the photos. She begged off saying it was so long ago she had forgotten who they all were. Again I didn't press.

After her death, I shared the story with her surviving sister, Rose. She said she had always wondered why Aunt Esther didn't marry Louis. Her surviving brother didn't remember anything. Not knowing the story of Aunt Esther and Louis saddens me as do the other secrets that have left holes in our family history.

— SANDY RUBIN, personal story

Religion or Spirituality

As a full-fledged adult, what role did religion or spiritual beliefs play in your life? Did you find that raising children pulled you back to the religion you grew up with? Or did it cause you to explore beliefs for the first time?

FACTS ABOUT YOUR RELIGIOUS OR SPIRITUAL BELIEFS

❦ Describe briefly the beliefs that were important to you, and how they changed, if they did, during your adult stage.

❦ Describe briefly what practices you followed in conjunction with your beliefs, such as attending services, meditation, observing holy days.

❦ Describe briefly any specific religious experiences you had as an adult.

MEMORIES OF YOUR RELIGIOUS OR SPIRITUAL BELIEFS

Think about your beliefs at this time. Were they central to your life? Did they change in any way during this period? Did your faith grow stronger, or did you question more? How did you try to resolve any doubts? Did you have any discussions with anyone about your beliefs? Did you ever try to convert anyone else to your beliefs?

Think about your religious or spiritual practices as an adult. Reflect on the practices that you identified above and recall any events surrounding them that were memorable.

Recall any religious or spiritual experiences you identified above. What happened? What preceded and followed each experience? How did the experience change you? Were others involved?

What role did religion play in your daily life? Did you and your spouse share beliefs? Did you carry any religious practices into your home? Did you have any religious family rituals or practices? Were any of these occasions memorable? If you and your spouse did not share the same beliefs, what happened around those differences? Did you raise your children in your beliefs and practices?

I began keeping Passover, and hosting an annual Seder. I get ready for Pesach, little by little, and do a little more each year. Some of it is spring cleaning: I dust and wipe and shake out the rugs, and in a good year, I get to the windows. Then I get rid of improper food, the crumbs and crusts and anything not kosher for Passover: the hametz. *I line drawers and shelves with new paper, and fit them out with Passover dishes. I scour the sink and clean the oven. I cover the countertops and kitchen table. All for a span of eight days, and then I box up Pesach again for another year.*

The preparations are insane. They get under your skin. One night in September, near on to the children's back-to-school, I dream Passover will begin in one hour, and I have done nothing. I have not cooked, cleaned, covered surfaces, shopped. Many guests are expected. As with a math exam for which one hasn't studied, I have failed at the geometry of switching dishes, lining shelves, at counting out place settings, estimating servings, timing errands. To a dazzling repertoire of anxiety dreams, add this.

— ELIZABETH EHRLICH, *Miriam's Kitchen*

Work/Career

By your thirties you probably had settled on a career, or at least a line of work, and were focused on advancing in your particular field. Was this a time of real striving for you in your career? Did you struggle to balance work and family? Was work the center of your life, or merely an important part? Was there some particular goal you strongly wanted to achieve by forty or shortly after?

FACTS ABOUT YOUR WORK/CAREER

❦ List the jobs you held in this period—the organization that employed you, what it did, where it was located, when you worked there, and what you did (duties, titles, etc.). (Treat self-employment or running your own company as a job.)

❦ Note any *career* milestones from this stage—moments, events, opportunities, promotions, disappointments—that marked your career progress.

MEMORIES OF YOUR WORK/CAREER

Did you begin a career or line of work at or prior to this stage of life? Were you achieving the goals, making the progress you wanted? Was there a traditional career path you were on? What were the stepping-stones along the way? Were you where you should have been? Was there something important you wanted to accomplish by a certain time in your life at, say, around forty? How did you define "success"? What did you do to advance in this career—programs or projects you led, presentations you made, organizational changes you led, and so on? Recall the career milestones you identified above and the events or moments surrounding each. Were you having second thoughts about this career?

Think about the following questions for each job you held in this period.

- *How did you get the job?* Did you seek it out? Were you recruited? Was it a promotion?
- *How was this job related to your career?* Was it a typical stepping-stone, or did it represent a career risk (i.e., it might not have advanced your career)?
- *Recall the business or organization you worked for.* What did it do? Did you believe deeply in what it did, or was it just a job or a stepping-stone? What kind of company was it to work for? How did it treat people? What were the other people there like? Recall the people who ran the place. Did you have any contact with them? What were they like?

Life in an advertising agency is like being at a dull party, interrupted by more serious moments. There's generally a kind of convivial attitude. Nobody's particularly uptight. Creativity of this kind flourishes better.

They're aware that they're talking about the little bears capering around a cereal box and they're arguing which way the bears should go. It's a silly thing for adults to be doing. At the same time, they're aware that the client's going to spend a million dollars on television time to run this commercial. Millions of dollars went into these little bears, so that gave them an importance of their own. That commercial, if successful, can double salaries. It's serious, yet it isn't. This kind of split is in everybody's mind.

—JOHN FORTUNE, in *Working*

- *Recall the place where you worked—the location, the building, where you sat or did your work, the tools or equipment you used.* Imagine walking through the work spaces. Who was there? Where did you eat lunch? With whom? What were the meeting rooms like that you used?

- *Recall the work that you did.* What was a typical day like? What were your responsibilities? What people did you tend to deal with? Were you good at what you did? Any moments when things went especially well? When things did not go well? What did you accomplish that you were proud of? Did you get any recognition or promotions? Were you ever passed over for a position? What was the most difficult part of the work? The part you found most satisfying? Did you deal with customers or other outsiders? What special projects or events did you work on? What training did you receive?

- *Did you become expert at something?* What was that, and how good were you? How did you gain that level of expertise? Did you have to work hard to achieve it? Where and when did you have a chance to use it? Were you proud of it?

- *What happened when the business struggled—say, in a recession?* Did your company ever get sold or merge with another? Were there ever layoffs? Re-organizations that affected you?

- *What was your boss like in this job?* Competent, knowledgeable, or not? How did he or she treat you? What did he or she think of you and your work? What did you learn from working for this boss? Did you ever have any hard meetings? Did you ever win praise, and if so, for what? Did you ever socialize with your boss?

- *Were you a boss?* Did the burden of responsibility for others come naturally to you? Recall any people you hired or had to let go. Who was the best employee who worked for you? The worst? What was the biggest employee problem you ever faced and what did you do? What did those who worked for you think of you? Why? Subordinates always talk about their boss—what do you think yours were saying about you?

- *Did you have any mentors?* Did anyone, your boss or someone else, take you under his or her wing and advise and help you with your work?

- *Recall your colleagues.* Think of their offices or where they worked. What were they like? What did they do? How did you work with them? Did all of you get along? Did you socialize outside work?

- *Did you manage to strike a work/life balance in this job?* How good were you at fulfilling all your roles—parent, employee, boss, community volunteer, church member, and so on? Did you ever have to make adjustments or changes?

- *How did this job end?* Did you leave the company? Were you recruited or promoted out of it? Did you quit? Were you laid off? Were you fired? How did you feel? What did you learn from that experience?

If you were a woman. Did your gender ever become a factor or play a role in events at work, or in what happened to you in your career? Did you hold a traditionally female position? If you held a position most often held by a man, what was that like? Were you ever treated unfairly by the organization or by colleagues because of your gender? What were your career ambitions and how were they affected by your gender? Did your gender ever work in your favor?

Were you ever discriminated against? Did your gender or racial or cultural background or other difference change anything about this work—how you did it, how others treated you, what others expected of you, your prospects for succeeding and advancing? What did you do or not do because of your status?

I had seen anti-Semitism downtown when I was selling stocks because at times I would go out with the people and they worked for major institutions and at that time, it was extremely common to have a drink at lunch. I mean, that was part of doing business. You'd have a drink or two at lunch. And give somebody a couple of drinks and they would talk about the Jews. And I had a greeting card that I used for those occasions. It went like this:

> *Roses are reddish*
> *Violets are bluish*
> *In case you don't know*
> *I am Jewish*

I had that card delivered to them by hand, and I said, "Enjoyed lunch, Mickie."
They got that card in the afternoon, and I never had to take any of that nonsense again.
And I never embarrassed anyone, either.

— MURIEL SIEBERT, in *Geeks & Geezers*

Did moral or ethical or fairness issues ever arise in your work? Did you ever feel that the requirements of your work conflicted with your sense of ethics or morals or fairness? Were you ever expected to do something that seemed to you unfair or dishonest? How did you resolve this dilemma? Did it affect your career, or your motivation?

Were you the same person at work and in your personal life? Did you have the same standards in both parts of your life? Did you treat people the same? Or did you think different standards applied in the two places? Did you ever work with or for personal friends?

Did you start and/or run your own business in this stage of life? What was the business? If it was new, how did you get into it? Imagine yourself back in your place of business—walk through it at this time in your life: what scenes and moments and occasions come to mind? Did the business grow and prosper? Did you or it ever struggle? Did you have a partner or partners? Did you sell it or close it down? Why—what happened?

If you chose the military as a career, think about the ways your military work was different from civilian work. For example, were you in combat, or on dangerous missions? What memories do you have of those experiences?

Friends and Other Memorable People

The importance of close relationships never diminishes, but was it difficult for you in your thirties to find the time needed to maintain close relationships apart from family and work?

FACTS ABOUT FRIENDS AND OTHER MEMORABLE PEOPLE

❦ Identify the few people from this period whom you would call close friends. List these people, where and when you knew them, and in a word or two the nature of your relationship.

❦ For each, note anything significant that happened in their lives during this time—marriage, divorce, births, promotions, changes in fortune, etc.

❦ Identify your mentors, the people from this period who took you under their wing and provided important guidance—when and where and how you knew them and the nature of your relationship.

❦ Identify anyone who served as a significant model for you in some way—when and where and how you knew them and the nature of your relationship.

❦ Identify anyone else who stands out in your memory, including strangers who touched your life in some important way, even if only for a moment. Note where and when and how such people entered your life.

❦ Describe briefly the circle of people (or circles, if they changed over time) with whom you tended to socialize as an adult, including groups at work. Note the names of the most memorable people in each group. Describe briefly the kinds of things you did together.

❦ Note the places you tended to go to socialize—like a club or a neighborhood bar or even a gym where you worked out. Who was generally there and what made this place feel comfortable to you?

MEMORIES OF FRIENDS AND OTHER MEMORABLE PEOPLE

Recall your friends, one by one, and see what memories come to mind. Think of things you did together, problems you helped each other solve, support you gave each other, and things you confided in each other. Recall each of the milestones you identified from their lives and see what memories you have of them.

The other person who stiffened my back was Luvie Pearson, who was the closest, most helpful, most ever-present friend. . . . The most important moment, one I will always remember, took place when the two of us were walking in Montrose Park, across the street from my house. I was talking about hanging on to the paper [The Washington Post] until the children, especially the boys—since in those days that's how I thought— were old enough to run it. I recall Luvie firmly and distinctly saying, "Don't be silly, dear. You can do it."

"Me?" I exclaimed. "That's impossible. I couldn't possibly do it. You don't know how hard and complicated it is. There's no way I could do it."

"Of course you can do it," she maintained. . . . And to counter my disclaimers of impossibility, Luvie added, "You've got all those genes. It's ridiculous to think you can't do it. You've just been pushed down so far you don't recognize what you can do."

That was the first time that anyone had mentioned the idea of my running the company, or that I had even contemplated it in passing. The whole notion struck me as stunning and ridiculous, wrongheaded but sweet, coming as it did from my good, loyal friend who was trying valiantly to buck me up but who obviously didn't understand what running the business was all about and what it would take.

— KATHARINE GRAHAM, *Personal History*

Recall anyone who mentored you. What were the ways and circumstances in which you knew each of these people? Was the relationship with each short, or did it continue over time? Recall the occasions when this person helped you. What was the outcome?

Recall those who served as role models in some way for you. Remember the situations in which you consciously used each person's personal example as a guide to your own choices and behavior. Role models aren't necessarily friends or mentors. Rather, they're people you admired in some way—perhaps the way they handled problems or pressure.

Were there other memorable people in your life at this time? Who else played an important role in your life that you haven't already identified? Who else gave you some great gift, or you to them? Someone memorable might be a person you met only once, who made a deep impression on you for some reason. Did you ever experience the simple kindness of a stranger?

Not long ago, I traveled with my son and daughter to my sister's 40th birthday in California. Mathew and Toby were then four and two years old. The first leg of the red-eye home, Los Angeles to Detroit, was blessedly uneventful, but the second leg quickly developed all the ingredients of a travel nightmare.

As we taxied out in Detroit, the plane suddenly turned around and headed back to the terminal to fix some kind of sensor, according to the pilot. As others deplaned, we stayed on board to chat with the co-pilot, who was a mom with her own four- and two-year-olds at home.

The problem with the plane was serious, so we were all asked to deplane. Hours later, when we re-boarded and buckled up, Mathew suddenly realized he'd left his new toy jelly fish inside the terminal. Tears in his eyes, he pleaded to go back. Before I could reply, the plane turned around again and headed back. More problems. I rushed to the cockpit, found the co-pilot. She immediately called the terminal, confirmed a strange plastic object under one of the chairs, and then left the plane herself and returned with Mathew's jelly fish. She understood how important it was to him, and to me, the mother traveling with a distraught four-year-old.

Finally, the plane was grounded. As I was collecting our belongings, the co-pilot came up to us and said, "I thought you may need this." She had our stroller. She had gone to the trouble of retrieving it from the plane's cargo hold.

When people comment on how awful this trip must have been, I tell them a kind co-pilot made all the difference in the world.

— SUSAN HUTER, personal story

Recall the group of people you tended to socialize with. Think about the specific activities and events you enjoyed with this circle of acquaintances. What did you have in common? Bring to mind some of the people. What did you do together? If you met any of these people today, what memories would you talk about? Did people ever fall out?

Other social occasions. Recall any other social moments or events that were especially memorable. Did you ever go to a high school or college reunion? What was that like?

After you got married. If you got married or engaged at this time, recall how your social life changed. Did you try to maintain an active relationship with friends? How did that work? Did you seek to make new friends? Try to remember events and moments from that period.

Education

By one's thirties, most people have completed their formal education. But for some it is a time for returning to school, perhaps for an advanced degree or to pursue a second or belated career. However, "education" can include any formal learning programs, including training and development at work.

FACTS ABOUT YOUR EDUCATION

❦ Note the name of the school or program you attended, its location, and the dates you attended.

❦ Identify the specific course of study you pursued, your purpose or goal in attending, and the outcome—such as a diploma or certificate.

Imagine yourself back in this school or program. In your mind, return to this place and walk through it, whether it was one building or an entire campus. What does that place bring to mind? What events and moments and people? Was there a final ceremony, a graduation, a diploma or certificate? What memories do you have of that day? How did you do in your classes and overall? Any awards or recognition?

Recall what you were doing there, your purpose or goal. Were you there to advance at work or to learn a new field or develop new skills? What people were involved, such as an adviser of some kind? What decisions did you make or change while you were in this place?

Recall your classes and professors. Put yourself in each of those classrooms. What happened there? Who was teaching? What fellow students were there? What was your favorite class? Favorite professor? Least favorite professor? Did you have any mentors in school? Did any classes or professors change your mind about what you wanted to do?

What classmates stand out in your memory? What happened with them? Did you do anything together?

Was any of your social life centered around school or training? Who were your friends in this school? What did you do together? What social group did you belong to?

What school clubs, groups, organizations, or causes did you participate in? Why did you join this club or organization? What did you do in the group? What events or occasions stand out in your memory of this group?

Did you participate in any school-related sports? Recall the sports, the games or tournaments, and how you or your team did? Who else was involved with you?

Causes, Community, and Politics

Did you find time as an adult in her or his thirties to pursue causes of some kind or help with community projects? Perhaps you worked in PTA because of your children, or helped coach a children's team of some kind. Perhaps a political cause retained or captured your interest.

FACTS ABOUT CAUSES, COMMUNITY, AND POLITICS

❦ Identify any causes—social, political, or whatever—that you supported and tried to advance during this time. Name each cause and its purpose, the time of your involvement, and the basic facts of what you did.

❦ Identify any community work you did—what it was, its purpose, when you did it, and your role or involvement.

❦ Identify any ways that you got involved with politics—getting yourself or someone else elected to office, or supporting a political cause or agenda. Note who or what you supported, its purpose, when you did it, and your role or involvement.

MEMORIES OF CAUSES, COMMUNITY, AND POLITICS

Recall the causes you supported. It could have been any cause—civil rights, the environment, abortion rights, some local movement. Think of the moments, public or private, associated with each. Who else was involved? Were there any causes you'd long supported and that still engaged your time and interest?

Recall any community work you did. What occasions or memorable people come to mind that are linked to each? What goal were you and the others trying to achieve? Did you succeed?

Recall your involvement with politics. What moments or events come to mind when you think about the candidates or political causes you worked to advance? If you ran for office, recall the events surrounding this effort.

Interests and Activities

What arts or sports or hobbies or other personal interests did you pursue in your thirties? How important were these interests in your life—major passions or merely pleasant ways to relax?

FACTS ABOUT YOUR INTERESTS AND ACTIVITIES

❦ Note any sports you played or pursued seriously as an adult, such as golf, tennis, fishing, hunting, hiking, or other active outdoor pursuits.

❦ Note any pro, college, or local teams you followed closely—how they did during this period, and any factual highlights about them from this period that seemed important to you.

❦ Name any social clubs or other organizations you joined—include what each did, when you belonged, and what you did with each.

❦ Identify pets you or your family kept. Note any other animals you were somehow involved with.

❦ Note any involvement you had with the arts: music, theater, dance, poetry, or some other art form. Note the art, the group, if there was one that you tended to enjoy most, and generally what you did.

❦ List any books or stories from this time that stand out in your memory and had special meaning for you.

❦ List any movies that remain vivid in your memory.

❦ List the television or radio programs that meant a lot to you.

❦ What hobbies did you pursue earnestly? Did you collect something, make something?

❧ Identify any games (such as chess) you played seriously. Note any accomplishments or recognition from your playing.

❧ Note any memorable trips you took—business or personal—in this period. Record where you went, when, and briefly what you saw.

MEMORIES OF YOUR INTERESTS AND ACTIVITIES

Recall any sports you played. For each sport, recall any memorable games or practices or other events linked to it. What moments gave you genuine satisfaction? Which were disappointing?

Think about the teams or sports you followed closely. What appealed to you about each of them? Did you ever attend games or events? Do you remember any memorable games?

Recall what you did in or with the arts. Think of each form of art—dance, music, theater, etc.—that interested and engaged you. Did you enjoy live theater, art galleries, museums? What specific performances or exhibits do you recall? Are there people you remember? Were you involved in fund-raising for any of these groups? If you performed in some way, were there memorable performances?

Recall the pets and other animals in your life at this time. What moments or occasions do you remember? Recall moments of pleasure, and moments of worry or sadness, with each.

Nowadays my affections, and most of my bed, are taken up by a blond and boxy Labrador named Barnaby, whose thick, many creased neck you want to roughly cuddle. Barnaby's idea of activity is to go and stand sentry for a half hour by the front gate, and once he is satisfied the perimeter is secure, go for a dip in the pool. Cocking his head slightly to the right, he pretends to give a sympathetic hearing to everything I have to say, and only once has he let me down—and then only under circumstances that would have desperately tested any dog. Barnaby and I had been invited to have Christmas Eve dinner with Annette and Oscar de la Renta at their home in Kent, where they had just added a new wing for their bed-sitting room. Brooke Astor was there with her little dachshund and schnauzer. Carolyn Roehm had her four dogs. The Kissingers were there with their Lab. And, of course, Annette had her terriers. Don't ask me how many dogs that was. It was cozy. Annette had set up the tree at the end of the room, with a nativity scene under it. There were carols and fun presents for everyone. And then, in the middle of all this, Barnaby went over to the tree and lifted his leg. Bang! There went two of three wise men.

—BILL BLASS, *Bare Blass*

Think of each of the hobbies and games that interested you deeply. Were there other people involved? What were they like? What times and events do you remember around each of these hobbies or games or people? Memorable losses? Victories? Milestones, such as memorable "finds"?

Remember each club or social organization to which you belonged. Recall the purpose and activities of the organization. What meetings or events did you attend? What was your role? Recall the other people in each group.

Think of the entertainment—books, movies, TV programs, dining out—that you enjoyed. What were your reading preferences? Did any book or movie leave a lasting impression? Think of the occasions or events or moments associated with ways you sought entertainment. Were others involved, or were these solitary pleasures?

Think about any traveling you did. Recall the trips you took at this time. Recall where you went, who you met, and what you saw. Did you face any problems or experience any particular surprises? What happened to you in different cultures?

NOTABLE EVENTS

As you lived through your thirties, what events outside your control—whether great newsworthy occasions or local occurrences—touched and influenced your life?

FACTS ABOUT NOTABLE EVENTS

❧ What historical or newsworthy events affected or touched you when you were an adult? Describe briefly what happened and when.

MEMORIES OF NOTABLE EVENTS

Recall any historical or noteworthy events. Recall how and when you first learned about each one. How did each affect or change your life? Did you somehow participate in any of them?

Recall any other outside events that touched you. What events out of your control, even if they weren't large and newsworthy, touched and changed your life? Perhaps someone's house burned down. What happened and how did your life change?

Other Voices

Contact some people who have memories of you, or memories that include you, from this time in your life. Their memories of you can enrich the picture that emerges of you as an adult.

   If you want to include other people's memories of you as an adult . . .

1. Make a list of people from your time as an adult and ask them to share their memories with you, in their own words.
2. Record each memory on a separate sheet of paper. Label each memory "A Memory of Me" and include the memory teller's name, as well as the approximate date and location of the memory.
3. Add these memory sheets to your own memories in your *My Life Story* notebook.

THE MEANING OF YOUR ADULT STAGE

In the introduction to this stage, we called adulthood a time of striving and un-remitting effort. We don't mean by that to imply it was a time of boring drudgery. On the contrary, to those of us for whom this was a time of great effort, it was a time of working toward something we considered deeply worthwhile, whether that was the achievement of some career goal or the successful raising of one's children.

It was striving, then, full of significance and meaning, which sprang from the ends we were trying to achieve. Think back over this stage and recall not just the striving but its purpose. There you will discover a rich vein of meaning.

Defining Moments

For many, this was a time of settling down and working hard to make your place in the adult world. What were the key choices you made—perhaps they were reaffirmations of choices made (maybe tentatively) earlier? What moments sym-bolized or signified those choices and your subsequent efforts to carry them through?

If this was a time of striving for you, your goal or dream can define this stage too, even if it would be attained (or not) later. If you had an overarching career or family or other goal, name it here, for it defined you and this time as surely as any more tangible aspect of life.

Consider anything that made a difference, whatever it was. Think of yourself at the beginning of this stage, in your early thirties, and then think of yourself at the end, somewhere around forty, or shortly thereafter. How were you and your life different then? Where and how did those differences or changes occur? Those are the defining or pivotal moments you should note here.

My grandmother was one of the loveliest women I have ever known. Her sweetness touched everyone she knew. Even as she was dying, her every waking thought was for others. This would sometimes enrage me—"Say something angry!" I would think to myself after listening to her tell me how everything was wonderful. While I admired my grandmother's ability to see the good in everything and everyone, I privately believed that somewhere, deep down, she harbored feelings of anger and injustice as many of us do, she simply wasn't sharing them. How could it be otherwise, since I knew her life had not been easy, and since she'd been diagnosed with cancer that was scheduled to take her life prematurely? My grandmother's goodness felt like a barrier to me. I felt like I could never truly know her because she never revealed her true feelings to me.

It occurred to me many years after her death that my grandmother was a person who chose to focus exclusively on the beauty and goodness in the world—it's who she was—and she was sincere in her loving kindness. It was, perhaps, something I couldn't relate to, given that I spent my life reading such fare as The Journal of Genocide Studies *and teaching the causes of war. But just as I, insistent on seeing the world through my jaded lens, opted to see humanity for what I believe it was, my grandmother chose to see things her way. I did know her.*

Since that realization, I have found myself many times in the years since her death confronting a difficult situation, taking a deep breath, and thinking about what Grandma Ruth would have done. I will never be the sweet and kind woman that she was. But her enduring influence has helped me avert confrontational situations by applying a heaping dose of kindness, empathy, and understanding whenever I invoke her memory.

— PATRICIA WEITSMAN, personal story

Values—What Mattered

Your life dreams are especially important in this stage. Reflect on your dream and on how it helped define what you considered important. What was your highest ambition? What did you hope to accomplish at home or at work or both, or somewhere else? Did it have to do with your career, your children, your social standing? What gave you the greatest pleasure at this time? The greatest satisfaction? The largest sense of pride? The most frustration? Disappointment? All these provide clues to what mattered most to you.

Think of the two or three or four big decisions you made as an adult; consider, for example, the big commitments you made for work and life partnership. Take each decision and try to recall how you made the choice you did. That "how" almost certainly reflected your values, even if at the time you didn't express them explicitly. Alternatives *not* chosen or opportunities refused—a job declined, for example—could also reveal your values. Think of such negative choices and what they revealed about your thinking and values.

How did you as an adult try to connect yourself and your life and work with something bigger and more important than yourself, something that would live on after you? This is the way many of us seek to give our lives meaning. What you considered "bigger" and "more important" than you revealed your values.

Think of yourself at the end of your thirties or thereabouts—call to mind where you were then and what you were doing at work and home—and compare what was important to you at that time with what had been important when you were approaching thirty. Did you want the same things, spend your time in the same ways? Surely not, and the differences reflected many changes, not least changes in what mattered to you.

[My] father, Milton, is considered one of the ten living masters of his craft—neurosurgery. He designs surgical instruments used by brain surgeons around the world. Directly and indirectly, he has saved thousands of lives.

When Milton retired, he returned to one of the activities that he loved in his youth—stargazing. But finding the range of books on stargazing unsatisfying, he decided to write a book of his own. Written with children in mind, Milton dedicated the book to his seven grandchildren, which of course included our two kids.

On Halloween night, soon after the book's publication, my parents were visiting. The children went out trick-or-treating with an old family friend, Rick Stemple. . . . At the end of a lively evening, as Rick was about to leave, I decided to give him a copy of my father's new book as a gift. As the family all crowded around, Rick thumbed through the book and then turned to Milton and asked him for a pen. Milton smiled, thinking about what he would write as he autographed the book for Rick.

Rick took the pen, but he did not hand the book to Milton. Instead, he got down

on one knee, opened the book to the dedication page where the names of the grand-
children were listed, and asked the kids to sign the book.

I looked over and saw tears come to my father's eyes as he watched his young grand-
children sign their names, in their one-inch-high script, on the dedication page. After
forty years of clinical medicine, with all of the lives he had saved, nothing for Milton
could compare to the meaning of that moment.

—RONALD A. HEIFETZ, *Leadership on the Line*

Love

Erich Fromm defined love as taking delight in the existence of someone else. Whose existence at this time of your life truly delighted you? For whom was your existence a delight? Who devoted themselves to you in times of adversity or pain? Who sacrificed themselves on your behalf? For whom did you do these things yourself?

Again, these few people will likely be ones you've already identified in earlier pages. The purpose here is simply to highlight those few with whom you had this special relationship. No period of life can be completely and fully recalled without acknowledging such people and such relationships.

We hope by now that this concept of love is a familiar one. As we age we become more comfortable with it and able to recognize its power. As we age, too, we come to realize that little in life matters more than loving and being loved.

It was still the days when you didn't know the sex of a baby until the moment it was
born, and on this day, August 16, 1973, Linda and I were about to find out. It was a
high forceps delivery and the doctor, a burly guy, was pulling with all his might, for the
cord was around the baby's neck and he had to get it out right away. In a few moments
he reached in with his gloved hand and slipped the cord aside. Out popped . . . Lesley,
yelling appropriately, slightly delayed but hale and hearty.

She was our third child but the first whose birth I witnessed. I'd intended to be
there five years earlier when Eric arrived. I was there for much of Linda's heroic 24
hours of labor but left when hospital staff said I should get some rest, since delivery

looked a ways away. I went home for a few hours and, of course, Eric decided to depart the womb then. I learned of his birth by phone. A real disappointment. Lauren, our second, arrived a year later (actually 11 months) with a bit more excitement. A separated placenta, dangerous for both child and mother, brought her forth six weeks early. "Poor sight," her grandmother said on seeing her. Lauren had to spend her first days alone in one of those little boxes with windows.

I remember the precise spot on the road in Carlisle where, pondering the new and strange feelings I felt for these children, I realized they were in fact love. So that's what love is, I thought. It was hard to describe, but it had a sense of bedrock or of an unchanging ocean current far below the surface. It didn't depend on anything the child did. Love was always there, deep beneath everything else, no matter what roiled the surface.

— KENT LINEBACK, personal story

Learning and Wisdom

In the previous section on values, you looked at key choices you made to discover what was truly important to you. Recall those same choices, but think now of how they turned out. Did each turn out exactly as you hoped and expected? Probably not. What did you learn, what wisdom did you gain, from the ones that didn't quite work out? And from the ones that did? What did you learn, especially about yourself, from the way you responded to disappointment, and success? Did you act on it? Did you live with it? Did you accept it? Did you struggle against it without really changing it?

What choices might you have made differently? What in general would you have done differently or not done at all? Did you ever say or think, I wish I'd known then what I know now? What was it you wished you'd known?

As adults we have many new sources of learning. The effort we invest in a lifetime relationship teaches us something. The time and effort we devote to our careers teaches us something. Children teach us something, both from our efforts to raise them well and simply from watching them and being aware of our feelings for them.

What about adversity, illness, or accident? Did work, marriage, the arts, friends, travel, or anything else lead you to insights about how to live? Who taught you something of special value—either something they told you or something evident in their actions, or both?

It may sound odd at this stage of life to ask the following questions that we've suggested you ask in previous stages, but they still make sense here: think of a child or grandchild who now faces the great challenges and tasks of the adult stage of their lives. What could you tell them that might help? What advice would you, knowing what you know now, have given to yourself as an adult?

When I started out as an actor, I thought, Here's what I have to say, how shall I say it? *On* M*A*S*H, *I began to understand that what* I *do in the scene is not as important as what happens between me and the other person. And listening is what lets it happen. It's almost always the other person who causes you to say what you say next. You don't have to figure out how you'll say it. You have to listen so simply, so innocently, that the other person brings about a change in you that* makes *you say it and informs the way you say it.*

The difference between listening and pretending to listen, I discovered, is enormous. One is fluid, the other is rigid. One is alive, the other is stuffed. Eventually, I found a radical way of thinking about listening. Real listening is a willingness to let the other person change you. When I'm willing to let them change me, something happens between us that's more interesting than a pair of dueling monologues. Like so much of what I learned in the theater, this turned out to be how life works, too.

—ALAN ALDA, *Never Have Your Dog Stuffed*

Summing Up

Capture here in a few words the adult stage of your life. How did this time of life feel to you? What was it like overall? Do you remember it fondly? Or was it a difficult time you struggled to get through? What role did it play in your life?

What kind of person were you and what kind of person did you become by the end of it? What should someone who's just read the story of your adult years think of this time in your life? If there was a time or moment or condition that to you characterized this time, describe it and explain how it seemed to sum up this time.

STAGE 5

———————

middle adult

Middle age!

Remember the moment you noticed it? It didn't

happen overnight, but many of us didn't see the

earliest signs until one day we looked in the mirror and there it was. A wrinkle. A gray hair, maybe one of those stiff curly ones that stick out. A little potbelly that wouldn't go away. Did you ever think you'd be shaving your ears?

It wasn't always something we could see. Maybe we were sore or tired after a morning of brisk tennis, or some other activity we'd done a thousand times that never bothered us before. Or we couldn't remember a name of an author or book or movie, something we knew well.

Then, once we noticed that innocent little sign, we began to look for more and suddenly they were all over the place. Before we knew it we were racing to the drugstore or standing anxiously at the cosmetics counter searching for something to make the problem go away. Vitamins. Herbs. Wrinkle creams. A little hair dye to banish the gray. Bases and blushes and a dozen other tubes and vials to pre-serve the bloom of youth.

Maybe we took it all in stride. Accept the inevitable, we thought. Let nature take its course. Still, we noticed one day that we had crossed a line, from youth to no-longer-young. Kent first noticed he'd passed that line when he went back to eat dinner in his old college dining hall, something he'd done periodically since gradu-ation. Only this time he noticed that the kids in the dining hall weren't that much older than his son, and suddenly they seemed a lot younger than he was. On pre-vious visits, he'd been able to maintain the myth that he was still "one of them." No more. They called him "sir." Sir! he thought. Why are they calling me "sir"?

Once over that line, life was different. Before it, we spent birthdays thinking about how many years we'd lived. After it, birthdays became a time to contem-plate how many we had left.

Consider all the ways our lives changed just in the opening years of middle adulthood:

We began to think about time differently. Time suddenly became important, because we realized we had only a limited amount of it left and we began to think of using it carefully, like some finite hoard of gold.

At work, in the community, we became "senior." At work we were no longer "lean and hungry" or "up and coming." Instead of being mentored, we became mentors ourselves. Colleagues in their twenties and thirties began to look to us for our expe-rience and insight. In the community, we were expected to take on leadership roles and assume authority. Along with some extra pounds we seemed unable to lose (a bad thing), we took on gravitas (a good thing). If we didn't, we were expected to. At-titudes, ideas, clothes, and speech that were previously acceptable now seemed immature. If we forgot ourselves, our teenage children would tell us to act our age.

We could see the day when children would leave home and make their own lives, with all the implications that would have for us and our lives. By the end of this period, for most of us, the nest would be empty. In fact, watching our children grow up was a constant reminder of our own increasing age.

Our relationship with our own parents and extended families began to change as well. Beginning in our early forties, and stretching through this long stage, family leadership passed naturally from the older generation to us. We went from being "kids" to being family leaders others turned to for guidance, advice, and direction. Sadly, this was the time we began losing forebears. Early in the stage (if not earlier), we typically lost our grandparents, and by the end of it we were dealing with the decline of our mothers and fathers, aunts and uncles. For by the time we were sixty, our parents were in their eighties, and we were caring for them.

These changes were only the beginning.

Do this little exercise: compare your life in your late thirties with your life in your late fifties—your work, where you lived, health, how you spent your time, what interested you, what you thought about, and so on. Large differences, right?

Now think about some of those changes. Did they occur with great noise and tumult? Or did they unfold in a quiet, orderly way? For some of us, this was a time of crisis, the infamous midlife crisis. For others, life simply went on naturally. Changes occurred, but quietly and without turmoil or fanfare. There was no screaming and yelling, no sleepless nights.

However change occurred, the fact is our lives changed profoundly in this stage. Children grew up and left home. Most likely, we changed our work too, in some way. That could take many forms, from a change of career, to a change in jobs, or simply but significantly a change in the way we thought about work and what we expected from it. Many of us expanded our interests, too. Or we simply changed how we preferred to spend our time.

The process of life change typically began in our early forties and proceeded either quickly or slowly, loudly or quietly, through the remainder of this period. We might have made some changes early, lived with them for a few years, and then concluded they didn't work as intended. So we made adjustments in our early fifties before settling into the life we would live through our remaining fifties and even into our sixties.

Behind all this change was a lot of questioning. Most of us spent our thirties striving, striving, striving, without much thought or self-examination. Now we began to ask basic questions, spurred on by growing appreciation of our mortality and the sense that time truly was a limited and precious commodity. We asked, Am I living the life I really want? and, How do I want to spend the rest of my time? and, most basic of all, What's truly important to me?

At the core of this questioning stood our life dreams. We—some lucky few of us—had achieved our dreams by this time and were beginning to ask, is that all there is? For our dreams had always been more than mere goals. They were supposed to transform us. Having fulfilled them, whatever they were—happy, high-achieving children, a big promotion, publication of a book, some other form of recognition—

we believed they would convert us forever into happy, satisfied, and fulfilled people. Our lives thereafter would be made. So we were frustrated to find that achievement and success hadn't brought the sense of profound satisfaction and fulfillment we'd expected. Whatever need had driven us to achieve still ached within us.

More likely, though, we began to realize that our life dreams would never be fully achieved. There were only a limited number of big jobs, for example. Or our children perversely insisted on living their own lives, instead of the ones we'd dreamed for them. We began to realize we were probably on the road to disappointment. The window of opportunity (with children, for example, or for some big promotion) was closing, probably forever. We could see the broad shape of our future and it didn't include the fulfillment of the dreams we'd carried forward from our youth.

So, in both cases—frustrated success or looming disappointment—we began to question our dreams themselves. Were they what we truly wanted? Would they really make us magically satisfied, and let us live happily ever after? Was pursuing them how we truly wanted to spend the limited time remaining to us?

Pondering these questions, we realized that the life we'd been living had been a life aimed at satisfying many people, including not just ourselves but also our parents, our spouses, our children, our culture, our mentors, our social circles. We'd been seeking to satisfy a complex set of expectations, which we'd internalized from many people and influences from childhood on. Those expectations got all wrapped up in our dreams, the life and goals and self we'd been striving to achieve.

So, here in mid-age, we began to think, Forget everybody else! What do *I* really want? That was the suddenly urgent question, whispered or shouted, explicitly expressed or only sensed, that characterized our middle adult years. Working out the answers and then acting on them was what bound the twenty varied years of this stage into a single epoch. Carl Jung said we spend our first forty years living the lives others expect of us, and the next forty years living the lives we want.

Our questioning most likely produced a combination of change and continuity. Some parts of our lives we changed and other parts we left the same, and some parts we retained, but for reasons and goals entirely new or renewed. We may have stayed in the same job, for example, but found different sources of satisfaction in it. Or we may have come to enjoy watching our children blossom as individuals in their own right, rather than vessels of our ambition and need. Some of us even abandoned our dreams as a vestige of immaturity. Others of us retained our dreams, but stripped them of pieces that weren't our own. Others kept our dreams unchanged and continued pursuing them.

Of course, it was also possible to pass through this period of questioning, emerge with a strong desire to make changes, and then do nothing. The changes felt painful or risky or tumultuous, and we didn't have the stomach for any of that. Such was the outcome chosen by many of us. It was a safe outcome, but not always a happy one. Eventually many of us who chose this alternative would have to deal with the sources of dissatisfaction in our lives—if not in midlife, then later.

Out of this questioning often came significant personal change as well. We began to feel increasing freedom to be ourselves, to reveal sides of ourselves seldom expressed before. Women learned to speak out. Men learned to respect and reveal a softer side. Both became less concerned, perhaps, with playing the roles of "men" and "women." Perhaps we began to explore an interest, like music or art, that we'd never before felt was appropriate, or that we had valued once but given up as we "matured." Perhaps we became more mellow, more tolerant of different points of view. Perhaps we became less competitive, more willing to give others a helping hand or the benefit of our accumulated wisdom. Perhaps our marriages became more tender and loving.

As we underwent these personal changes, many of us became more interested in self-expression, and, with the weight of growing age, more interested in what legacy we would leave. We thought less of what *we* would accomplish and more of how we could help someone coming behind us or support something bigger than ourselves, something that would outlive us. Many of us talked about "giving back," which referred not just to money and goods but also to the experience and wisdom we'd accumulated along the way.

As you recall the facts and memories of your middle adulthood, include any questioning and changes that occurred at that time in your life. "Oh, he was just going through his midlife crisis," is an unflattering comment we sometimes hear. It somehow seems to imply that the questioning that occurred at this time of life signified personal weakness and immaturity. We were supposed to have figured out our lives in our twenties and then pursued unswervingly the paths begun there for the next many decades.

That's silly. No one could or should live all those decades without continuing to question, change, and grow as a person. There's accumulating evidence that so many of us pass through this questioning period that it must be a natural part of life. Think about it. What could be more appropriate, once we fully grasp our own mortality, than asking how we want to spend the finite time remaining to us?

So don't hesitate to reveal yourself and your stories of this fascinating period in your life. Those who read your story—children, grandchildren, and others— will be passing through this very period themselves one day. They will need your wisdom, just as you benefited, or could have benefited, from the experience of others as you passed through it yourself. Share your hard-won wisdom and, above all, enjoy the process of remembering.

FACTS AND MEMORIES FROM YOUR MIDDLE ADULT STAGE

This time of life—roughly your forties and fifties—typically bustles with fundamental questions and change and new directions, all driven by a newly urgent sense of time passing and growing age.

As already noted, the middle adult stage lasts longer than previous stages, its double decades highlighted by efforts to cope with the many changes it includes, and to build lives different from the ones you lived through your twenties and thirties. Because of its length and all that occurs in it, you may find that it contains distinct sub-eras. Its first years, for example, could be years of transition into "middle age."

Indeed, most likely you spent your forties making this transition as you became aware of passing age, children left home, and your own needs and desires of life changed as well. You gradually settled into new patterns, which may have required continuing change and adjustment. This ongoing change, and the time needed to consolidate your life after each change, may create in your memory sub-eras within this lengthy stage.

In fact, throughout this chapter, you will be asked to think of yourself at forty, at fifty, and at sixty. The purpose of this recurring request is to help you think about the changes that occurred throughout this stage, all bound together in their diversity by efforts to find and settle into the mature life you want, a life true to who you are.

As always, record the facts as requested for each life segment. Then see what memories are stirred by the many provocative memory questions that follow each set of fact questions.

You in Middle Adulthood

For most who pass through these middle adult years, they're an era of significant personal change. Increasing age alone guarantees it. So the following questions will lead you to reflect on the changes that occurred at this fascinating time.

FACTS ABOUT YOU IN MIDDLE ADULTHOOD

❦ Note or describe when and how this stage began for you. Was it noticing the signs of age or some outside event or the growth of children? Did it happen in some sharp turning point, or did it creep up on you? How old were you when this happened?

❦ Now, without thought or reflection, just off the top of your head, note the highlights of your middle adult years. These are the major changes and significant events that occurred in these years.

❦ Note when you began to question some key parts of your middle-aged life, or when you began to think of changing that life in some significant way, by retiring or moving, for example. How old were you?

MEMORIES OF YOU IN MIDDLE ADULTHOOD

What events and moments first gave you a sense of growing older? Was there a time when you seemed to cross that line from "young" to "no longer young"? When were you first aware that others saw you as someone "older"? How did you feel when you first received a solicitation from AARP, or when a clerk first gave you a senior discount without your asking?

At approximately 3:45 on a Tuesday in late April it happens. John Steinbeck flies out of my head.

It is so disturbing I call a friend. "Who is that author," I ask, "who wrote about migrant laborers in the Depression . . . ? One book was really famous. . . . This family travels across the country to California—"

My friend interrupts, a note of horror in her voice. "The Grapes of Wrath? By Steinbeck?"

"Right," I say in equal horror.

—ELIZABETH COHEN, *The House on Beartown Road*

Did you begin to think differently about the passage of time? When did you begin to think about the amount of time remaining in your life, instead of the amount of time you'd already lived? When did you realize that time was truly limited and precious? What led you to that realization? How did it change the way you thought and acted?

Did you begin in general to question the way you were living your life? Did you begin to wonder why you'd been struggling so hard for so long? Was there something missing in your life that you wanted to add, or pieces you wanted to change or remove? Did your questioning cause turmoil in your life or in the lives of those around you? Did you try to push those questions aside, or did you take steps to explore and address them?

How did you define success at forty and at sixty? What were your life goals at forty? What were they at sixty? What caused any changes in the way you thought about personal success? Did your definition become less defined by others and more specific to you personally? If you changed your definition, did that lead you to change your life in some way?

What happened to your life dream in this period? Was there some important milestone that was to signify fulfillment of your dream, which was the life and self you'd been striving to achieve? Did you achieve that milestone and your dream? If so, did it bring the long-term satisfaction you'd expected? Or did you come to realize you probably would never achieve it? How did that change your life and your goals? Did you drop your dream, or change it in some way?

How did your personality—outgoing, quiet, warm, aloof, thoughtful, spontaneous—change through these years and why? Did you, for example, become less or more tolerant, less or more shy or outspoken? How did you handle stress or pressure? Recall times and occasions when you felt most like yourself. When did you feel least yourself?

How did your physical appearance, including the way you dressed, change during this period? How did age most show itself in your appearance? Try to be objective—describe yourself at forty and at sixty the way an honest friend might. If you believed your appearance was an asset before, did you continue to believe that through this stage? Do you think you aged well or not? Did your clothing and personal presentation change from forty to sixty? What were the clothing fads and fashions of the time and how did you follow them (or not)?

What were your primary strengths and weaknesses at the beginning and end of this stage? How would an honest friend have described your strengths and weaknesses at forty and at sixty? What incidents come to mind when you think of those characteristics? If they changed through your middle years, how and what caused the changes?

How were you trying to change yourself in your early forties versus any similar efforts in your late fifties? What personal skills or characteristics were you trying to improve? Were these related to your perceived strengths and weaknesses? In each case, why did you think you needed to change? How did you go about trying to change yourself? Did you take courses or seminars, read self-help books, use counselors or coaches? Did you succeed at making changes in yourself?

How self-confident were you? Did your self-confidence grow or diminish as you advanced through your forties and fifties? What did you do or not do because of your self-confidence? If it changed, what caused the change? Did your sense of what was important and what you cared about change?

Was something from the past still part of your life? Did any problems or questions or matters from your past life still play a definite role in your life in this period? Troubled relationships with your parents, an ex-spouse, other relatives, or past associates, for example? Perhaps it was something you'd done (or not done) in the past, which was still playing out in your life.

I was the youngest of four children—the "trailer"—born five years after my youngest brother. They had more years with my father who died when I was fifteen.

I became an only child at home when my siblings went off to boarding school. By that time, my father was already suffering with the heart condition that would cause his early death. He had worked very hard in a family business during his lifetime and had little time to enjoy home life. My mother, meaning well, sheltered him from the chaos of four children to try to give him peace when he came home late each night. It was the era in which children were to be "seen but not heard." To be brief, it was a remote father-daughter relationship. He was certainly not unkind, but quiet and—I think now—shy.

One evening, not long before he died, when my mother was not at home, my father and I were sitting on our couch in front of the television. I don't remember what we were watching. My hand was resting beside me. During the program I noticed that my father's little finger was touching my little finger. He didn't move his hand away and neither did I. We just sat there, silent and barely touching . . . but touching. This image is etched in my mind.

I'm a grandmother now, well beyond the age he ever achieved. Last summer, I had a dream. In it, my father is driving and I am in the passenger seat beside him. I am silent and looking straight ahead. As he drives, he apologizes for not paying enough attention to me, for neglecting me. Then he hands me a pile of old magazines and family photographs. Life Magazine *is on top.*

I felt the absence of a father during most of my life. It contributed to my making poor choices in men, including my ex-husband. There is no formula for repairing early deficits. A loving man helps, and I was fortunate to have found one, after fifty.

— MIRIAM REEDER, personal story

Compare your daily routine at forty, fifty, and sixty. When did you usually get up? How did you typically spend your mornings? Your afternoons and evenings? When did any changes occur in your routine and why? How did these changes reflect other changes in your life?

How did you prefer to spend your free time? Reading? Sports? Talking with friends? A hobby? Did the way you spent free time change over this period? How and for what reason? Did you discover new interests? Did you find you had more, or less, free time as you got older?

What possessions were most important to you at forty and at sixty? A memento? A ring? Something someone had given you? How did you get it? What was the story embodied in that thing that gave it meaning to you?

What did you worry most about through your middle years? Children? Money? Marriage? Work? Something about yourself, like health? Did you tend to worry a lot or a little? Compare your chief worries at forty with those at sixty.

Recall any health issues—illnesses or accidents—that you faced in this period. Did your health change over this period? Did you develop a set of physical problems that you increasingly had to accommodate in your life?

Did you ever suffer discrimination in this time of your life? Was it because of your race, your religion or beliefs, your looks, your health, something else? If it was something you'd suffered earlier in your life, was it different now? What form did it take?

What was it like to be a woman in middle age? How did you find your gender made a difference? If your children were now going out on their own, or were already gone, how did that change your life and your role and your whole sense of yourself? Did you try to enter or reenter the work world? What was that experience like? Did being a woman have any specific effect on your reaching or not reaching your personal dream, whatever that was? Did you have to give up or change your dream because of your gender?

What part of your life—e.g., work, family, religion—was most important to you when you were forty? Children, work, marriage, something else? Was the same part still most important at fifty and sixty? If not, what changed and what parts were more important at those later ages? Did the circumstances of your life cause any change, or was it a choice on your part? Was there ever a conflict between what you thought or said was most important and where you actually spent your time? How did you resolve any conflicts?

Recall your most intense moments and events in middle adulthood.
- Recall a time or times when you *laughed* and *laughed* and *laughed*.
- What caused you to feel *sad*?

One of the hardest things I've had to accept as an adult is the fact that my ex-husband doesn't want any kind of relationship with me. After 24 years of marriage, I hoped we could be friends or, at the very least, communicate from time to time about the two best things we did together—our daughter and son. I even thought we might get together from time to time—him, me, our new partners, and our kids. I never had any illusions about heart-to-hearts or financial advice or gift giving, but I hoped we might share concerns and joys as the kids' lives developed. After ten years of hoping and trying, he gave me a strong signal that was hard to ignore. Last winter, when I'd decided to visit old friends who live on the same street as he, I sent him a courtesy e-mail about my visit so he could drop over to say hello, or not. He was furious that I was coming to 'his' neighborhood and made sure he was out of town the day I arrived. My friends were baffled by this behavior, but I got the message. It still saddens me that he doesn't want to be friends. It is a huge loss in my life.

— KARIN BARTOW, personal story

- Recall moments of *joy* and *happiness*.
- When did you experience *doubt* and *uncertainty*?
- Recall times when you felt *romance* and *passion*.
- Were there times when you *connected* with another person?
- Recall experiences of *physical pain*.
- Recall a time or occasion when you felt a strong sense of *physical well-being*.

- What happened to *surprise, shock,* or *amaze* you?
- When and why did you become truly and deeply *angry?*
- What caused you to feel a sense of *despair?*
- What happened to make you feel *regret?*
- When did you have a sense of *being loved?*
- What caused you the most *disappointment* and *frustration?*
- What was your greatest source or occasion of *pride?*
- When did you feel *embarrassed* or *ashamed?*
- What were your most intense experiences around your senses: *sight, sound, smell, taste,* and *touch?*

Did you take up some form of creative, expressive activity in this period? Did you try writing, woodworking, photography, or some other craft? Did you feel some urge now to express yourself creatively by making something of your own? Did you take any courses or buy any books on some such subject? What came of these activities?

Did you face any hardships at this time? Was there ever a period when you truly struggled? Was your trouble financial? Emotional? What did you have to endure for a time? How did you do it? How did it change you?

What difficult choices or decisions did you make at this time? Did you ever feel torn between two or more choices, each desirable in some way? How did you resolve these dilemmas? Did you ever face a dilemma and do nothing and let it resolve itself? Did you ever choose the more difficult alternative? Were you happy with the outcome?

What did you fear most in your forties? Failure? Embarrassment? Being alone? Being poor? Aging? Think of times when this fear determined or affected a major decision, or when it changed your behavior. Did your fear change as you progressed through middle age? What did you fear most at fifty? At sixty? What did you do, or not do, because of fear?

What did not happen that you wished had? Did you or someone near you *not* get something desired? How did you deal with the disappointment? How did it affect your life?

What experiences did you have of life and death? Did you start to lose family members? Parents or grandparents? Siblings? Friends or colleagues? How did it affect you or those close to you? How did you deal with loss and grief? How did you help others deal with their grief?

Mom and Dad picked me up at the West Palm Beach airport. They hadn't expected me until the next day, but I convinced them that I'd completed my work and was able to catch an earlier flight. I told them I wanted even more time with them to celebrate their sixtieth wedding anniversary.

As we began the short drive home from the airport, Mom leaned over the front seat and began with a battery of questions: "When will Toby get here?" "Do you think she's feeling better?" "Where should we go for dinner when she arrives?" "How long is she planning to stay?" They hadn't seen her for a while.

Toby was my older sister. She called me her "little wish" because she badgered Mom and Dad to have another child. She assumed I'd be a girl. Our brother, Allen, five years her junior, wasn't interested in country music and resisted being dressed up.

A few days before my flight home, I'd learned that Toby was in the hospital again and that she was having trouble breathing. She had quit smoking, finally, after her doctor said he wouldn't see her again unless she stopped. This time, what appeared to be bronchitis was rapidly turning into pneumonia. I called the airlines and moved up my trip home.

The flight to Florida felt long, and I was glad for that. The flight attendant was very kind and offered me a seat in first class where I could be alone. She brought a pillow and blanket in an effort to make me comfortable. I spent the entire flight rehearsing what I would say when I arrived home. I tried it every way, with every intonation, using the most soothing words I could muster. I tested phrases, pauses, and imagined hearing myself speak the words. To relax, I tried to read to pass some of the time, but my mind would drift back to the challenge ahead.

As we reached the gates of Century Village, where my parents had retired twenty years earlier, Dad circled the bend and parked in front of their condo. As always, he insisted on carrying my luggage into the house. Mom no longer offered to help because she'd been diagnosed and operated on for stomach cancer the summer before. I was care-

ful to lead the way into the house, and grateful that it was already dusk and the lights in-side dim. I didn't want either of them to get a full look at my eyes, at least not yet.

"Mom and Dad, please sit down," I began, when we entered the living room. "What is it?" they said. Their initial excitement faded. Their expressions turned to concern, their faces softening and sinking as their breathing stilled. They became quiet. I tried to recall all the words and phrasing I'd chosen, all the practicing and rehearsing I'd done in preparation for this moment, but now that the moment had arrived, all I could manage to say was, "She didn't make it."

— CAROL FRANCO, personal story

Did you rethink the way you were living your life? What conclusions did you reach? What caused this reconsideration? What did you do as a result?

Did you begin to think of your legacy, or how you would be remembered? Was it important to leave something that would survive you? Was it money or goods or property, or did it include something less tangible, like your wisdom or knowledge or your life story? How did this interest in legacy begin, and what did you do to pursue it?

Children and Family Life

These middle years are often times of great change in family life. Children begin to grow up and leave home. Think now of your children and family and the lives you lived through your middle adult years and the changes you all experienced.

FACTS ABOUT YOUR FAMILY LIFE

❧ List the names and ages of family members who were living at home at the beginning of your middle adult years.

❧ Note any changes or turning points that occurred in the lives of those family members—for example, a child going off to school, a major illness or accident.

❦ Note the name, date, place of birth, and gender of any child born during this period.

❦ Note the names, ages, and parents of any grandchildren born during this stage of your life. Note briefly as well any factual highlights in the young lives of each of these grandchildren.

MEMORIES OF YOUR FAMILY LIFE

For each of your children, reflect on the following, as it applies to that specific child in this period:

- *Infancy and childhood:* What was it like to have young children when you were middle-aged? Did you wish you'd had them earlier? What memories do you have of this child's young years, at home and in school? Did you face any problems with him or her?
- *Adolescence:* Did you find the teen years enjoyable, or were they a difficult time for you and this child? Were you much involved in this child's life? Did you talk much? When did you feel closest? Did this child ever get in scrapes? What kind of personality did this child develop? How did the two of you get along? How did this child get along with his or her brothers and sisters?
- *Adulthood:* What was your relationship with your adult child? What gives you special pleasure to recall? Is there anything you feel you did particularly well with this child? Did you have any hopes or expectations for this child's life—what he or she would do, for example? Were there any times when you expressed your feelings to this child, and he or she to you? If this child was a stepchild, or an adopted or foster child, recall incidents related to that status.
- *Leaving home:* What was the occasion of this child's leaving home—the military, getting married, taking a job, going off to college? Was the leave-taking difficult for you or the child?

So, here we stand, Kurt and I, in the middle of the street, watching our oldest child leave home. Braving it out, on the verge of tears, we make jokes, trying to act normal. After all, this is as it should be. . . .

I try to speak, to say something funny and glib like my father would have. "Don't pick your nose in public. And remember to put the butter back in the icebox." But I can't find the words. I squeeze Kurt's hand, knowing that he is feeling the same way. Where did the time go? How did Oliver speed through his childhood at such a pace? At this moment, we both want to turn back the clock and start all over again. . . .

Oliver takes one last look at Kurt and me, standing arm in arm in the street. I know he is capturing this snapshot moment in his memory, just as I had done. Now it's my turn to stand and wave.

Oliver guns the engine, lays some rubber for laughs and peels out down the street. He is the joker, just like his grandfather, Rut, always breaking the tense moments with a flourished smile.

Kurt and I lean against each other, waving and smiling, smiling, and waving, until our son's car finally disappears from view. . . .

Kurt and I walk quietly through our front door, unable to speak just yet.

Taking my hand, he leads me upstairs to Oliver's bedroom. Pushing open the door against a tide of abandoned sneakers, jeans and T-shirts all heaped on the floor, we walk in and sit on his bed. Looking around at his belongings—his picture of Kurt and himself white-water-rafting in Colorado, a marlin he caught that we had stuffed, a photo of me holding him when he was a baby, an old fisherman's lamp I bought him, trophies from karate and his hockey stickers—we sit in silence, letting the tears flow, wallowing unashamedly in the sadness of this passage in life.

—Goldie Hawn, *A Lotus Grows in the Mud*

Establishing his or her own life and home: How often did you and your child see each other or talk? If this child got married, recall the courtship, engagement, and wedding. Think about times and occasions spent with your child's spouse or significant other. Did you get along? Recall times with your child's family—holidays, birthdays, for example. How did you get along with your son and daughter-in-law's family?

As a woman, how do you look back on childbearing and child rearing? Was bearing and raising children what you'd expected or hoped or feared it would be? If you devoted full time to housekeeping and child raising, did you have any regrets that you didn't also pursue other interests, too, like work? How did you handle the empty nest?

As a man, how do you look back on child rearing? How did your experience fathering children differ from your expectations? Were you actively involved in the daily work and activities of your family, or was being breadwinner your primary involvement? Do you wish you had been more involved?

How did you feel about becoming a grandparent? If your child had children at this time, recall any moments or occasions from the pregnancy and birth. Recall the grandchild and any time you spent with him or her. Were there any special occasions, like holidays or birthdays?

Recall a typical day in your life as a family through this period. What usually happened each morning? Each afternoon and evening? How did this routine change over time, particularly as children grew up and left home? Were there chores assigned to different family members? Did you expect children to take on more family responsibilities as they grew older? How did you handle money with the children? Did they get allowances? Where did they get spending money?

How did family members generally get along with each other? How did you and the children get along when you lived together? Was there generally good interaction or some ongoing friction? Did children compete with each other? Recall some typical, day-to-day spats and what they were about.

Recall memorable times spent together as a family. Were there any family rituals, such as dinnertimes, or family games? Did you play games? Did you go on holidays or take trips together?

What problems and crises did you face as a family? Recall serious illness, accidents, injuries, personal problems, problems at work or school, and so on. Did your family ever pass through a time of hardship of any kind—economic, social, and so on? Recall how you as a family dealt with problems and crises. Did you share and come together, or did you or others in your family remain silent? Did your children know what problems you were facing?

Were you a single parent? Did the responsibility of raising your children fall on you alone at this time in your life? Recall those moments and that life of single parenthood. What memorable times come to mind? Did you get any help from the absent parent? Did you try to compensate for the lack of a parental partner?

Marriage/Partnership

How did your relationship weather these sometimes turbulent middle adult years of change, as you came to terms with an empty nest and perhaps with changes in outlook and life goals?

FACTS ABOUT YOUR MARRIAGE/PARTNER

❧ Note your spouse's age at the beginning of this stage and any factual highlights in his or her life through this period.

❧ Note any changes in your relationship with your spouse that occurred during this stage.

MEMORIES OF YOUR MARRIAGE/PARTNER

Did you pass through the aging process of middle adulthood together? How did you each react to the growing signs of age you saw in the other? Did aging affect your relationship in some way? How about the reexamination of life and life goals that people typically do in the early part of this stage? Was this something you shared and experienced together?

How would you describe your relationship in this period? Close? Contentious? Loving? Distant? Were the two of you good at working through differences now? What did you learn over the years that you didn't know when you married? When you ate dinner together, did you have a lot to talk about, or was it generally a quiet time? How would each of you at that time have completed this statement: You always . . .

"Why do you always have to be right," I remember John saying.

It was a complaint, a charge, part of a fight.

He never understood that in my own mind I was never right. Once in 1971, when we were moving from Franklin Avenue to Malibu, I found a message stuck behind a picture I was taking down. The message was from someone to whom I had been close before I married John. He had spent a few weeks with us in the house on Franklin Avenue. This was the message: "You were wrong." I did not know what I had been wrong about but the possibilities seem infinite. I burned the message. I never mentioned it to John.

—JOAN DIDION, *The Year of Magical Thinking*

What happened to your life dreams? Did either or both of you examine and revise or drop your individual or joint life dreams, the sense each of you had of what you wanted to become and accomplish in life? What changed, and did you change together or apart? Was a particular kind of marriage or partnership relationship part of that dream? Did one of you have to change his or her dream for the other? Did you two develop basically the same dream for the rest of your lives?

What was your daily life together like? What was a typical day like then for the two of you? Did you have any routines or rituals? If life changed through this longish period, think of each part separately: early, middle, and late. What did you do together? How did you each spend spare or leisure time? What did you do on holidays, vacations, or special occasions? Did you share a group of friends? What did you do together socially? What hobbies or interests did you share?

What specific life challenges did you face together? Did any problems emerge in this period—physical health, depression, alcoholism, economic problems? If so, how did you face those as a couple?

Were you and your spouse in basic agreement about dealing with your children in this period? Did you support each other and present a more or less united front? After your children left, how did you and your spouse react to the empty nest? How did you and your spouse like your children's significant others or their spouses? How did each of you respond to becoming grandparents?

If you were both remarried and had children from previous marriages, what challenges did you face melding two families? Did the children have problems getting along? Did you or your spouse have difficulties treating all the children equally? Recall any problems and what was done to alleviate them.

How were your relationships with your in-laws? How did you get along with your in-laws? How did you and your spouse handle issues of aging parents?

What about ex-spouses? Did either of you have a continuing relationship of any kind with an ex-spouse? How did this affect the relationship between you and your spouse?

Was the relationship ever in danger? Did you somehow seek to save or renew the relationship during this period? Did you as a couple ever seek outside help, such as from a marriage counselor? What forces held your relationship together? What forces pulled you apart? What got you through whatever troubles you faced in the relationship?

> *On Saturday morning, August 15th, with the grand jury testimony looming and after a miserable, sleepless night, I woke up Hillary and told her the truth about what had happened between me and Monica Lewinsky. . . .*
>
> *Hillary and I . . . began a serious counseling program, one day a week for about a year. For the first time in my life, I actually talked openly about feelings, experiences, and opinions about life, love, and the nature of relationships. I didn't like everything I learned about myself or my past, and it pained me to face the fact that my childhood and the life I'd led since growing up had made some things difficult for me that seemed to come more naturally to other people. . . .*

In the long counseling sessions and our conversations about them afterward, Hillary and I also got to know each other again, beyond the work and ideas we shared and the child we adored. I had always loved her very much, but not always very well. I was grateful that she was brave enough to participate in the counseling. We were still each other's best friend, and I hoped we could save our marriage.

Meanwhile, I was still sleeping on a couch, this one in the small living room that adjoined our bedroom. I slept on that old couch for two months or more. I got a lot of reading, thinking, and work done, and the couch was pretty comfortable, but I hoped I wouldn't be on it forever.

—BILL CLINTON, *My Life: The Presidential Years*

Home

What was your home like in your forties and fifties, as children left and you, perhaps, began to wind down your career? Imagine yourself back there in that place (or places) as you lived through the great sea changes that occurred in this long period of middle age.

FACTS ABOUT YOUR HOME

❦ List the address, town or city, and state (and country, if not the United States) of each place you (and your family) lived in this stage, including a second, vacation home.

❦ Briefly describe each physical place—house, apartment building, etc.—and the neighborhood, town, or city.

MEMORIES OF YOUR HOME

Imagine yourself in the physical place where you lived. If it was the same home as before, try to remember it from this time in your life. Enter it in your imagination, in middle adulthood, and walk through it, space by space, room by room. What highlights, memorable moments, of your life occurred there? As children left, did the place start to feel too big?

Imagine yourself walking around the outside of the house or building. Again, what moments and events come to mind from that space?

Think of yourself back in the neighborhood. Who were your neighbors? Were you close to any of them? What houses or buildings were next to yours? What stores and businesses were nearby? Who lived there? What happened there?

Remember the town or city where you lived. What kind of place was it when you were in your forties and fifties? Where did you usually go? Who did you go with? Did you feel connected to this place? What happened to make you feel that way? Were you involved in your community in any way?

Recall any moves you made. Think back over each move and what it involved and what happened. Was it difficult to leave the home you left? What was the adjustment like in the new home?

If you had a second or vacation home. Recall this place and imagine yourself back in it. Use the physical spaces to recall people and incidents there. How often did you go there? Was it a special place, somewhere to relax and get away?

Romantic Relationships

There is romance in middle age! If, for whatever reason, you found yourself alone at this time of middle age, recall the relationships you had. How were they different from the romantic relationships of youth?

FACTS ABOUT YOUR ROMANTIC RELATIONSHIPS

❦ Name the individuals with whom you were involved.

❦ Describe each of these people briefly (age, work, background, relevant other facts), and note the location (city, etc.) and approximate beginning and ending dates of each relationship.

MEMORIES OF YOUR ROMANTIC RELATIONSHIPS

Think of each person with whom you had a relationship.

- *Where and how did you meet?* What attracted you to each other? How did the first date, or time together, happen? Where did you go?
- *What did you especially like about him or her?* What did you dislike? What is he or she doing in your memory? What places are linked in your mind with this person?
- *When did you know this was a special relationship?* Did the other person share your feelings? When did you first make your feelings known to each other? Did you ever consider marrying?
- *Recall highlights of the relationship.* Recall the most romantic moments. What other moments or events or occasions do you most remember from this relationship?
- *When did the relationship end (if it did)?* What caused it to end? Did you have any regrets?

Did you use a matchmaking service? Recall incidents around that process.

What did you want? Were you looking mostly for a good time and companionship? Or was your goal to get serious and find a mate? Did you ever go with anyone whose goal was different from yours? Did your goals change over the course of this period?

Getting Married (or Entering a Committed Relationship)

Every day people in their middle years get married. If you were one of them at this time in your life, think back to that occasion and the events surrounding it.

FACTS ABOUT GETTING MARRIED

❦ Note the name of your new spouse or partner, and briefly and factually describe the person's background—where he or she grew up, and his or her education, and work or career.

❦ Note the date and place you were married.

MEMORIES OF GETTING MARRIED

What was your courtship? How and when and where did you and your spouse meet? How and when did you decide to get married? Did you live together before getting married? How long was your engagement?

What was your wedding like? What was the planning and preparation like? Did you and your spouse create your own ceremony, or did you use a traditional program? Recall the location and building where you were married. Who was in the wedding party? Who officiated? What family members were there? Recall that day and walk through it in your mind. Who else attended? What were the highlights of the ceremony? Did anything go wrong, or threaten to go wrong? Where was the reception? How did your two families—the bride's and the groom's—get along? What were the highlights of your honeymoon?

How about you and your new in-laws? How did you get along with your spouse's family, especially as you were getting to know your spouse before marriage? Did you see his or her family often? What did you do together? How did your spouse and your family get along?

If this was a second marriage. Did you or your spouse have children from a previous marriage? How did they react to your marriage? Were they supportive, or did they object? How did your children get along with your spouse's children? Recall any memories from this experience.

What kind of adjustments did you and your new spouse go through in the first year of marriage? What changes, discoveries, surprises occurred in the first year or so of your marriage? Was it a time of significant adjustment? What was the first real challenge of any kind that you faced together? What did you learn about each other in those early days? How did your experience with a previous marriage change or affect your behavior or expectations in this marriage?

Divorce/Splitting Up

If one of the midlife changes you faced was a divorce or the breakup of a longtime relationship, recall those events here.

FACTS ABOUT YOUR DIVORCE

❧ Note the date and place of your divorce.

❧ Briefly describe the terms—who got what, what happened with children, and any other factual highlights.

MEMORIES OF YOUR DIVORCE

What caused your divorce? What were the patterns of behavior that contributed to the breakup? What was the immediate cause—that is, what events actually precipitated the split? Was the divorce by mutual agreement? Or did the breakup surprise one or the other of you? What part do you think you played? Was there a turning point when you realized that divorce was inevitable?

Recall the divorce process—the steps you and your spouse went through from the decision to divorce through the formal divorce itself. Negotiating the divorce and navigating the various issues that arise during this process could be difficult and contentious. Was it that way for you, or was your divorce relatively amicable? What moments do you especially remember from that process?

The morning was quite cold for April—April 12th to be exact. I picked Carol up at the apartment where she had been living for the past six months and we headed for City Hall. After four years of sustained effort, we'd finally decided to go our separate ways.

A group was gathering around Room B, where the divorce proceedings were to take place. At around 9:30 we filed into the room silently and found seats along long rows of benches. Carol and I weren't the first up, so we waited and watched as lawyers battled lawyers for alimony, child support, or custody, finally reaching some resolution. She rested her head on my shoulder until we were called to the judge's podium.

We rose, hand in hand, and came before the judge, a woman in her sixties and obviously familiar with the agonies of divorce. We had no lawyer, having addressed all of our issues through a mediator. She began to review our docket, raising her head from time to time to ask us a question, increasingly surprised by our composure and obvious concern for each other. Midway through the process she paused, looked up, removed her glasses, and called the entire courtroom to attention. "Never in my thirty-eight years of presiding over divorce cases have I ever had a couple come before me holding hands. You might all take a lesson from these two people."

When it was over, Carol and I left the courtroom in silence. We'd managed to go through the trauma, pain, and finally the divorce and come out the other side, still hand in hand.

—Zack Gould, personal story

How did others react? How did your children take the news? Were they surprised or did they see it coming? How did your family react? Your in-laws? Did you get emotional support from any of them? Did your friends help you through? Did any of them take sides?

How did you find life as a divorced parent? Did the children stay with you, primarily, or your spouse? How often did you, or your spouse, see them? What moments stand out in your memory around this arrangement? How did you and your spouse try to minimize the effects on your children? Did your relationship with your children change? What kind of continuing relationship did your ex-spouse have with you and your children?

How did you find life as a single person? What do you remember most vividly about adjusting to your new life? What friends stood out as particularly helpful at this time? Where did you live—in the same residence or somewhere else? Did you remain in touch with your ex-spouse or his or her family? Did you start going out again? Did you do all right economically? Were you relieved or sad to be single again? Did you hope to find another partner soon, or did you question whether to get involved again? If you wanted a partner, how did you pursue that goal?

How long did the healing and adjustment process require? Was your primary reaction a feeling of relief, sadness, or anger? How long did you look backward at what happened and why, rather than looking forward to the future?

Birth Family

Now, as you passed through your forties and fifties and your parents entered their sixties and seventies and beyond, the family baton truly did pass from the previous generation to yours—at least it did in most families. How did that transition happen for you, your siblings, and your parents and their generation?

FACTS ABOUT YOUR BIRTH FAMILY

❦ Note the names of those who remained in your birth family at the beginning of this period. Note the ages of each and very briefly describe his or her life at that specific time.

❦ Note anything factual and significant, with year of occurrence, that happened in each of their lives—death, illness, accidents, accomplishments, marriage, divorce, and so on.

MEMORIES OF YOUR BIRTH FAMILY

Recall your relationship with your parents when you were forty and when you were sixty, and reflect on the changes that occurred in that period. What occasions did you and your family spend with them? Did they live close by and remain part of your life? Did you ever express your feelings to each other? Was there anything left unsaid, or aspects of their lives that remained a mystery to you? How were they financially—did you or others help them? What did you worry about most in regard to them? Were you involved in any health issues they faced? Did you take on the responsibility of caring for them?

> *When we worked together on M*A*S*H for the second time . . . I wrote a show for him [my father] in which his character, Borelli, is so controlling that it drives Hawkeye crazy. It gave us a chance to play out the tensions between us as other people. . . . My father loved it. He even had an idea for the resolution of the story. "What do you think of this?" he said, his eyes glowing. "Hawkeye and Borelli are both hurt when the aid station is shelled. They have to do surgery, and one of them can only use his right hand and the other can only use his left. They each become the other's hand."*
>
> *I didn't tell him, but the idea sounded corny to me, too much like the neat ending of a Tin Pan Alley song or a burlesque sketch. But for once I didn't hold myself above him; I decided not to be so precious about my elevated taste, and I wrote his ending into the script.*
>
> *It wasn't until we were actually shooting the scene, sewing a stitch with one hand each—two men having to work together in spite of themselves—that I realized what my father had given us to play. Like the two characters, we were working hand in hand— and it had taken a few wounds to get us there. It was as though the scene were a wish on his part and a gentle nudge to us both, delivered through the medium of play. I felt his shoulder against mine; my father's arms entwined with mine. We tossed the scene back and forth between us, and over our masks our eyes locked and we were playmates again.*
>
> —ALAN ALDA, *Never Have Your Dog Stuffed*

What were your parents' lives like in this period? They probably progressed through their late adult years (roughly sixty to eighty) and into their elder years as you advanced through your middle adult stage. What happened with them at work—did they retire? How did they adjust to retirement? What did they do with their time? What happened to them at home? Socially? Did they still live where they'd always lived? Did they struggle in any way, physically or mentally? Did their relationship with each other change or stay the same?

If either of your parents died at this time, recall those sad events. What events led to his or her death? Recall the death itself and burial. Were you there? How did you handle this loss and your grief? What effect did it have on your relationships with other members of your family? What of him or her did you miss most?

Think about your brothers and sisters at this time. What was happening in the life of each? What was your contact with each of them now? How often did you talk and what did you talk about? Were you comfortable together? Did you do things together? Were there any issues between you? Did you agree about your parents and their lives? If your parents died, how did that affect your relationship?

Remember your grandparents. If your grandparents weren't already gone when you entered middle age, you almost certainly lost them during this stage. If they were still alive, how were they coping with old age? Did you worry about them? Recall times when you saw them. Did you have any special times with them? Did you help take care of them? If any of them passed away at this time, what memories come to mind of that sad occasion and the events surrounding it?

When I found out my sweet grandma had inoperable cancer, I was devastated. The same grandma who was up at the crack of dawn (or before) baking cookies and who seasoned everything she made with a special ingredient: L-O-V-E.

So I did what I often do with my tortured emotions. I wrote a song. I recorded it so I could present it to her when I went to visit. It's called "Your Star in the Sky" and we did in fact purchase and name a star after her.

When she heard her song, she was deeply touched. She invited all her friends and neighbors to stop by to listen to it. But most often she would listen by herself. She would excuse herself, take her tissue and her tape into the bedroom, and let us know that she just needed to cry a little bit.

—STACY YOUNG, personal story

Recall members of your extended family. Who still played a role in your life? What kind of ongoing contact did you have? Did your relationship with them change over the roughly two decades of this stage? If they were older, did you help care for them? If any of them died, recall the events surrounding that sad occasion. Were there any unresolved issues associated with any of them?

Religion or Spirituality

What role did religious or spiritual beliefs play in your life in middle adulthood? As your life went through the significant changes of midlife, was religion a part of those changes in some way? Recall that part of your midlife now.

FACTS ABOUT YOUR RELIGIOUS OR SPIRITUAL BELIEFS

❦ Describe briefly the beliefs that were important to you, and how they changed, if they did, through your middle adult years.

❦ Note briefly what spiritual or religious practices you followed, the activities you did, based on your beliefs.

❦ Describe briefly any specific religious or spiritual experiences at this time.

MEMORIES OF YOUR RELIGIOUS OR SPIRITUAL BELIEFS

If you questioned and examined your goals and purposes at this time in your life, did that exercise include your religious beliefs? Did that questioning serve to underline the importance of religious beliefs to you, or did it lessen their importance? How did your beliefs change from the time you were forty to the time you were sixty? Did anything happen in this stage—the death of someone close to you, for example—to cause you to doubt your beliefs, or make them even stronger? Did you become more or less tolerant of people whose beliefs differed from yours?

Reflect on the practices you performed, related to your beliefs. Was your religion an integral part of your life, or simply one, albeit important, part? Did you carry any religious rituals and practices into your home? Did you and your spouse share beliefs? If not, what happened around those differences? Did your children take with them any of the beliefs and practices they learned in your home as they established lives and homes of their own? Did you ever try to convert anyone else to your beliefs?

Think about any religious or spiritual experiences from this stage of your life. What brought them on? What happened in them? What difference did they make in your day-to-day life?

Work/Career

The middle years see the culmination of career for many people. Was that the case for you, or did you continue to progress through these years and even beyond? Did your reexamination of life and goals at this time in your life lead to any changes in your work and career?

FACTS ABOUT YOUR WORK/CAREER

❦ For each job or different position (including different jobs within the same organization), list the name of your employer, where you worked, your title, what you did, the name(s) of your boss(es), and whether you supervised others.

❦ Identify each business you started and ran. What was it and how long did you run it?

MEMORIES OF YOUR WORK/CAREER

As you entered this stage, was your career or work life turning out the way you wanted?

- *If you had any career goals in your thirties, did you reach them by your early forties?* If you achieved them, what did it take? Did they bring the satisfaction you'd expected? What was the high point of your career? Any setbacks? If you didn't achieve them, or weren't likely to, what did you think and feel about that?

- *Did you spend any time in this stage reappraising your basic work or career goals?* If so, what did you decide? Were you doing what you truly wanted to do? Did you define yourself by your job? Did you consider circling back and trying to do something you abandoned early in your career? What came of this thinking and rethinking? Did you make work and career changes?

- *Were you apprehensive that when you retired you would regret not doing or achieving what you'd truly wanted?* Did you wish you had chosen different work, a different career? If you'd spent most of your work life with the same company, did you reconsider that, too?

How did your work and career change as you progressed through middle age?

- *Compare your work circumstances (the work you did, where you did it, etc.) at forty and at sixty.* What were they at, say, thirty-five, compared with what they were at fifty or fifty-five? Did you shift careers, or make a significant change in your work?

- *Did your attitude about work change?* Did work and career move from the center of your life to a necessary but not crucial part of your life? Did your attitudes about working in an organization change? Did you worry less about organizational politics and rivalries?

- *Did you continue to be ambitious?* For the same things, or something different? Did you consider going to work for yourself? Doing what? Why did that sound attractive? Did you do anything about it?

Did you actually embark on a new and different second career? Recall the events surrounding that big step. How did you choose this career? Was it an actual choice or something that came up by chance? How difficult was it to make the change? How did it work out? How long did it take before others accepted you in this new career? Did you have any regrets—that you'd done it or that you hadn't done it sooner?

Were you exceptionally good at something? If you were an expert, or particularly accomplished, did you retain and increase that mastery in this period? Did you take pride in your expertise? Did your career ever take you in a different direction—for example, toward running something rather than personally *doing* what you were good at and enjoyed?

Recall each of the specific jobs or positions you held at this time.

- *How and why you got/took that job.* Did you seek it out? Were you recruited? Was it a promotion? Were you working for yourself? Did it work out the way you hoped?
- *The job and your career.* How was this job related to your career? Was it a stepping-stone? To what? How deeply did you invest yourself in this job? Why? Recall moments of hard work and dedication.
- *The organization or business where you worked.* If it was a new job, in a new company, what did it do? What kind of company was it to work for? What were the other people there like? How was management? Recall the people who ran the place.
- *Your work.* Recall the work itself—what did you do? Recall moments when things went especially well. What work goals did you have in this job, such as increasing sales or cutting costs? What did you do in a typical workday? What was the most difficult part? The easiest? The part you found most satisfying? Hated most? What problems did you typically have to overcome? What personal needs and goals did this work fulfill, such as the need to help others or to do something important or to make a certain amount of money? What did you accomplish that you're proud of? Did you get any recognition? Did you deal with customers or other outsiders? What special or memorable projects or events did you work on? What training did you get? Did you ever spend time working in a country and culture not your own? Was there ever a time the business went bad—a recession, a company problem, whatever? What happened and what did you do?
- *The place where you worked.* Recall the location, the building, the people, and where you sat or did your work, and what tools or equipment you used. Imagine yourself back in that place and what it looked like and how it felt. Imagine walking down the corridors. Who was there? What did they do? Did all of you get along? Where did you eat lunch? With whom? What were the offices and meeting rooms you used like?
- *Your boss.* What was he or she like—competent, knowledgeable, or not?

Recall times you interacted. How did he or she treat you? What did he or she think of you and your work? What did you learn from working for him or her?

- *Being the boss.* What was your biggest challenge as a boss? Recall any people you hired or had to let go. Who was the best employee who worked for you? The worst? What was the biggest employee problem you faced at this time and what did you do? What did those who worked for you think of you? How did you know? Did you enjoy managing people? Did your attitude about this change during this period?

The difficulties of my job remained enormous. I still had little idea of how to relate to people in a business environment, and no idea how closely I was being watched by everyone. Within the company, whatever I said or did, even my body language, sent a stronger message to people than I realized. In addition, I had spent a lifetime with dramatically impressive people and probably dismissed as unimportant too many quiet, unassuming, but hardworking people throughout the company. It took me a while to learn that certain people may have important skills that are not always blazingly apparent. Gradually I came to realize—slow as I may have been—that what mattered was performance, that sometimes people might have to be helped to develop, and that it takes all kinds to make an organization run properly.

I made mistakes and suffered great distress from them, partly because I believed that if you just worked diligently enough you wouldn't make mistakes. I truly believed that other people in my position didn't make mistakes; I couldn't see that everybody makes them, even people with great experience. What I did that I'm certain my male counterparts did not, and which was particularly tormenting, was to lie awake at night reliving events of the day, going over and over certain scenes, wondering how I could have managed whatever it was differently.

—KATHARINE GRAHAM, *Personal History*

- *Being a mentor.* Did you take anyone under your wing and advise and help that person with work or career?
- *If you were a woman, what was it like in this job and place, working for your particular boss?* What were your career ambitions? Were you frustrated in them, or successful, and did that have anything to do with being a woman? Did you bump up against the "glass ceiling"? Did you feel you needed to work harder because you were a woman?
- *Were you able to maintain a good work and home personal balance?* How good were you at fulfilling all your roles—parent, employee, boss, community volunteer, church member, and so on? Were there ever times of conflict and difficult choices?
- *The way this job ended.* Did you leave the company? Were you recruited or promoted out of it? Were you ever let go, fired, or laid off? How did you feel?

Did you start your own business, or continue a business you started earlier? If so, what motivated you to take this step? What did your business do? Where was it located? How did you raise money for it? Imagine yourself back in that place— walk through it at this time in your life. What scenes and moments and occasions come to mind? Did the business grow and prosper? Did you or it ever struggle? Did you have a partner or partners? How did that work out? If you closed it down, why—what happened?

Did you ever face ethical or moral issues in your work? Did you ever feel that the requirements of your work conflicted with your sense of what was right and wrong? Were you ever expected to do something that seemed to you unfair or dishonest? How did you resolve this dilemma? Did it affect your career, or your motivation?

Friends and Other Memorable People

Middle age can be a time when people discover anew the value of friends and relationships. What relationships outside family meant most to you through your forties and fifties?

FACTS ABOUT FRIENDS AND OTHER MEMORABLE PEOPLE

❧ List the people who were your good friends. Note any facts or highlights during this stage in your life that occurred in their lives or in their relationship with you.

❧ Identify people you mentored.

❧ Identify anyone here who served as a model for you, whose example was helpful to you at this time.

❧ Identify anyone else who stands out in your memory. List these people, where and when you knew them, and in a word or two the nature of your relationship.

❧ Describe briefly the circle of people with whom you socialized in middle age. Note briefly where you'd typically get together—at a local watering spot, a social club, even work—and what you'd do.

MEMORIES OF FRIENDS AND OTHER MEMORABLE PEOPLE

Recall, one by one, each of the friends you identified. Remember moments and occasions you shared. Why and how were you close? What events and circumstances led to your closeness? How did friends help you, or you them, through some of the questioning and turmoil of this stage? Did you confide in each other? Did a friend ever betray you or you them? Did a once-close friendship fall apart or even blow up? What caused that and what came of it?

Recall situations in which you mentored someone. Recall the people, our protégées, whom you helped and guided, at work or in any other life arena. How did you make a difference? If anyone mentored you through some or all of this stage, recall that person and what he or she did.

Were there times when you were guided by the example of someone else? It could have been anyone, even an historical figure, whose life or actions—or just one action—guided you at this time.

Bring to mind any others who stood out at this time of your life. Someone memorable might be a person you met only once who made a deep impression on you for some reason. Recall each of these people, if there were any, where you encountered them, and what effect they had on you.

Recall your social life and the people in it. Think about the specific activities and events you enjoyed with this circle of acquaintances. Did you play tennis and socialize afterward? Go to the movies? Eat out at a favorite restaurant? If you met any of these people today, what memories would you talk about? Recall any other social moments or events that were especially memorable. What other people did you see and do things with?

Learning

Did you continue to learn—through reading or programs of some kind—during your middle years? What programs did you attend? What did you learn? Did you still find it exciting to learn something new?

FACTS ABOUT LEARNING

❦ If you attended school of any kind in this period, name the school and its location, the dates you attended, what you studied and why, and any outcome, such as a diploma or certificate.

❦ If you attended some other kind of course, program, or seminar, note its name, the dates, and what you studied.

Did you actually go back and attend school? Perhaps you returned to finish college, for example, or get an advanced degree or some sort of certification.

- *The school building or campus.* In your mind, return to this place and walk through it. What events and moments and people come to mind?
- *Your purpose for being there.* Recall the program you attended or the degree/certificate you obtained. Did you enroll to advance in your work or fulfill a personal ambition or explore a new area?
- *Classes and teachers.* Recall the various classes you took. Remember a memorable class and imagine yourself back in it. Who was teaching? What other students were there? What was your favorite class? Favorite teacher? What happened in that class, or with that teacher?
- *Fellow students and social life at school.* What classmates stand out in your memory? What happened that makes them memorable? Did you do anything together? Who were your friends in this school? Was any of your social life centered around school? What school clubs and groups did you join?

Remember any other courses, seminars, or other educational programs you took. For each, put yourself back in that place and time and recall any people or moments that stand out in your memory. What caused you to take this program or seminar? What did you learn and how did you use that knowledge or skill in your life?

Causes, Community, and Politics

As you reexamined your life and values in these middle adult years, did you become involved in new causes or community projects or politics? Perhaps you continued to advocate the causes and projects that occupied your time and interest before.

FACTS ABOUT CAUSES, COMMUNITY, AND POLITICS

🍁 Name each of the major causes, community projects, or political campaigns that you tried to advance in this period.

🍁 For each, include its purpose, the time of your involvement, and the basic facts of what you did.

MEMORIES OF CAUSES, COMMUNITY, AND POLITICS

What causes or movements took up your time and effort as you lived through middle adulthood? Think of the occasions or moments associated in your memory with each. What other people were involved? What did you accomplish? Was there a thread that wove through all of them, some common concern or desire or passion? Compare your involvement in these causes at forty and at sixty.

For years I had thought of adopting a little girl from China. But the timing wasn't right, or maybe I was too committed to my traveling job. Adoption was an idea that I kept choosing not to pursue, but that kept tugging at my heart. When I turned fifty, and began to think seriously about how I could give back, especially from the heart, I realized that I could do volunteer work with Chinese orphans. It would be a way to help—and I knew, too, that it would crystallize the adoption issue for me. I was thrilled to learn about a children's home outside Beijing where I could work with special-needs babies and toddlers for a few weeks.

On my arrival at the home, I could hardly wait to see the little ones. There were so many precious babies that I felt a little overwhelmed trying to figure out how I could possibly help each one, twenty in all. Kai Jian, for instance, was a healthy, happy, beautiful two-year old whose clubbed feet were almost completely healed; on my last day, his shoe bar was removed. I'm confident he'll be readily adopted. I think Yu Min, a cuddly four-month-old from Mongolia, will be okay, too; despite spina bifida, his legs were in good shape and he should be able to walk. I realized fairly quickly that the love went both ways, that there was so much these children had to offer; I was not the only one doing the giving.

It was fascinating, too, to see how my thoughts and feelings evolved to the point where I realized where my deepest connection lay. It was tiny Xiao Hua, one year and three months, smart and curious, awaiting her third cleft palate surgery, who pulled me most strongly. She had arrived my first night, and with her sweet and independent nature, captured my heart.

As I was leaving the toddlers' house on my last day, Xiao Hua crawled all the way to the door for the first time. She was poised on the threshold, as if waiting for a sign that she could follow me outside into the cold night. It seemed that she knew I was truly leaving, and she wanted to come, too. It broke my heart to have to close the door.

When I got back to the States, I planned to let my emotions settle; I was determined not to rush to any conclusions. But it became clear immediately that I could not stop thinking about Xiao Hua, and that not only did I want to adopt, but I wanted to adopt her. Even though I knew that the Chinese government did not allow foreigners to identify specific children they want to adopt—even though I knew the rules from the very start—I had to follow my heart, and do everything I could to try to bring Xiao Hua home.

—LESLIE ZHEUTLIN, personal story

Imagine yourself back involved in any community groups or activities that took your time and effort in middle adulthood. What occasions or memorable people come to mind in each? What goals were you and your associates trying to achieve? Did you succeed? Did your interests or involvement shift between the ages of forty and sixty?

Think of the ways you actively participated in politics in middle age. Did you campaign for a candidate? Did you participate in politics yourself?

INTERESTS AND ACTIVITIES

Middle age can be a time of exploring new areas or rediscovering interests from an earlier time. Did either of these happen to you? Did you continue pursuing some longtime interest?

FACTS ABOUT YOUR INTERESTS AND ACTIVITIES

❦ Name any pets or animals that were important to you or your family.

❦ Name the clubs or organizations you belonged to in middle adulthood, the times you were involved, the purpose of each and your role.

❦ Note which of the arts—music, theater, dance, poetry, or some other form— seriously engaged your time and attention. Note as well the nature of your involvement.

❦ Name any hobbies or games (e.g., bridge) you pursued seriously through your forties and fifties. Include when and where you were engaged and any accomplishments or recognition you achieved.

❦ Identify any sports you either played or followed seriously in middle adulthood. Note any highlights or accomplishments of your own playing, or of the team or teams you followed.

❦ Name the various forms of popular entertainment, such as movies, reading, and radio, that you followed through this period. Note any specific examples of each that were important to you—movies seen or books read, for example.

❦ Note any memorable trips you took in middle adulthood—where you went, with whom, when, and briefly what you saw.

Recall each pet or animal. Recall moments of pleasure, and moments of worry or sorrow, with each.

Just weeks after the milestone of my 40th birthday, my 29-year-old horse, Rikki, whom I'd owned for 26 years, fell ill. I kissed my husband and three-year-old daughter good-bye, and bundled our baby into the car to drive 200 miles to my mom's house, where I still kept Rikki.

On that long drive home, I reminisced about the first time I'd seen him. I was 14 years old and just coming off a bad experience with another horse. I wasn't sure I ever wanted to ride again. Despite his youth, Rikki had already given up on people. The breeder had beaten him and locked him up in a stall for hours in the Midwest heat, often with a heavy western saddle on his back. He was 200 pounds underweight with an abscess in his front right hoof. It was love at first sight.

The breeder wanted far more money for Rikki than we could afford. So every afternoon after school I'd secretly (or so I thought) walk the mile up the country road to spend time with him. When no one was around, I'd soak his foot in Epsom salts. As he improved, he'd follow me around the pasture, nosing for carrots, a taste he'd never experienced.

One afternoon when I came home from school, my mom told me she needed my help urgently in the barn. I rushed to assist her only to find, peeking out from one of the stalls, my chestnut prince!

When the vet told me that nothing could be done to save Rikki, my heart nearly broke. The most beautiful moments of my childhood and adolescence were wrapped up in that horse. I shared every trauma and drama with him—he was the wisest horse I ever knew, and my closest confidante. As the vet administered the shot, I stood stroking him, whispering in his ear, reminding him one last time of our shared memories. I told him I loved him, and would always miss him. And I will.

After saying good-bye to Rikki, and with him, my childhood and youth, I walked back to the car where my eight-month-old son slept. I looked down at him and realized that for all of the pain of saying good-bye to the past, there were exquisite moments ahead.

— PATRICIA WEITSMAN, personal story

Think of each club or organization to which you belonged. Recall what each did. Are any of its activities or events still vivid in your memory? What meetings did you attend? Recall the other people in each group. What aspect of this organization gave you particular satisfaction?

Were there any memorable events or moments in the arts that interested you? What performances or exhibits or other occasions do you remember vividly? Are there people you remember? Where did you go for each? If you performed in some way, were there memorable performances or highlights?

Think of each of the hobbies or games you enjoyed and recall moments from each. How did you choose to spend your leisure time? Did you garden? Cook? Did you develop some new interests such as photography? Remember times of great satisfaction or accomplishment. Were other people involved?

What forms of popular entertainment do you recall with fondness (or otherwise)? What radio or television programs did you make sure you watched or listened to through this time in your life? What movies remain in your memory? Did you enjoy any specific actors (male and female)? If reading was important to you, what did you read that was especially memorable? Did you belong to a book club? Did any book have the power to influence you in your personal or work life?

What sports did you play or follow actively through middle adulthood? Did you take up any new sports? Think of each sport and recall any that stand out in your memory. If you were a serious sports fan, recall any important games. How did your favorite teams do?

The lure of the sea, in all its forms, is probably the strongest urge in me. It is a silent world. I am always fascinated, as one is with a favourite poem. It is the indescribable beauty down there that makes you want to go to it and hold it. It is an exercise in quick reflexes. Your mind sharpens, it snaps, it works like an automatic pistol. It is an exercise in self-control too, for you have to breathe half the number of times you do normally. The oxygen-tank is on your back. It is a new, a different, a fallible lung, and you go with dread and expectation and a sense of danger, and you hope you'll live.

This sport keeps me alive, but there are those who know me who say I am trying to kill myself this way. I wouldn't say no. I just don't know. I know that when I get down a hundred feet or so, and the air in the tank is gone, and I have only a two-minute or three-minute reserve supply left, and I pull the lever that sets this free, and I start my swim back up to the surface—then I am living—and if not, I am dying as one who has, just before, been living intensely.

—ERROL FLYNN, *My Wicked, Wicked Ways*

Think back over each trip. Where did you go and what did you see that has stuck with you? Did you face any problems or experience any surprises? Did you meet anyone interesting? What happened to you in different cultures? Was there a special vacation destination you especially enjoyed and visited often?

Notable Events

What noteworthy events touched and influenced you in these middle adult years?

FACTS ABOUT NOTABLE EVENTS

❦ Identify any historical or notable events that touched you in middle age, including what happened and how it affected you.

❦ Do the same for any local events.

MEMORIES OF NOTABLE EVENTS

What historical or noteworthy events touched you or your world? Think back to the years of this period, your middle adulthood, and the great events of that time. Recall how and when you first learned about each. How did each affect or change your life? Did you somehow participate in them?

On Tuesday, October 5, 2004, I received a telephone call from the Gallup polling organization asking how I was going to vote. I said I did not know. After twice giving the same response to the same query, I answered by saying, "I don't know. My choice is between a fraud and an incompetent." That answer produced another question—would I be interested in participating in the presidential debate scheduled for Friday, October 8, at Washington University in St. Louis, Missouri. They were looking for undecided voters, and I certainly qualified.

All participants received a FedEx package on Thursday telling us what time to be where and what to expect when we got there. Also included were four 3 x 5 cards; we were to write our question for Bush on two of the cards and our question for Kerry on the other two.

When I arrived at the Radisson Hotel at 8:30 Friday morning, along with 139 other undecided voters, we were organized by name and told to stay next to our alphabetical neighbors for the rest of the day. People from the presidential debate team thanked everyone for their willingness to participate and explained the schedule. We were allowed to use our cell phones to keep our families informed of the day's events, but were asked not to have any contact with any media. Those of us who had assumed cameras would not be permitted were given cameras to take as many photos as we liked. Once the debate began, there would be no restroom breaks, so we were encouraged to make use of the facilities as often as necessary. Charles Gibson, the debate moderator, then gathered one copy of our questions, and we kept the second copy. He spent the rest of the day reading all 280 questions, choosing the questions and the order in which they would be asked.

When we finished the buffet lunch they provided, we were taken by bus to the university campus where there were a lot of men in black and the security was extremely thorough. We spent the afternoon sequestered in a large room with tables and chairs where board games and cards had been provided. At midafternoon we had a dress rehearsal to be sure we could enter the auditorium and be seated in the allotted time. Seven cameras televised the debate and we were told to assume that at any given moment we could be in one of the viewfinders. We were also told to show no reaction to any Bush or Kerry answer. In the unlikely event someone became ill and had to leave, we were told how to exit and that we would not be readmitted. Before going back to our room, Charles Gibson addressed each member of the group and made notes on how to pronounce our names and everyone's location.

After our buffet dinner, it was showtime! We were seated by 6:30 p.m. (as luck would have it, I was seated on the aisle where Bush entered at 7:45), the debate began at 8:00, and was scheduled to end at 9:30. The closer it got to 9:30, the less likely it was that my question had made the cut . . . but THEN I heard my name! and the first thought that went through my head was, Please, God. Let me get out of this chair without looking really stupid!

I asked my question: "President Bush, you have made hundreds of decisions that have affected thousands of lives. Please list three instances in which you came to realize you had made a wrong decision and what you did to correct it. Thank you." He responded with a canned answer about Iraq, and the debate was over. We had been told that we would know if the candidates would be willing to mingle, but that we would not be allowed to leave until the candidates had left. By this time I just wanted to go home. My back hurt, my tush was numb, and it had been a really long day. I positioned myself at the front edge of the aisle so I could make a quick getaway. There was a lot of mingling and photo taking, but Bush began to work his way toward his exit aisle. When he saw me (in my red sweater), he stopped and said, "That was a good question. It was a difficult question." I intentionally chose my tone of voice (pleasant with a smile) and facial expression (also pleasant with a smile), but my response just came out: ". . . and you did a fine job of avoiding answering." He said he knew I had meant Iraq, and I said, "No, Mr. President. I didn't mean Iraq and I wasn't referring to the appointments you mentioned. We all go through our days, and every once in a while we realize some decision we'd made wasn't the right one, and we go back and try to fix it." The expression on his face changed in such a way that led me to believe he had a different understanding of the question, but someone asked a question about his wife, and our exchange ended.

When I got home, there were 25 messages on my answering machine, including ones from The New York Times; Good Morning America; Fort Worth Star-Telegram; The Wall Street Journal; St. Louis Post-Dispatch; *and a reporter from a newspaper in Sweden! Believe it or not, Matts Larsen, the reporter, persuaded his paper to pay for a trip to St. Louis (for him and his photographer, Finn) to interview me. My 15 minutes of fame was more like half an hour, and the very best part was being parodied on* Saturday Night Live *and inspiring a* Doonesbury *strip. Don, my late husband, would have been so pleased.*

—LINDA GRABEL, personal story

What local events played a role in your life? Did any other events, even if they weren't large and notable, touch and change your life?

Other Voices

If you want, contact any people who knew you and were part of your life during this stage. Ask them to record any memories of you from this important part of your life.

If you want to include other people's memories of you as a middle adult . . .

1. Make a list of people from your time as a middle adult and ask them to share their memories with you, in their own words.
2. Record each memory on a separate sheet of paper. Label each memory "A Memory of Me" and include the memory teller's name, as well as the approximate date and location of the memory.
3. Add these memory sheets to your own memories in your *My Life Story* notebook.

My father is not always right. I remember the moment this was made clear to me like a lightning bolt. I was around 15 (maybe it took me longer than others to get to this point?!) and being a chubby adolescent, my father was nice enough to take me to a nutritionist (and to pay for it) weekly.

This one day, we were driving on a very familiar road into town. As we rounded the bend at the bottom of the hill, I was telling him something my nutritionist had taught me: food is energy for the body. The body needs this energy to be sustained and to run. It is literally the fuel for the car.

"No, no!" my dad insisted. "That is not correct." And something else along the lines that this lady was saying nonsense. I was silent. I believed what she had said and further, I knew she was right.

My dad is not always right, I thought. He does not always know all the answers. This was life altering. I spent the next five years looking for proof that he was wrong and

I was in fact right. He does not remember this but has not yet lived it down. For me, I may as well be driving on that road right now, I remember it so clearly.

—LESLEY SHEARER, personal story

THE MEANING OF YOUR
MIDDLE ADULT STAGE

If any life stage should make talk of meaning easy, middle adulthood is the one. For most of us it was a time when we naturally asked questions about what we wanted from life and what we must do with the remainder of our lives to find satisfaction.

As you work on middle adult meaning, compare your thoughts here with your recollections of meaning from previous stages. You might even go back and see what you wrote about meaning in earlier stages. It's always fascinating to see how we grew and developed (and sometimes regressed), as we passed through the great phases of life. It's hard to believe that most students of human nature, until the twentieth century, thought human beings stopped developing and changing shortly after reaching physical maturity. Anyone who follows a process like the one outlined in *The Legacy Guide* soon realizes how much virtually everyone continues changing throughout the adult years.

At the same time, it's also true that we carry forward certain beliefs and issues from our youth. Kent, who's just exited this stage, recalls a recent conversation with a thirty-year-old who said something that revealed a big assumption: by the end of middle adulthood, according to this thirty-year-old, all life issues from one's early days would be happily resolved. "Wait until you're sixty and see what you think then," was Kent's response. He recalled his own mother who, to the day she died at eighty-six, believed fervently that she was her father's favorite child (he died in the 1916 flu epidemic when she was five).

Defining Moments

If this was a time of self-examination for you, as it was for many of us, there were perhaps events or moments of insight when who you were and what you wanted became clearer. Do any of those moments stand out in your memory? Sometimes these moments are more obvious in hindsight than they might have been at the time.

As always, it's a useful exercise to think of yourself at the beginning of this stage, in your early forties, and then think of yourself at the end, somewhere around sixty, or shortly thereafter. As you do that, ask: How was I as a person different at sixty than I was at forty, and where and how did those differences or changes in me occur? Those are the defining or pivotal moments you should note here.

Isn't one of the difficulties knowing who should make the first move? The child is angry because the parent hasn't been what he or she should have been, and the child waits for the deficient parent to admit he or she was terrible and to ask forgiveness. But it's harder to change when you are older. You know you've made mistakes, but you don't understand this new generation and you're stuck in your ways (unless you keep working on yourself to not get stuck). Playing Chelsea in [the movie] On Golden Pond *and paying attention to the advice her mother gives her allowed me to see that it has to be the child who makes the move toward forgiveness and that if it is done from a loving place, the parent will almost always be there to receive. One important caveat that Ethel gives Chelsea: "Sometimes you have to look very hard at a person and remember he's doing the best he can."*

—JANE FONDA, *My Life So Far*

Values—What Mattered

Did you think through in this period what you most wanted to do with your life, what would provide for you the most meaning and satisfaction? If you did, try to capture what you discovered here. Think of your values, what mattered most to you, at forty and then at sixty. What were the differences, and what made them change? Perhaps, somewhere in this stage of life, you discovered not what was providing the most meaning but what *would* provide meaning if you made appropriate changes. If that was the case, what were those changes and did you make them?

Here are some other ways of looking at this question, through different metaphors: where was the center of gravity of your life? What kept you anchored and steady, as the world swirled around you? What was your compass and where was north? What was your North Star? Again, think of these questions at forty, and then at sixty.

Look at the major components of life—work, relationships, family, marriage, the world of ideas, community. Which of these, or some component not listed, was most important to you? Where did you spend your time and effort and money? What about that part of life compelled you to devote such time and attention?

One other idea: recall two or three or four big decisions you made in middle adulthood. For each decision recall whatever choices you had, and then recall how you made the choice you did. That "how" almost certainly reflected your values.

The three of us were together for the last time on a late morning in winter: my father, my eldest son, and me. Three generations gathered in the basement of the funeral parlor, in Brookline, Massachusetts.

My father was laid out on the table, dead, in the parlor's basement. He had been a tall, handsome man. Now he was probably less than 5'10" and his emaciated body weighed less than a hundred pounds. He was so very still. You view a loved one's corpse as much to let it sink in that they're gone as you do to say goodbye.

Community elders had washed his body and wrapped it in a plain white burial shroud. The funeral home wanted to know if they should provide the tallis, prayer shawl, as his outer wrap, or would we. His tallis was in a blue velvet bag in his dresser. It was large, of fine yellowish-white wool with black stripes across at the ends. He bought it in Jerusalem, on a trip several years ago. He was more a traditional man than a religious one, and had not worn it too often. I had a similar blue velvet bag and tallis in my own dresser at home. He had given it to me 47 years earlier for my Bar Mitzvah. It was a smaller, satiny version, equally given only occasional use. Rick and I decided we would wrap mine around my father, and I would keep my father's. Then, when I died, Rick would repeat the process, wrap me in his tallis and assume his grandfather's prayer shawl. There, in the basement, we felt we had started a tradition. We will pass it on through the generations.

—STAN DAVIS, *Tall Tales*

Love

Identify the love that helped make this time of your life what it was for you. It could be someone you'd known for years, or a stranger who did something truly generous.

The few people you identify will be ones you've already named in your facts and memories. The purpose here is simply to highlight those few with whom you had this special relationship. No period of life can be completely and fully recalled without acknowledging such people and relationships.

As you identify each person, briefly describe the relationship between the two of you and the ways you each took care—you of them or they of you.

We hope by now that this concept of love is a familiar one. As we age we become more comfortable with it and able to recognize its power. As we age, too, we realize more and more that little in life matters more than loving and being loved.

The problem when someone loses his memory is that people start reinventing him. They have their own versions. And you can't ask the person who is forgetting for help. They become a disputed territory.

I start looking through boxes. I want my version—the Daddy I remember—to be the real one. I have kept old letters, but I can't find any from him. I read my old diaries. I read about the time I went to Israel with my father when I was thirteen, right after my Bas Mitzvah. It was an awkward trip; we didn't know exactly how to be together, what sorts of things to talk about. But of course he knew my name. He had to have known it, to get through customs, to check into the hotel.

Finally I find it. Across from the contents page of Issues in Labor Policy, *a book he edited in 1977, he lined up our names in a single column. . . .*

Like a blind person, I run my fingers over the pages of Issues in Labor Policy. *I want to feel the pages in the dark that way, because in that book he is still and will always be the other Daddy, smart Daddy, before Daddy. I touch the soft paper as if brilliance were Braille or sunshine or sex, something that goes in through your skin and ends up in your heart.*

—ELIZABETH COHEN, *The House on Beartown Road*

Learning and Wisdom

If this was a time of rethinking your life and what you wanted, what did you conclude after making (or not making) any choices or changes based on that reexamination? How did those decisions and changes work out? What would you do differently, if anything?

As we age, our sources of learning become richer and more diverse. We have more experience, meet more people, read more books, see more art and beauty, have more opportunities to feel and react and think. What did you take from all this rich, raw material flooding over you?

As we've advised in past stages, you can look here at your choices and how they came out. You can also look at mistakes and errors, yours and others, and what happened and how you reacted. Look at adversity, bad luck. Every experience has the potential of teaching us something.

Don't forget the wisdom part of learning. It's one of those words we know but can't define clearly. To us it's a distillation of learning. It's the essence of what we know and have experienced. Think of it as advice you might give to yourself and others.

Remember yourself in some important moment or occasion in middle adulthood—when you were hurt or happy or embarrassed, for example. If you, knowing what you've learned, could now enter that scene and say something to that person you were then, impart some wisdom that might have helped you then, what would you say? Would those words have been useful only to you, or would they now help others, too? Share that wisdom with those coming after you. This is your true legacy.

Summing Up

Rise up from the detail of your middle adult years and look at them whole. How would you characterize this time in a few words? What role did it play in your life? Was it a time you questioned the life you'd been living and the goals you'd been pursuing? Did you try to discover what was truly important to you and how you should spend the rest of your life? What was it like overall? How did this time of life feel to you? Do you remember it fondly? Or was it a difficult time you struggled to get through?

Try to remember a time or moment or occasion that best characterized this whole era for you. If there was one, describe it and explain how it seems to you to sum up this time.

STAGE 6

late adult

Remember those old maps you saw in school books, the drawings of the world from four or five hundred years ago? Large parts of the planet then were still unexplored. But instead of simply labeling these vast mysterious territories "Unknown" or "Unexplored," early mapmakers presumed them to harbor untold dangers, filled them with fancy drawings of terrible monsters, and warned, "Here be dragons!" Of course, as courageous explorers ventured into these unknown parts and found no monsters, the fear of dragons faded away.

Much the same thing is happening now with society's view of the life stage we're calling late adult. It begins roughly at age sixty, and more and more of us are living into it and bringing back stories of aging without terrible monsters. If you've passed through this stage already, or are passing through it now, you're one of those explorers. What have you found? We hope no dragons.

Until only a few decades ago, certainly until the middle of the twentieth century, age sixty was considered the gateway to old age. For good reason: it *was* for most people the onset of old age, with its monsters of inexorable decay, decline, pain, and loneliness. It was not so for everyone, of course, because some lived sprightly decades beyond that milestone. But such ancient mariners were the exceptions. Back then most people at sixty could expect to begin soon an irreversible slide into the final years of life. Someone who died in his sixties then was thought to have lived a full life.

No longer. A revolution is under way. More and more of us are demonstrating that life after sixty can routinely be a time of continued vitality and productive activity. An astounding statistic appeared recently in *USA Today*. It said that, of all people who have reached age sixty-five *in the entire history of the world,* roughly two-thirds are living today. If true, that's partly a result of today's larger world population and partly a function of the very point we emphasize here—the increasing longevity and vitality of people over sixty. Roughly half the baby boomers—some seventy-plus million Americans just approaching sixty in 2006—are predicted to live to age eighty-five and beyond. Because there are so many baby boomers, their experience will probably change society's perception and definition of "old age" forever.

Part of this old-age revolution is the fact that most who live well past sixty will do so in relative good health. As revealed by studies that tracked large groups of people from age twenty or so through the late stretches of life, most people today do not roll into old age on a hospital bed. The norm is to remain in relatively good health until coming down with whatever ailment finally kills us. "Good health" does *not* mean a total absence of any ailments. Many and perhaps most of us at sixty and beyond have something physical gone awry. Health is "good" when illness does not prevent us from living more or less the lives we want. Living the lives we want in the face of ailments does require courage, however, which is a personal quality that helps those of us over sixty, as someone said, "keep on going on."

What all this means is simple: until recently, there was only one stage of life after middle age and that was old age. Now that's no longer true. There is a new period among the "ages of man," a time of continued vitality beyond sixty that can hardly be considered old age in its traditional sense. So in *The Legacy Guide*, life after sixty is divided into two stages—late adult and elder. Late adult is the period of continuing vitality after middle age, and elder is the following, final stage that leads to the end of life itself. The elder stage has been with us throughout human history, and we will explore it in the following chapter.

Given that the late adult stage is new and largely unexplored territory, what can be said about it? Most obvious, it is by definition the last great *active* epoch of life. So why not simply consider it a part or extension of middle adult? Because certain events and passages occur in it—notably sea changes in our work lives, including retirement—that separate it from the middle adult years. Perhaps when the baby boomers are done with it, society's conception of age will truly change and the late adult stage will indeed become simply the latter part of middle age. For now it seems different enough to be treated separately.

This late adult stage is unique among life stages in one key way: its length can vary widely from person to person. It may last only a few years, or it may extend decades. All other stages tend to end at or around a certain age, even though it is not age itself that moves us from stage to stage. Adolescence ends right around twenty or shortly thereafter. Middle adult begins somewhere around the early forties. The late adult stage, though it begins around the early sixties, will end only when the effects of infirmity and age diminish our vitality and drive.

For some of us, that point was reached not long after sixty, particularly in the case of serious illness. But for many of us, that point was only reached much later, perhaps not until our late seventies or early to mideighties, or even later. For those of us who die with our boots on, it literally never ends. A recent *BusinessWeek* article told of a ninety-three-year-old social worker who still carried a full caseload and lived a life more active than those of her far younger colleagues. Age alone might define her as what some call "old-old," but the reality of her life says otherwise. It's likely that only death will end her late adult stage.

For others of us, our late adult years began with a real rite of passage, such as retirement or some other significant life change—for example, moving to another part of the country. But more often, the late adult stage began more quietly. We simply started to feel dissatisfied with some part or parts of our middle adult lives. Perhaps we grew impatient with those pieces of life that increasingly seemed burdensome, like winter snow and cold, or the endless meetings and politics and budget games at work, or the need to put up with individuals we didn't like in our social life or neighborhood. Or we jettisoned entire parts of our lives, or simply changed a few aspects slightly. We dropped out of social groups we belonged to for years. Or we joined new ones. Maybe we changed jobs to something less stressful. Perhaps nothing changed except our attitude; for example, our job became less important to us. We went to work, enjoyed the parts we liked, and went with the flow on the rest of it. Change like that could occur in any part of our lives, not just work.

Many of us at this time also began to look back on our lives and try to make sense of them. Some call this the search for integrity, which simply means we tried to make a story of our lives; we looked for the oneness in the life we lived, rather than let it remain in our minds a series of unconnected events. As we lived our lives day by day, the underlying patterns were hard to see. Now we have the vantage point of looking back over our whole lives, and we want to see them as having been more than "just one darn thing after another," as one person put it. So we looked for the themes, the unifiers, the patterns that somehow weave together all the disparate pieces into something we each can call "my life." Perhaps your work with *The Legacy Guide* is part of that. It certainly can be.

With these years often came as well an increased desire to create and play, to make something. Many of us in late adulthood took up painting or writing or some other form of self-expression and creativity. We learned to play again, to enjoy some activities for their own sakes, rather than the ends or purposes they serve. In fact, this desire may even have been the catalyst that began the stage itself—a longing for something missing, rather than unhappiness with what we already had. The distinction between work and play diminished at this time of life, or we strove to eliminate it. We wanted to remove as many of the *have to do* parts of our lives as possible and replace them with *want to do* parts.

This is the period of life, for example, when we moved off center stage in all parts of life, in the work we did, in our families, in our community groups. Moving through the late adult stage was a process of stepping out of central and crucial roles and into parts less commanding and demanding. Indeed, it was a time when we *should* have been making room for younger successors. This kind of change may have worked against our human need to feel important, and so many of us might understandably have found it difficult. The good of those around us and of society in general, however, behooved us to move away from center stage gracefully and take on roles still valuable and valued, still full of what gives life meaning—people and purpose—but no longer so much at the center of things.

No doubt about it, this is a time of great adjustment and personal change. If we were lucky, we got to do it more or less on our own terms and timetable.

For late adulthood was ultimately a time of transition. Yes, every life stage represents a transition, but this one brought a greater magnitude of change from beginning to end than all others, except adolescence. In one great leap of only a few years, adolescence took us from child to adult. Decades later, the late adult stage took us from vital middle age to true old age.

Focusing on the changes and turmoil of this period might have led those of us passing through it to overlook the freedom it offered. Because it is a new stage in human history, society has developed few expectations around it. In each previous stage, there were social standards—for example, by age thirty we were supposed to have started a family and career—and we lived in the context of those standards, even if we chose to ignore them. Here, as each of us lived through the late adult stage, we were relatively free to make of it what we wanted, limited only by our personal circumstances, inclinations, and attitudes.

Consider two of our acquaintances and the wide differences between their approaches to this time in their lives. One, we'll call him Richard, is a lawyer who continues to work actively and full time in a law firm where he's a partner. In fact, he's striving to become the managing partner of the firm. He still relishes high-profile cases and loves to take on pro bono work for the environmental causes he supports. There's no mandatory retirement age in his firm and he plans to continue working as long as he physically can and so long as he feels he's making a genuine contribution. Growing age and some ailments, such as arthritis, have begun to slow him down, and he's had to adapt himself to the limitations they impose. But so far he's still been able to do the work he wants to do. For him, his work is life itself, and he will put it aside only when he absolutely must. The other acquaintance, we'll call him Bill, devoted his career to work for a large East Coast city, where he headed the Public Works Department for fifteen years before his retirement at sixty-two. Now he lives with his wife on the Gulf Coast, where they're near most of their grandchildren. He spends his days deep-sea fishing, golfing, acting as a pro bono adviser on some local municipal projects, telling stories to his grandchildren, and doing some volunteer work at a local hospital.

Richard and Bill represent two different ways of living the late adult stage. Both are vital and active, and engaged with the world around them. Neither approach is inherently better than the other. The difference is in striving and ambition. Richard still wants to have an impact, make a difference, in a world broader than family and friends and immediate community. Bill is done with that. He lived many years with the pressure of a highly visible position, often caught between political pressures. Now, knowing he did what he did well, he wants to take his ease and enjoy a life of freedom from responsibility. He helps those around him, he contributes to his community, but striving—changing the world beyond family and community—no longer matters to him.

With the freedom offered by this stage also comes the ability to address new personal needs that rise in importance to us. For many of us, like the stories Bill tells his grandchildren, and the mentoring Richard offers young lawyers in his firm, these needs often include a concern for the legacy we leave. This concern often arises in the middle adult years and becomes more urgent here. More and more, we want to leave behind something of value that will outlive us. Perhaps, as one way to do that, we grow increasingly concerned for instructing and preparing the generations that follow us, particularly our children and grandchildren. We want to pass on whatever wisdom we've gained and we try to pass on the traditions and customs and lore of the past to those coming after us.

As you look back on this stage in your own life—or perhaps you're still in the midst of it—try to capture your approach, your attitude, toward this period. How did you make it, how are you making it, uniquely your own? Capture both the sea changes that occurred in it and the continuing vitality, along with the bittersweet, paradoxical sense that indeed it is the last great active stage of life.

FACTS AND MEMORIES
FROM YOUR LATE ADULT STAGE

You most likely entered late adulthood, somewhere around sixty, still engaged with life but unhappy with some features of your middle-aged existence. Somewhere around your early sixties, you started to feel the need for adjustments. Perhaps you wanted to customize your life. You wanted it to be more to your liking. So you tried to remove those parts you found less palatable, and most of all you tried to focus more on those parts that gave you the greatest satisfaction. Late adulthood ends when you become elderly and infirm.

If you're currently living through this late adult stage, do proceed with this chapter. Consider the fact and memory questions to the extent you can. For example, when you're asked to compare yourself, say, at sixty and at seventy-five, simply compare yourself at sixty and your current age.

Record the facts as requested, as best you can, given your current age. See what events and moments and occasions come to mind as you ponder the many memory questions.

You in Late Adulthood

Who were you in late adult life? What kind of person did you become? Were you the same person you had been in midlife? In your thirties? Your twenties? Do you believe what once was conventional wisdom—that after becoming adults we stop developing and changing as people? As you work through these pages, consider how you answered many of the same or similar questions for earlier stages in your life.

FACTS ABOUT YOU IN LATE ADULTHOOD

❦ Note the year, your age, and the events (if any, such as moving or retirement) that marked the *beginning* of this time in your life. What was it you wanted to change, or did actually change? Your work? Where you lived? Some other aspect of your middle adult life that no longer appealed to you?

❦ Note the major changes and key moments that highlighted your late adult years. Just list them as a way to help you get this stage clearly established in your mind.

❦ If you completed this stage, note the year, your age, and the events (if any, such as illness or simply the process of aging) that carried you into your elder years.

MEMORIES OF YOU IN LATE ADULTHOOD

Think about the parts of your middle adult life that you changed as you entered this late adult stage. How were you different in your late sixties from the person you were in your midfifties? What adjustments or changes in priorities did you make? What did you allow yourself to do that you would not do in the past? Did you enjoy a slower pace, or were you as busy as ever? What were some of the best parts of this period? Greatest challenges? Reflect on the two or three or four key ways you and your life changed.

Recall any specific rites of passage or explicit turning points that initiated and highlighted this stage of your life. Did you formally retire? Did you move to a different home or even a different part of the country? Did your work change significantly? Did you join new clubs or social groups, take on new interests? Did you celebrate milestone birthdays? Perhaps you rediscovered old interests. Did your life routines change significantly?

How were any midlife changes you'd made earlier working out in this stage? If, in middle adulthood, you reexamined your life and aspirations and made changes, how did those changes work out? As you passed sixty, were you still pursuing them? Did you regret any of these changes?

Were you still trying in your sixties and seventies to "change the world"? Were there still things in this stage that you wanted to accomplish? Did you feel your life's work was not done? Were you pursuing the same life dream you'd long had, or had you taken on a different dream?

Even if you weren't trying to change the world, did you still have broad goals—personal, work, social, other—for the remainder of your active life? What were they? Did these goals represent fundamental or minor changes in the components of your life—your work, where you lived, your interests, how you spent your time? Were there still things in life you wanted to do, like travel or some different kind of work, that you hadn't been able to do previously?

How did you think and feel about time as you continued to age? Did you sense even more that time was fleeting? Were there occasions or events associated with these thoughts? What precipitated them? Did you start seeing or thinking of yourself as "getting old"? When did you start saying things like "at my age," "when you start getting old," or "when I was young?" Did the aging process upset or frustrate you?

How was your health in these late adult years? Did you suffer any specific, serious health problems? Were these problems acute (serious but they went away) or chronic (you had to live with them, at least for a while)? Were you in any accidents? Did you experience any physical disabilities? Did you have to start coping with any conditions that would remain with you for the rest of your life? What did you do to stay healthy? Exercise? Practice yoga? Meditate?

Compare your personality in your late fifties and at seventy or seventy-five. How were you the same and how different, as others saw you? It's said that our personalities, what others see of us, become more distinct and sharply defined as we age. Was that true for you? Did you become a "character," a little eccentric, a little less inhibited? That's often part of the freedom society grants those of us in this time of life. Think of how a good but candid friend might have described you at those different ages.

What had you discovered by this age of your temperament and character? Character is the part of our personalities that is learned and can change with time and experience and conscious effort. Temperament is the part of our personalities that we're born with; it's the personality every newborn baby starts to exhibit within hours and days of birth—fussy, sweet-tempered, placid, loud, demanding, happy, and so on. Temperament comes from our genes and the way our brains and neurons work. It's much less likely to change through life. By this time in your life, what insights had you gained as to your temperament versus your character? Of all your personality traits, which ones stayed fairly constant through life and which ones were you able to develop and change?

Were there times in this stage that required from you great courage and endurance? Were they times of illness or accident, or something else, such as a great loss? What were the conditions or events that called on courage and a strong sense of persistence from you? Did you ever do something despite everyone's advice to the contrary? How did you come through? Did you have help?

Recall your most intense moments and events in late adulthood.
- Recall moments of *loss* and *grief.*
- When did you feel *love* and *closeness* with someone?
- Were you ever *ignored* or *misunderstood*?
- When did you experience a real *sense* of *freedom*?

- Were there ever times of deep *despair,* a sense of *hopelessness.*
- When did you feel particularly *impatient* or *frustrated?*
- When did you feel deep *disappointment?*
- Did you ever experience a feeling of *peace?*
- Recall moments of *embarrassment* or even *shame.*
- On what occasions did you feel *joy* and *happiness?*
- When did you feel particularly *angry?*
- Were there moments when you felt you had been *heard* and *understood?*
- What caused you to feel *proud?*
- Remember moments of real *laughter* and *amusement.*
- On what occasions did you feel especially *satisfied?*
- What were your most intense experiences in late adult life around your senses: *sight, sound, smell, taste,* and *touch?*

But all the memories return, especially the sharp-set memories of youth. For more than twenty years I had not thought of Gerald. He had ceased, even as a recollection, to have a part in my life. He was gone. He was finished, with my first love, with my girlhood. If he were to come back to me, I should scarcely recognize him, for he would be old. Once he had meant to me all the youth of the world; and, now, he would be old, and forgotten by time. So much had happened since I had known him. . . . Then, when I was nearly sixty, I went out, one evening in New York, to a foreign restaurant in a strange street, which was yet vaguely familiar. I smelt the scents of crushed apples and crowded places; and, suddenly, I remembered. I saw him again, clearly. . . .

— ELLEN ANDERSON GHOLSON GLASGOW,
The Woman Within

Were you ever discriminated against? As we age, many of us who never experienced discrimination before begin to face age discrimination. Did that happen to you, that you were treated differently or unfairly because of how old you were? Were there other ways you experienced or suffered from discrimination in late adult life? What form did it take? Was it because of your race, your religion or beliefs, your looks, your health, something else? How did it affect or change your life? If it was something you'd suffered earlier in your life, was it different now in any way?

What was it like to be a woman in late adult life? Did you find gender differences even here in late adulthood, in your work, in your social or religious life, or in any other way? Did you have to fight to be heard or recognized?

Did you care more or less about your appearance and your clothing as you passed through late adulthood? Was your appearance still important to you? What did you see at sixty when you looked in the mirror? What did you see at seventy and seventy-five? Do you think you aged well? Were there times or moments when you felt your appearance was an issue? What did you think it meant to "look your age"? What changes, if any, did you make in your clothing and personal presentation from sixty to eighty?

Was it difficult as you passed through late adulthood to move off center stage? This is typically the time of life when we gradually give up positions of authority and importance, at work, at home, socially, and make room for others who follow us. How did this happen for you? How did you feel about it?

Did any possessions, large or small, have particular meaning for you at this time? Did some object or thing help define your life now or give you special pleasure? A book? A vacation home? China? Some piece of art? A piece of jewelry? A gift of some kind? A keepsake from your mother or father? Why was it valuable? How did you get it?

What occupied your thoughts most in this time of life? Was there any part of life that demanded more of your attention than before? Did you still daydream? What about? What did you worry about most? What did you dream about at night? Did these preoccupations change over this period, through your sixties and seventies?

What did you fear or feel most anxious about at this time? What did you do, or not do, because of fear or anxiety? Were you ever afraid of something that turned out not to be a threat? Were there times and situations in which you should have been more fearful? Were there any times when you acted in spite of fear?

How did you spend your time? What was your daily routine in your early sixties? When did you get up? What did you have for breakfast? Did you exercise? What was your morning typically like? Your afternoons? Where did you go? How would you get there? What was a typical evening? Think of those questions for when you were in your early seventies, in your early eighties. Which daily, routine activities did you most enjoy? Least enjoy?

How did you spend your time alone? Did you enjoy such time? Or did you usually seek out the company of others? Were you lonely? Was there a place or a time of day that was your own, a haven or sanctuary where you could go to be renewed and refreshed?

Did you nurture others? Were you nurtured? What did you do to help, mentor, and nurture others in this period of life? Was it people at work? Family members? Grandchildren? Whom did you help through problems and hard times? Who nurtured you and helped you through your hard times?

What specific satisfactions, and regrets, stand out from this time of your life? What deed, what outcome, what decision gave you the greatest pleasure and contentment? What regrets do you have? Did you ever go back and try to correct or remedy what had happened?

It is not unusual for Americans who visit North Vietnam to be taken to see Vietnamese military installations, and when they do they are always required to wear a helmet like the kind I have been given to wear during the air raids. I am driven to the site of the antiaircraft installation, somewhere on the outskirts of the city. There is a group of about a dozen young Vietnamese soldiers in uniform who greet me. There is also a horde of photographers and journalists—many more than I have seen all in one place in Hanoi. . . .

What happens next is something I have turned over and over in my mind countless times since. Here is my best, honest recollection of what took place.

Someone (I don't remember who) leads me toward the gun, and I sit down, still laughing, still applauding. It all has nothing to do with where I am sitting. I hardly even think about where I am sitting. The cameras flash.

> *I get up, and as I start to walk back to the car with the translator, the implication of what has just happened hits me.* Oh, my God. It's going to look like I was trying to shoot down U.S. planes! *I plead with him.* "You have to be sure those photographs are not published. Please, you can't let them be published." *I am assured it will be taken care of. I don't know what else to do.*
>
> *It is possible that the Vietnamese had it all planned.*
>
> *I will never know. If they did, can I really blame them? The buck stops here. If I was used, I allowed it to happen. It was my mistake, and I have paid and continue to pay a heavy price for it.*
>
> —JANE FONDA, *My Life So Far*

Did anything from your past get resolved at this time in your life? Were there any friends, colleagues, or family members with whom you had a misunderstanding or falling out? Did it get resolved here? How did the resolution occur?

Did you start to think about the story of your life? As you moved through this stage, did you begin to reflect on your life and try to make sense of it? Did you look for the themes and deep goals and underlying purposes and patterns that tied together many of its disparate parts?

What did you want to be remembered for? Was your legacy important to you? Did you think about what you could leave behind that would survive you? Did you make any efforts, like telling stories of your youth to your grandchildren, to create and preserve your legacy? Did you do anything in the community to remember and preserve the past and the people in it? Did you begin to think of your material legacy (money or property, for example) and what you should do with it?

Marriage/Partnership

How did your marriage or partnership flow into late adulthood, following the changes of midlife? Did it move ahead seamlessly, or was there a time of adjustment? Did your relationship continue to develop, or did the two of you settle into, or simply continue, a comfortable routine together that seemed to work?

FACTS ABOUT YOUR MARRIAGE/PARTNERSHIP

❧ Note your spouse's age and any factual highlights, milestones, major events, turning points in his or her life in this period.

❧ Note any highlights or changes in your life with your spouse that occurred during this stage.

MEMORIES OF YOUR MARRIAGE/PARTNERSHIP

What was happening in your spouse's life in this period of your life? Review the highlights you identified under facts, above, and let them bring back memories.

What was your relationship like through this period? Did you remain close? Did you share the same goals and outlook on the rest of your lives? What was a typical day like for the two of you? What did you do together? What did you typically talk about—at dinner, for example? What daily rituals and traditions did you practice? How did you each spend spare or leisure time? Did you share a group of friends? What did you do together socially? What hobbies or interests did you share? What did you do on holidays, vacations, or special occasions?

Was there anything new in your lives as a couple? Did your lives change in any way? Did you move? Did you develop any new rituals? Did you take on new interests or hobbies? Did you share new goals or aspirations? Did you make new friends? If both of you were home, how did you adjust to being around each other all day? Did you learn new aspects of each other? What did you do together that you hadn't done before?

What specific life challenges, such as an illness or loss, did you face together? Did any problems emerge in this period, and, if so, how did you face those as a couple? Were there any sudden changes in fortune—a job loss, an accident, a stroke of luck—that changed your lives? Did you face any difficult choices as a couple?

Did you lose your spouse at this time? Was your loss sudden, or the result of a long illness? Were you there at the time? How did you handle it? What was life alone like? How did you adjust? How long did it take? Who helped you through the loss? What were your fears? What did you miss most? What would you tell a friend about him or her?

> *When the twilights got long in June I forced myself to eat dinner in the living room, where the light was. After John died I had begun eating by myself in the kitchen (the dining room was too big and the table in the living room was where he had died), but when the long twilights came I had a strong sense that he would want me to see the light. As the twilights began to shorten I retreated again to the kitchen. I began spending more evenings alone at home. . . . One night I found myself taking from the cupboard not one of the plates I normally used but a crackled and worn Spode plate, from a set mostly broken or chipped, in a pattern no longer made, "Wickerdale." This had been a set of dishes, cream with a garland of small rose and blue flowers and ecru leaves, that John's mother had given him for the apartment he rented on East Seventy-third Street before we were married. John's mother was dead. John was dead. And I still had, of the "Wickerdale" Spode, four dinner plates, five salad plates, three butter plates, a single coffee cup, and nine saucers. I came to prefer these dishes to all others. By the end of the summer I was running the dishwasher a quarter full just to make sure that at least one of the four "Wickerdale" dinner plates would be clean when I needed it.*
>
> —JOAN DIDION, *The Year of Magical Thinking*

Children and Grandchildren

Just as family leadership passed to you from your parents in midlife, it now over the course of your late adulthood begins to pass to your children. Was that a normal transition for you, or was it something of a struggle?

FACTS ABOUT YOUR CHILDREN AND GRANDCHILDREN

❧ Note the ages of each of your children at the beginning of this stage in your life, and the ages of your grandchildren.

❧ Note for each child or grandchild any significant events, highlights, or milestones that occurred in his or her life during this period—the date (year) and the event briefly.

MEMORIES OF YOUR CHILDREN AND GRANDCHILDREN

Think of each child and grandchild and recall times you spent together. Did you live far apart and see each other only rarely, or close by and see each other often? Did you do things with your grandchildren you wish you'd done with your child? That you wish your parents had done with you? What did you do? Did you spend holidays together? Did you babysit? Think of where each child lived and let thoughts of that place bring back memories of what happened there.

I literally cannot take my eyes off my grandchildren. When they both sit on my lap (ages five and seven), I am at peace and filled with a joy I have never known.

Then the war breaks out!

I am on the front lines. I am a mediator; I hand out candy; I make funny noises with my vibrating lips (my best trick). When the conflict subsides, I escort them back to the Parental Command Post. And then I go to bed and sleep like a baby.

—PHIL DONAHUE, in *If I Knew It Was Going
to Be This Much Fun, I Would Have
Become a Grandparent First*

What was your relationship with your children and grandchildren? Did your relationship with your children change when you became a grandparent? Were you close to your grandchildren? Were you involved in their lives? Did you want to be? Did they want you to be? What did you enjoy most?

Think of the milestones and highlights you identified in the lives of each child or grandchild from this period. Did you participate in any of those events or occasions? Did anyone in your family struggle with hardship or loss at this time, or enjoy great success and good fortune?

I came back from his wedding in Guadalajara with a new perspective on my son and on myself. . . .

The ceremony took place outdoors, with the guests sitting on the lawn, on blankets and on chairs. The parents and siblings walked the couple in. Aní wore a white floor length dress, with a garland of yellow flowers on her head and the same in a handheld bouquet. Len wore a traditional white Guayabera shirt and slacks. They sat with ankles crossed on low cushions and hands held in the prayer position.

The ceremony was completely bilingual, so what would have been a half-hour took twice as long. The woman who officiated was straight out of central casting, a Mexican psychotherapist in her early fifties, dressed in white cotton serape and pants, with a blue beaded necklace and an Indian rattle of feathers in her hand. She lit a charcoal brazier on the floor and sprinkled incense over the fire, fanning the smoke towards the couple. She only spoke Spanish. Standing next to her, one of Len's college roommates repeated all in English.

Everything was said gently and quietly, at a leisurely pace, with great sincerity. First, she asked everyone attending to put their right hands over their hearts, then their left hands on top, and to close their eyes. She asked us all to take a few minutes and send our best feelings, thoughts and prayers to the bridal couple.

Music was playing gently, from across the lawn at the bandstand. Birds seemed to be chirping everywhere. Very tall palm trees were swaying. The sky was a clear blue. The afternoon sun was almost setting. At the same time, a full moon was almost rising. And the tears were streaming down my face. I was cleansing out every nook and cranny of good will in my soul and sending it to them. I was silently saying that my life was complete and theirs together was beginning, and they should have every good thing I could teleport to them. Afterward, some woman—I don't know who—said to me, "I'm glad to see you're the kind of man who cries at weddings."

— STAN DAVIS, *Tall Tales*

Home

For many people, home changes as they pass through their sixties and seventies. Perhaps you downsized to a smaller home that was easier to care for. Perhaps you moved to a more temperate part of the country. Where was home for you in your late adult years?

FACTS ABOUT YOUR HOME

❦ List the address, town or city, and state (and country, if not the United States) of each place you lived in this stage.

❦ Note a brief description of the physical place—house, apartment building, etc.—and the neighborhood or town.

MEMORIES OF YOUR HOME

Recall each house or building where you lived. Recall the physical structure of this place. Enter it in your imagination, in late adult life, and walk through it, space by space, room by room. What happened there? Who was there with you? What highlights, memorable moments, of your life occurred there? If you were still in the same home as before, think of it in this time in your life. Did you begin to think of moving someplace smaller or warmer? Did anything become difficult about your home—going up and down steps or stairs, or the amount of maintenance required? Don't forget to think as well about a vacation home, if you had one.

Imagine yourself at this time walking around the yard, or the outside of each place you lived. What moments and events come to mind from that space?

Remember the neighborhood and the town or city of each place you lived. Put yourself as a late adult in your neighborhood. What houses or buildings were next to yours? What stores and businesses were nearby? Who lived there? What happened there? If this was the place you'd lived for a long time, think about what changed in this period. Imagine yourself back in the city or town.

If you moved in this period, bring that series of events to mind. What was the move and the preparations for it like? Did it go smoothly? Did you want to move? What was it like to leave a home where you'd lived a long time, if that was the case? What memories do you have of adjusting to a new home and neighborhood?

Romantic Relationships

What was said before still applies: it's never too late for romance. If you found yourself unattached for some reason in your sixties and seventies, recall now that part of your life.

FACTS ABOUT YOUR ROMANTIC RELATIONSHIPS

❦ Note the people with whom you had romantic relationships in your late adult years.

❦ Note the location and approximate beginning and ending (if it ended) dates of each relationship.

MEMORIES OF YOUR ROMANTIC RELATIONSHIPS

Think of each person with whom you had a relationship. Bring each of these people before your mind's eye. Where are you with this other person? What is he or she doing in your memory? Where and how did you two meet? What attracted you to each other? How did the first date, or time together, occur? Where did you go? When did you know this was a special relationship? Did the other person share your feelings? When did you first make your feelings known to each other? What did you especially like about him or her? What did you dislike? Did you ever consider marrying this person? Recall the most romantic moments. What other moments or events or occasions do you most remember from this relationship? When did it end (if it did)? What caused it to end? Did you have any regrets?

Getting Married (or Entering a Committed Relationship)

If you married or remarried during your late adult years, recall the occasion, what led up to it, and the events around it. If you were previously married, how was this time different? How much of the difference was age, and how much simply different expectations based on prior experience?

FACTS ABOUT GETTING MARRIED

❧ Note the name of your new spouse and briefly and factually describe his or her background—where he or she grew up, education, and his or her life (work, major interests, activities, etc.).

❧ Note the date and place you were married.

MEMORIES OF GETTING MARRIED

Remember your courtship. How and when and where did you and your spouse meet? How and when did you decide to get married? Did you live together before getting married? How long was your engagement? How was it different from relationships or marriages you'd had earlier in life?

Recall your wedding day and the ceremony. Did you make an occasion of it, or did you get married quietly and without much fanfare? What was the planning and preparation like? Did you and your spouse create your own ceremony or did you have a traditional ceremony? Recall the location where you were married. Who was in the wedding party? Who officiated? What family members were there? Recall that day and walk through it in your mind. What moments stand out? Who else attended? What did they do? What was the highlight of the ceremony? Did anything go wrong, or threaten to go wrong? Where was the reception? Did you go on a honeymoon? If so, what were the highlights of that trip?

It was a Sunday morning in May and Carol and I were spending it as we often did, working at her office. As a writer, I worked at home, but when she went to her office on a weekend to catch up, I would keep her company. This Sunday our work was different. We were laboring in a little windowless room to plan our wedding ceremony.

It would take place in a month at the picturesque seaside home of our dear friends, Marjorie and Michael, who in addition to being hosts would officiate our vows. They would be, according to the Commonwealth of Massachusetts, our "solemnizers." There we would gather in a simple ceremony with family: Carol's brother, Allen, and his wife, Wei; Carol's cousin, Sandy; my three children, Eric, Lauren, and Lesley, with Lesley's husband, Rich, their son Teddy, and newborn Phoebe; and my sister, Marcia, and my brother-in-law, Robert.

Both Carol and I had been married before, and both of us had simply used traditional—Jewish and Catholic—ceremonies. This one would be our own. In preparation we'd bought an armload of books at Barnes & Noble. We'd also gathered a lot of language, especially certain poems, that had meant much to us as we fell in love and created a life together.

Our task this Sunday morning was to put it all together. We laid out the various parts of the ceremony on the whiteboard—convocation, readings, invocation, remembrance, expression of intent, vows, and more—and plugged into the proper places the various beautiful words we'd collected.

When we'd organized it all on a laptop computer and thought we were finished, we realized we had to read it through aloud. It was a ceremony meant to be heard.

We began to speak it, taking the parts we actually would in the ceremony. As we read, we found ourselves filled with feeling. For both of us, the road to this moment had been long and filled with both joy and pain. The words reminded us of all that. We found ourselves holding hands as we read, tears in our eyes, choking on words like Yeats's lovely,

> *"I have spread my dreams under your feet;*
> *Tread softly because you tread on my dreams."*

Or Pablo Neruda's luminous piece that opens,

> *"Maybe nothingness is to be without your presence,"*

and ends,

> *"and through Love I will be, you will be, we will be."*

By the end of that Sunday we realized there would be two ceremonies, the one we'd just had, our own, the two of us alone in that windowless room, celebrating the "we" the two of us had found in each other. The second, equally important and no less heartfelt, would be (and was) with family in sunlight, by green salt marsh and blue sparkling sea.

— Kent Lineback, personal story

If there were children. How did your and your spouse's children respond to your marriage? Were they happy for you, or did it take some time for them to come around? How did they get along with their new siblings, if there were any?

Recall the period of adjustment in the early days of marriage. What changes, discoveries, surprises occurred in the first year or so of your marriage? Was it a time of significant adjustment? What was the first real challenge that you faced together? How did your experience with a previous marriage or relationship change or affect your behavior or expectations in this marriage?

Divorce/Splitting Up

It happens. Married couples, committed partners, even in their sixties and seventies decide they want to go their separate ways. If that happened to you, consider the questions below.

FACTS ABOUT YOUR DIVORCE

❦ Note the date and place of your divorce, and any related factual highlights worth noting.

MEMORIES OF YOUR DIVORCE

What led to your divorce? What were the underlying causes of the breakup? What was the immediate cause—that is, the events that actually led to the split? Was it by mutual agreement? Or was it driven by one or the other of you? Did it surprise you?

Remember the divorce process. Was it difficult and contentious, or relatively amicable? What moments do you especially remember? How did your children, family, and friends handle your breakup?

How did you find life as a single person at this stage? Were you relieved or sad to be single again? Did you and your ex-spouse remain friends? Did you continue to have any contact? What was your relationship with your children after the divorce? What do you remember most vividly about adjusting to your new life? Did you have any fears about the future and being alone? What friends stood out as particularly helpful at this time? What did they do? Did you start going out again? Did you hope to find another relationship, or were you resigned to remaining single? Where did you live—in the same place or somewhere else? Did you do all right financially?

Birth Family

If your parents were alive at the start of this period, you likely lost them as you passed through your sixties and seventies (and they entered their eighties and nineties and beyond!), or you dealt with them as they became truly elderly.

FACTS ABOUT YOUR BIRTH FAMILY

❦ Note the names and ages of those who remained in your birth family at the beginning of this period—parents, brothers, and sisters.

❦ Note any turning points or life events, with year of occurrence, that happened in their lives during this period—death, illness, accidents, accomplishments, marriage/divorce, and so on.

MEMORIES OF YOUR BIRTH FAMILY

If your parents were still alive, what were their lives like in this period? How was their health? Did they struggle with old age? How did their lives change through this period? If they remained vital, think of their lives—where they lived, their daily routines, their interests, the way they passed time.

What was your relationship with your parents at this time? Was it different from the past? Remember occasions when you were together. How were they financially—did you or others help them? What did you worry about most in regard to them?

I kept my promise to my mother on November 2, 1996. I took every dollar I had and bought her a house, a good house, the first thing of any real value she has ever owned. She never had a wedding ring, or a decent car, or even a set of furniture that matched. Or teeth that fit. But she had a home now, a home of her own. I was happy and sad at the same time as I handed the realtor the money, happy that it had finally come true, sad that it had taken so long to accomplish. . . .

"Did you know it had a doorbell?" my momma asked me, right after we bought it. "I never had a doorbell." I asked her if the sound of it bothered her, and she shook her head. "I kind of like it."

Some weeks later I was talking to Sam on the telephone, asking if she had settled in. She has, he told me, but he was a little worried about one thing. "She rings her own doorbell," he said.

I told him to let her ring it till she wore it out.

— RICK BRAGG, *All Over but the Shoutin'*

If either of your parents died at this time, recall those sad events. What led to his or her death? Recall the death itself and burial. Were you there? What happened? How did you handle this loss and your grief? What effect did it have on your relationships with others in your family? What of your father or mother did you miss most?

Recall each of your brothers and sisters at this time. One by one, bring them to mind. Where did each live? What was each doing? Recall the major events you identified in the lives of each. Did you see them often and were they part of your life now? How often did you talk and what did you talk about? Were you comfortable together? Were there any issues between you? Had your relationship with them changed now that all of you were getting older? Did you agree on what to do with aging parents?

Recall other members of your extended family. What memories come to mind? Think of when and where you came into contact with this relative. Were your lives in some way linked? What moments of happiness or sadness and pain were connected with each? Did your role change as you passed through this period?

Religion or Spirituality

As you passed through your late adult years, did religion still play an important role in your life? Were your religious beliefs and views still what they had been, or did they change and moderate, or become sharper and more defined? What effect, if any, did growing older have on your beliefs?

FACTS ABOUT RELIGIOUS OR SPIRITUAL BELIEFS

❦ Note in brief the beliefs that were important to you, and how they changed, if they did, through these late adult years.

❦ Describe in brief the spiritual or religious practices you followed based on your beliefs. Did they change at all with growing age?

❦ Describe briefly any specific religious or spiritual experiences you had during late adulthood.

MEMORIES OF RELIGIOUS OR SPIRITUAL BELIEFS

Reflect on your beliefs at this stage in your life. What effect did advancing age have on those beliefs? Did they change from the time you were sixty to the time you were, say, eighty? Did anything happen in this stage—the death of someone close to you, for example—to cause you to doubt your beliefs, or to make them even stronger?

Did your religious or spiritual practices change in this period? Did you practice or observe with your spouse? With others in your family? With friends? What moments did you share around these beliefs and the practices based on them? What was the highlight of your religious or spiritual life in this period? Think of any holidays or festivals or holy observances that stand out. Did your practices change in any way at this time?

Recall any religious or spiritual experiences you identified. What happened? Were you alone? Did anything change as a result of the experience?

Work/Career

If you worked for an organization, you almost certainly retired at some point in this late adult stage. If you kept working, very likely the nature of your work, or even your career, changed. Were you happy to be rid of work, or did you want to work on as long as you could? Was this because you loved your work, you needed to work, or you weren't sure what else to do?

FACTS ABOUT YOUR WORK/CAREER

❦ In brief and factual form, as you might on a resume, summarize your work history through this period: positions held, when and where you held them, and a brief description of the work you did.

❦ If you retired, note your retirement date.

❦ Note also any incidental or part-time work you did after retirement.

MEMORIES OF YOUR WORK/CAREER

If you continued to work in your longtime field or to pursue a life career, recall the highlights. Were you still striving for some professional or career goal? What were you trying to accomplish, personally in your work and for your organization? Recall any events or moments or people linked to these goals and accomplishments. Instead of retiring outright, did you take on reduced responsibilities? Did you start something new?

Being the boss. Were you still the boss? Recall any people you hired or had to let go. Who was the best employee who worked for you? The worst? What was the biggest employee problem you faced at this time and what did you do? What did your subordinates think of you? Recall the highlights of your relationships with them.

We got feedback from our annual motivational and job satisfaction surveys, from pre-sentations made at planning meetings and individual critiques, at the periodic "town meetings" we held in all departments, and from just walking around. . . .

Most of the feedback was positive but some not so. An unsigned planning meeting questionnaire came back criticizing "Leon's foot-dragging leadership." Not a bad metaphor although I wouldn't have used it myself. Another time I got a letter from one of our warehouse workers. He said, "I think if you did not inherit L.L. Bean you would have been a farmer selling vegetables on the roadside. Don't get me wrong. I think you would have a swell farm." He offered to have a talk with me, which we did, and it was a nice conversation. Unfortunately I thought his grievance was not justified and he probably still thinks I should be running a vegetable stand.

— Leon Gorman, *L.L. Bean: The Making of an American Icon*

If you are a woman, what was it like to work in this period of your life? If you faced any gender-related issues, were they the same as in earlier stages, or were they new to this period?

Recall each job or position that you held.
- *Recall what you did and where.*
- *Recall the people you worked with.*
- *Try to remember any big projects or problems you worked on.* What happened? How did they come out?
- *What were you proud of?* Something accomplished by you or your group? Some problem prevented or solved?
- *What did you enjoy most about this work?* Did you continue to learn and do new things?
- *Did your age and experience give you any special status at work,* or was age a negative?
- *What problems or crises did you face?* Did you resolve them? Did anything happen in your work that you regretted?
- *Whom did you work for and what was your relationship with that person?*

If you retired, recall the incidents leading up to and surrounding that life event.

How did you prepare for retirement? How did you choose the time to retire? Was it chosen for you (by company policy, for example)? Were you ever worried about finances after you retired? To whom did you pass on your work and responsibilities? How did others treat you once you announced your plans to leave? Did you stay in touch with former colleagues? What did people remember from working with you? How did you adjust following retirement? What was the hardest part?

If you took on part-time or different work after retirement, recall that work. What did you do? What was memorable about the work or the place or the people or what you did? Did you embark on a new career?

Friends and Other Memorable People

Friends probably became even more precious as you passed into and through your late adult years. Unfortunately, it's also the time you began losing them from illness and age. Did you retain long-standing friendships? Did you make new friends?

FACTS ABOUT YOUR FRIENDS AND OTHER MEMORABLE PEOPLE

❦ List the people who were your good friends in this time of your life. Note any facts or highlights that occurred in their lives or in their relationship with you.

❦ Identify any people from your late adult years who qualified as memorable. Note briefly and factually what they did that touched your life, including when and where they did it.

❦ Describe briefly the circle of people with whom you tended to socialize in your late adult years. Note where you'd typically get together—at a restaurant, a social club, work, church—and what you'd do together.

MEMORIES OF FRIENDS AND OTHER MEMORABLE PEOPLE

Bring to mind each of your good friends and recall moments and occasions you shared with them. For each, recall why and how you were close. Is there anyone you spoke with every day? What events and circumstances led to your closeness? How did they help you, or you them? What did you do together?

New friends. What new friends did you make at this time? How did you meet them and how did they turn from acquaintances to friends?

Recall any friends who fell ill, or struggled with some hardship, or died at this time. Think of the circumstances surrounding the illness or death or hardship. Were you involved? How did you and others cope with this loss or the struggles of a friend?

Call to mind other memorable people and recall times and places and moments associated with each. Did you do things together? Did you share interests, like a hobby? Did you help this person in some way, or he or she you? Did anyone serve as a model for you? Did you ever seek advice from someone, or someone from you? Did anyone younger ever seek your counsel or help? What did you do for them? Did anyone ever cause you to change your mind? Did any professional, like a doctor or minister or rabbi, help you deal with a problem or get through a difficult time? Was there anyone you met whom you admired, and whose company you enjoyed?

After the speech, I left the hotel through a side entrance and passed a line of press photographers and TV cameras. I was almost to the car when I heard what sounded like two or three firecrackers over to my left—just a small fluttering sound, pop, pop, pop. . . .

We pulled up in front of the hospital emergency entrance and I was first out of the limo and into the emergency room. A nurse was coming to meet me and I told her I was having trouble breathing. Then all of a sudden my knees turned rubbery. The next thing I knew I was lying face up on a gurney and my brand-new pin-striped suit was being cut off me, never to be worn again. . . .

I was lying on the gurney only half-conscious when I realized that someone was holding my hand. It was a soft, feminine hand. I felt it come up and touch mine and then hold on tight to it. It gave me a wonderful feeling. Even now I find it difficult to explain how reassuring, how wonderful, it felt.

It must have been the hand of a nurse kneeling very close to the gurney, but I couldn't see her. I started asking, "Who's holding my hand? . . . Who's holding my hand?" When I didn't hear any response, I said, "Does Nancy know about us?"

Although I tried afterward to learn who the nurse was, I was never able to find her. I had wanted to tell her how much the touch of her hand had meant to me, but I never was able to do that.

— RONALD REAGAN, *An American Life*

For each of your social groups, recall the times and activities you enjoyed together. What was the glue that held you together? What did you usually do together? If you met any of these people today, what memories would you talk about? Who were the key people in the group—the ones who tended to be more visible and make things happen? Were you one of them?

How did the group cope with the changes and life events that occurred in the lives of its members? What changes were happening in the lives of people in the group? Did any members move away or die? How did that affect the group and what it did? Did members help and support each other in times of illness or loss?

What other social occasions do you remember from this time? Not everything involved the same group of people. Recall other social moments or events that were especially memorable. What other people did you see and do things with?

Learning

Few people in their sixties and seventies return to school, but learning never has to stop. What did you do in late adulthood to keep learning?

FACTS ABOUT LEARNING

🍂 If you attended a course, program, or seminar, note its name, the dates, what you learned, and why you attended.

🍂 If you attended school of any kind in this period, name the school and its location, the dates you attended, what you studied and why, and any outcome, such as a diploma or certificate.

MEMORIES OF LEARNING

Recall any courses, seminars, or educational programs you took. This can include almost any kind of program, something in your church, for example, or classes held in evening school or in a retirement community. What caused you to take this program or seminar? What did you learn and how did you use that knowledge or skill in your life after the course?

Did you actually go back and attend school? Think about the course or program you took, where you took it, the people who taught it, your fellow students, what you learned, projects you did, books and materials studied, tests, and so on. Who was your favorite teacher? Your favorite class? Did you make new friends among your fellow students?

Causes, Community, and Politics

As you passed through your late adult years, did your passion for some cause or for politics, or your interest in your community, continue and grow? As you retired from work, did you find you had more time to help others in some way?

🍁 What community programs or causes—social, political, environmental, or whatever—did you advocate and pursue actively in these years?

🍁 Name each, and its purpose, the time of your involvement, and the essential facts of what you did.

MEMORIES OF CAUSES, COMMUNITY, AND POLITICS

What memories of events or occasions or people come to mind as you recall each of the causes that you pursued? How did you become involved? What was your experience in pursuing this interest? Was it new or something of longtime concern? What did you and others associated with you accomplish? What moments of happiness or embarrassment or satisfaction or anger and frustration do you recall from this involvement?

> *It was never my intention to become a farm animal rescuer. I believe in fighting for the many, not saving the few. But when I took a crew to film pigs in intensive systems there was something about the pitiful frustration of Sow 206, gnawing the bars of her small stall, that just wouldn't shift from my mind. "What's happened to 206?" I would enquire as casually as possible at the end of subsequent conversations. She was pregnant. She was about to give birth. She was—horrors—about to be slaughtered in two days' time. I cracked.*
>
> *Suddenly I was engaged in a Hollywood-style death row drama, phoning, faxing and e-mailing to save her, begging and pleading to get someone to give her a home, weeping when the wretched woman who promised to do so let me down. Switch to final scene: Sow 206. Victoria as she has become, makes her stately way aloft a cart drawn down a country lane to take up permanent residence in a hastily fenced-off field*

on my own land. She lived there in perfect bliss for the next five years, foraging all day on roots, sweet chestnuts and acorns, wallowing in cooling mud in the heat, doing all the things that every factory-farmed pig longs to do, until her old legs gave out and, one beautiful summer evening, my vet put her gently to sleep as she contentedly munched Sainsbury's jam tarts.

—AUDREY EYTON, in *Reinvented Lives*

Recall the ways you actively participated in politics in late adulthood. Recall your work for the election of any political candidate, or the advancement of some political agenda. What did you do and how did it feel to win or lose? Did you run for office yourself or hold some form of public office, appointed or elective?

Imagine yourself back involved in the community groups or activities that engaged you at this time. Recall each of these community groups or activities. What occasions or memorable people come to mind that are linked to each? Were you and your associates trying to accomplish some goal? What was different because of the work you did?

Interests and Activities

Did you find yourself with more time in late adulthood to pursue arts, sports, hobbies, travel, or other interests? Did something new capture your interest?

FACTS ABOUT YOUR OTHER INTERESTS

❦ Name the clubs or organizations you belonged to in late adulthood, the times you were involved, the purpose of each, and the role you played.

❦ Name and briefly describe any pets or animals that were important to you.

❦ Note which of the arts—music, theater, dance, poetry, or some other form—seriously engaged your time and attention.

❧ Name the movies, books, and radio or TV programs that were especially memorable in this period.

❧ Name any hobbies or games you pursued seriously.

❧ Identify any sports you either played or followed closely in late adulthood, such as golf, tennis, fishing, or hiking. Note any highlights or accomplishments of your playing, or of the individual or teams you followed.

❧ Note any memorable trips you took at this time—where you went, with whom, when, and briefly what you saw.

MEMORIES OF YOUR OTHER INTERESTS

Recall each of the clubs or organizations you belonged to in late adulthood. Think about what each organization did and the activities each undertook. Why did you belong to it? What meetings did you attend? Recall the other people in each group. What aspect of each organization gave you particular satisfaction?

Recall each pet or animal in your life at this time. What moments or occasions come to mind with each? Recall times of pleasure, and moments of worry.

We've always been cat people. Sure, we had dogs—mother and daughter dachshunds— and every other kind of pet when our kids were, well, kids. But cats were our pet of choice. That changed in May 1999. We stopped at a trading post on Second Mesa, Hopi, Arizona, and when we came out, a small white ball of fur came up to our feet, sat down, and looked into my husband's eyes. She put up her paws and said, "Take me! Take me!"

We couldn't do it. We were on a trip with 36 other people, and we already had two cats at home.

Then the Indian trader said to me, "Lady, if you take this puppy, I'll give you a box of food and a blanket." "No, thank you," we said. But wherever we walked, there was the puppy. We put her in the garden, but before we knew it, she was among the cars and buses and under our feet. What could we do? We relented. Our lives have never been the same.

Hopi, as we called her, our miracle dog, grew a long coat of shining white hair, made friends with our cats, commandeered a spot between us in bed, and became a constant presence in our lives.

The proof of the pudding is that we've taken 10 trips across the country—between Santa Fe and two of our kids' homes in New Jersey—each trip four days and three nights on the road. We made those trips so that we didn't have to fly Hopi in a crate or leave her at home alone. Hopi has been with us to California, Scottsdale, Sedona, and other places. And our three kids recognize her as a real sibling—our fourth child.

— JANE AND BILL BUCHSBAUM, personal story

What memorable events or moments in the arts can you remember from this time? What performances or other occasions in each do you recall vividly? Are there people you remember? If you performed in some way, were there memorable performances or highlights?

Recall any popular entertainment you particularly enjoyed in this period. What radio or television programs did you make sure you watched or listened to through this time in your life? What movies from this time remain in your memory? Did you particularly enjoy any specific actors (male and female)? If reading was important to you, what did you read that was especially memorable?

What sports did you play or follow actively through late adulthood? Did you take up any new sports? Think of each sport and recall games and other occasions that stand out in your memory? Were there moments of happiness and celebration and elation? Moments of disappointment and defeat and frustration? How did increasing age affect the sports you played? Did you change sports, or adapt the way you played? Did you reach a point that you had to give up active sports? If you were a serious sports fan, recall any important games or occurrences involving your team or teams and/or the players. How did your favorite teams do? Did you attend games or practices?

Recall each of the hobbies or games you enjoyed at this time. Did you develop any new hobbies or interests? Remember times of great satisfaction. Were other people involved? Or was this a solo activity?

> *I have just purchased a second twenty-six-foot Nordic Tug, one for San Francisco Bay, my home, and one for Puget Sound and cruising the Northwest. I am a longtime solo-sailor, and still do most of my boating solo, as at my age, seventy-six, most of my long-time friends are interested in other things than bouncing around on the water. In searching for a name for the new Tug, one thing I kept hearing was "Two tugboats . . . ? We wonder if Old Joe is losing it." There was so much wonderment, I decided that I would incorporate it into the new name, and it became* Wee Wonder, *an appropriate name for a twenty-six-foot tugboat and for those who are still wondering. If you see me cruising in the Northwest in* Wee Wonder *or in* Little Toot *in San Francisco Bay, give me a wave—I'll be enjoying my son's inheritance.*
>
> —JOSEPH S. COLLETTO,
> in *The Older the Fiddle, the Better the Tune*

Recall the traveling you did at this time and imagine yourself back on each trip. Did you travel more often? Where did you go and what did you see that has stuck with you? Did you ever go with a tour group? Did you face any problems or experience any particular surprises? What happened to you in different cultures? What struck you? Did you own a vacation home? Or was there a special vacation destination you especially enjoyed and visited often? Remember any of those places, homes, or destinations, and recall special times and events or moments in each. Did you begin to consider the possibility of retirement in any of those places?

Notable Events

What notable events in your sixties and seventies touched your life in some way, directly or indirectly?

FACTS ABOUT NOTABLE EVENTS

❧ Identify any historical or newsworthy events that touched you in late adulthood, including what happened and how it affected you.

❧ Do the same for any local events that perhaps weren't newsworthy but touched your life nonetheless.

MEMORIES OF NOTABLE EVENTS

Recall any historical or noteworthy events that had an effect on your life or your world. Think back to the years of this period and the great events of that time. Recall how and when you first learned about each. How did each affect or change your life? Did you participate in them?

One fall day a few years ago, Robert and I flew from our home in California to Boston, en route to Turkey, where we planned to tour the country and take a cruise along the Turquoise Coast. It was the same coast Paul traveled in the early days of Christendom, and some of his letters that now make up part of the New Testament were written to churches in cities there.

It was actually our second attempt to make the trip. Robert, an engineer, had gone to Turkey a few years earlier to construct a power plant for Fiat at Bursa. I'd planned to join him there, but the day I left my mother died and we had to postpone all our plans.

Now we were stopping over in Boston to spend a few days with Carol and Kent before going on. We'd arrived on Thursday. Tuesday morning, as we were loading our bags in Kent's car for the drive to Logan Airport, Carol called from her office and said we should turn on the television.

It was September 11, 2001. We turned on TV just in time to see the second tower collapse. We watched in shock as the story emerged that terrorists had hijacked four planes, three from the same airport we had been about to use.

Our first impulse was to go home to California. But with airports closed and all flights grounded, our only choice was to rent a car and drive. We bought road maps and began planning the road trip, only to realize it wasn't a great idea. The airports had to reopen in a matter of days.

But if we were going to fly, where should we fly? Going home involved a long flight; some of the hijacked planes had been bound for California. Then we began asking ourselves, how much more risk was there if we went on with our trip? It seemed like a far-fetched idea at first, but the more we thought about it, the more sense it made. Robert had liked Turkey and its people a great deal and felt we would be completely safe there.

Then the key question was whether there was still a tour for us to join. As the days progressed we learned from our travel agency that everyone else on the tour, all or most of them Americans, had backed out . . . but the tour had not been canceled, we were told, and if we could be there the next Monday, it would go on. We held our breath waiting to learn when flights would resume.

Sunday morning we were on the first flight out of Logan for Dulles outside Washington, D.C., where we would go on to Frankfurt and Istanbul. On our flight to Dulles, we passed over New York City and saw the heartbreaking sight of the still-burning towers, a terrible image etched in our memories. At Dulles the entire United Airlines staff there applauded us as we deplaned. We were the first passengers since 9/11 to fly between the two airports from which the terrorist planes had taken off. We flew over the burning towers again on our flight to Europe.

Our stay in Turkey, though a sad time, was a lifetime experience. We had one-on-one guide service throughout Istanbul and the rest of Turkey, and when we boarded our beautiful wooden gullet—a Turkish boat meant for fourteen people plus crew—we were the only passengers. Many people there expressed sadness for what had happened to America. They said our coming honored them.

— MARCIA KEELINE, personal story

Did any local events touch your life? What other events, even if they weren't large and newsworthy, touched and changed your life?

Other Voices

Contact any people who knew you and were part of your late adult life. If you want, ask them to record any memories of you from this time.

If you want to include other people's memories of you as a late adult . . .

1. Make a list of people from your time as a late adult and ask them to share their memories with you, in their own words.

2. Record each memory on a separate sheet of paper. Label each memory "A Memory of Me" and include the memory teller's name, as well as the approximate date and location of the memory.

3. Add these memory sheets to your own memories in your *My Life Story* notebook.

THE MEANING
OF YOUR LATE ADULT STAGE

For many of us, the previous stage, middle adulthood, was a time of significant introspection, when we pondered and reexamined the sources of meaning in our lives. We questioned and made changes, large and small. We may even have realized that what we truly wanted to do and accomplish might not have been the same as the dream we grew up with, a dream often given us in part by others.

If you did reexamine your life in middle age, did any of that internal work pay off for you in this next stage? Did it, for example, help you understand where to focus your time and energy and resources? Did you emerge understanding better the real sources of happiness and satisfaction for you, so that here in late adulthood you could concentrate on them more? Did you emerge with a better sense of what was important to you?

If none of that applies to you, perhaps you were one of the lucky ones whose dream was your own and it continued to guide your life, both through midlife and here. The truly lucky among us discovered our calling as we grew up and it served as our North Star through the rest of life. The remainder of us had to find our own lodestar through constant struggle and experimentation and self-examination.

As we recommended in the previous stage, you might enjoy comparing your thoughts here about meaning with your recollections of meaning from previous stages, just to see how you changed and developed.

Defining Moments

Think of yourself at the beginning of this stage, when you were around sixty. Then think of yourself now (if you are still in this stage) or at the end of this stage (if you've progressed into your elder years). How have you changed? Where in late adulthood did those changes occur? What caused them? Did they happen all at once, or through a series of steps? What events, occasions, and moments come to mind when you reflect on how you've changed over that period of time? Those are the defining or pivotal moments you should note here.

Think of any major transitions you made in this period, such as a move or retirement or an ailment, or even something that happened to someone close to you. These are things that can shape or influence the person you became.

As we said in the introduction, this stage can cover a lot of territory. Many of us will enter it hale and hearty and leave it perhaps struggling or coping with some ailment, or just plain old-age infirmity. We may enter it still in the throes of a career or profession and leave it a retiree living in some distant place. Since the process of aging is a key factor that shapes this stage, many of our defining moments will be driven by the realities of getting older and by our responses to that inexorable process.

The defining moment of my mature adult life came on a summer's walk in the Forest Hills Cemetery in Boston when a wasp got between my leg and a picnic bag and stung my thigh. I knew I was in trouble because I wasn't carrying my epi-pen, which allows me to self-inject a counterserum. Two years earlier I'd gone into anaphylactic shock from a yellow jacket sting but got to the local hospital quickly and was treated successfully. I knew I had to be careful around stinging insects, but didn't take the threat seriously enough to remember the epi-pen and cell phone on all outings.

My life partner threw me into the car and rushed us to the nearest emergency room, driving through red lights, stop signs, on the wrong side of the road, and arriving at the Beth Israel–Deaconess Hospital just as I fainted. My blood pressure dropped to near zero and I was gasping for breath. Anaphylactic shock causes your throat and lungs to swell, and death can come within 30 minutes by suffocation or heart attack.

As the ER doctors and nurses hovered over me, I felt my soul leave my body in a near-death experience. I watched the scene from two or three feet above my body: my clothing was cut off and I was injected with the maximum dose of epinephrine. Then I heard God's voice asking me whether I'd like to check out or return to the living to do something worthwhile.

I chose to come back, determined that I would not waste the time left to me. From the wasp sting to an emergency room recovery just 15 minutes had elapsed. But that quarter hour led me to my life's calling, coaching, and grateful, meaningful days.

—JAMES BOTKIN, personal story

Values—What Mattered

What meant most to you through this time of your life? Health? Family? Friends? Some hobby? Your religious faith and practice? Identify those few things that you considered truly valuable?

Think of major, life-changing decisions you made in this stage. There're probably only a few of them. In each decision, what did you decide and why did you make that particular decision? The reason you made that decision provides a clue to what was important and significant to you at this time.

Your answer can be something on a grand scale, like religious beliefs or some great humanitarian cause. It can also be something on a smaller scale too, such as helping people in need, like an elderly neighbor who can't get out. It can even be about the more mundane parts of life, such as the way you spent your spare time, or what you read. These are values too. It can be whatever is important to you and gives you genuine pleasure.

Love

Love is a gift given from one person to another. It's not earned or justified. In some mysterious way, it happens and two people touch each other and in that simple process change each other's lives.

Where did this happen for you in these late adult years? Sometimes it happens in the most unlikely places and with the most unlikely people. As you identify each of these people, think about the relationship between the two of you and the ways you each delighted in each other and took care—you of them and they of you.

> *I wanted to speak at [my father's] funeral; I wanted to put into words who he had been—as a father and as an actor—but I didn't know if I could. Some of the best things about him couldn't be put in words: the performer's energy, the willingness to please, the frank gladness at contact with the audience. And how could I put into words the rude ambivalence I felt toward him, the way I had held myself above him for so long, in spite of his unconditional acceptance of me, the gentleness of his manner? None of that could be said in words.*
>
> *I got up in the chapel, walked to the front of the room, and looked at the people who had come to remember him. I said a few simple things about his kindness, the sweetness of the man, and then I just dropped the words and I did him. I walked over the side of the chapel and showed the people who had gathered to remember him how he used to make his entrance onto the vaudeville stage: the banana curve, the hand on his rib cage. And as I did this, my ambivalence evaporated. They smiled and chuckled in recognition, and he was there for a moment. For a moment, the performer and the actor came together in me, without conflict or judgment. I didn't just accept him, I was him. It brought him back. I could see him, smell him, love him; I could accept him as he was. And I could accept how much of him was in me. In my imagination, he was in the room with me.*
>
> —ALAN ALDA, *Never Have Your Dog Stuffed*

Learning and Wisdom

It's an irony of life that as we age we seem to remember less and understand more. Perhaps we just come to terms with things that confused or frightened or put us off earlier. Was this true for you? Was there anything in your life that, as you lived through this stage, became less of an issue for you? Did you learn to care less (or more) for what people thought of you? Did anything that seemed significant for you earlier become less (or more) so as you lived through this time?

Of course, this stage, like all the others, contained its own challenges and highlights. Recall some moment or event when things didn't go right. You were hurt or embarrassed or confused—or happy, satisfied, even ecstatic. What did you learn from that experience, or since then as you reflect on it, that might have helped? If you could go back and talk to yourself in that moment, to the person you were then, what wisdom would you impart?

Sometimes, when life gets too hard and crowds in on you and you become desensitized, you need to remember to just take time. Go away. Change your surroundings. Put yourself in a situation where the outcome is uncertain. Give way to the kindness of strangers. Humble yourself on your road untraveled.

I have found that when we go on a journey, we buy time, because we give our full attention. We are present and conscious because all the newness of our surroundings keeps us sparked and alert. Travel prolongs our time, I think. I like to call it "rubber time." How often do we say to ourselves, Where did that year go? Hey, where did that week go? But if we go away to some place that holds a little interest for us, every moment will be filled with wonder, and our brains will peak.

— GOLDIE HAWN, *A Lotus Grows in the Mud*

Summing Up

Here's your chance to talk about the big picture. Step back after all your remembering and capture now in a few words this whole period of your life, roughly your sixties and beyond, clear to your elder years. What was that time like overall? What should someone who's just read the story of your late adult years conclude about this time in your life?

STAGE 7

elder

We enter the elder stage when age or infirmity begins to restrict our lives and bound our worlds. Life here is life on a smaller scale.

Age itself, with its ultimate frailty, usually initiates these elder years, but illness can bring them on as well. Because each life can vary so widely in the effects of age, there is no typical time of life when the elder stage usually begins. It can start anywhere from the sixties, because of illness, to sometime in the nineties.

When we think of this stage, we think of a ninety-two-year-old friend who still lives by herself, though she does spend long visits with two sons and a daughter whose homes are spread across the country. Until three years ago, she played golf every day, until a broken hip ended that sport for her. Now she looks forward to her daily walks. Occasionally, when her heart decides to beat irregularly, she takes medicine and lies down for a few hours. She drives, though rarely, because she lives in a retirement community where most everything is nearby. She enjoys the company of many friends and an active social center, where she plays cards and attends lectures and listens to live music several times a week. Every day she reads the paper and watches television and keeps up with current events. She goes out to movies with friends once or twice a week and loves to talk about what she's seen. Someone comes in weekly to clean her small apartment, but she still prepares most of her meals herself.

It's easy to focus on the dark side of this final stage, like our friend's cranky hip and irregular heart. Physical limitations, loneliness, the steady loss of friends and contemporaries, illness and pain, the fear of becoming no longer valuable or valued—all these can make this stage a difficult time. Only those living through it can truly understand the courage, stamina, and mental toughness needed to cope with its challenges.

Fortunately, these negative aspects are far from the entire story. There is another side, a brighter side, of the elder years. For example, our friend's life, in spite of her ailments, remains rich with family and friends and laughter. Like all previous stages, the elder stage has its own life tasks and challenges, which represent opportunities for satisfaction, meaning, and even continued personal growth. It is, after all, a time of freedom—freedom from the endless striving of our adult years and from the lash of our own ambition. Our life work is done. No longer must we struggle each day toward some self-imposed goal or to satisfy some other person's expectations. Whatever aims and purposes we retain are entirely our own.

What are the tasks and challenges, the sources of meaning and satisfaction and growth, in this phase of life?

First, there is the task—perhaps *need* or *desire* describes it better—to look back over one's life and make sense of it. This urge probably began in our late adult stage, but here it often becomes urgent. We seek integrity in our lives, which means finding some sense of overall meaning and coherence. We try to answer such questions as: What did I do in my life? What contribution did I make? Was it worth something? What did I accomplish? What role did I play in the world, and how well did I play it? For some it's enough to say merely, "I was born and lived the life I lived." But many of us feel compelled to seek resolution, if only for ourselves, of these important questions.

Creating one's own story doesn't mean crafting a detailed narrative of one's journey through life. Usually our story, after reflecting on the life we lived, takes a form no more complicated than, for instance, I was a good mother. Or I was a good teacher who helped youngsters build important life skills. Or I carried my responsibilities—to my country as a soldier, to my family as a husband and father, and to those I worked for. I never let anybody down. Or, even, I wasn't perfect. But, given the circumstances, I did the best I could.

Remember the character played by Jimmy Stewart in the movie *It's a Wonderful Life*? As a young man, he dreamed of traveling the world and doing great things. Yet circumstances and responsibilities obliged him to live his life in the small town where he grew up. Finally, believing his life had been worthless, he was about to jump from a bridge when an angel appeared and took him back to view the community and people as they would have been if he'd never lived. Only in that way could he finally see the difference he'd made in other people's lives. It wasn't the contribution he'd dreamed about as a youngster, but it was real and good. The world was better off, he discovered, for what he'd done with his life.

The second task of the elder years is to bestow the gift of continuity on those who follow us. This involves telling them the story of the past, as it was told to us by our forebears and as we ourselves experienced it personally. Those who follow us want to understand how the past has unfolded into the present. Imagine a world without history, a world in which none of us had any sense of what or who came before. What a frightening and unpredictable world that would be. We did not come from nowhere and some large piece of who and what we are, and the world we now know, came from what has gone before. Even more important, the future will somehow flow from the past and present. So this task is more than a matter of merely recounting history. Much of the meaning in each moment arises from the tradition, custom, and lore of the past, all of which create the context in which the present occurs, and from which the future will flow.

Yet another task of the elder stage is to arrive at some resolution of the pain and hurt and grief we have experienced in life. Often, such resolution comes only through forgiveness. We forgive those who have wronged us, even if they remain unrepentant. And we ask others to forgive us for the pain and wrongs we have wrought on them. Perhaps as important, we forgive ourselves for the failures and wrongs we perceive in ourselves and our lives, for which we carry a burden of guilt and self-directed anger.

The final task, perhaps the most important of all, is to continue reaching out to others, to maintain and nurture connections. The need to love and be loved, to be heard, to feel valued and, in some way, important to others, does not diminish with age. It is a paradox of life that, as our world shrinks with age and infirmity, the need for connection and love and community often grows stronger. As we lose friends and acquaintances, we must grieve them and hold them in loving memory . . . and then replace them with new connections, including connections with younger people, if we are wise. The evidence from studies of aging is crystal clear: the secret of happy aging is the ability and willingness to stay connected with others.

So we hope you'll go ahead and tell the story of this stage of your life. Finish the story so those who follow you can learn how you lived this part of your life and faced its unique tasks and challenges.

FACTS AND MEMORIES FROM YOUR ELDER STAGE

The elder stage starts when age or infirmity begins to limit your life and world. Years can remain of life still rich in many ways, but it is no longer a life of activity and movement and energy.

Here the goal is to bring the story of your life to the current moment. Answer the various fact questions that follow for your elder years, up to the present time. See what memories come to mind as you ponder the memory questions. In earlier stages you recalled events that occurred decades ago. Here your memories can include events as fresh as yesterday.

You as an Elder

As always, facts and memories begin with you—who you are, who you've become— in your elder years.

FACTS ABOUT YOU IN YOUR ELDER YEARS

❧ Note the year, your age, and the events that marked the beginning of this stage in your life.

❦ Note any highlights of your elder years so far. Just list them as a way to help you get this stage clearly established in your mind.

MEMORIES OF YOU IN YOUR ELDER YEARS

Think about the turning points or rites of passage that have highlighted your elder years. Recall your transition into your elder years. Was it rapid, because of an illness, or did it occur slowly? Was there a moment or some "rite of passage" that marked the transition? Have there been any other such turning points in this period for you?

> *I always needed to have people around me. That's how I was. Something had to be going on all the time. If I was by myself, even for a little while, I'd get restless. I was out the door before you could blink. I'd rather do anything than be alone.*
>
> *But then I got to a certain age. Until then, I never knew that you could run out of people to see and places to go. My friends started dying off, and I wasn't able to drive at night anymore. It got to be there was nothing to do, and nobody to come over. I got stuck with my own company.*
>
> *At first, I hated it. Imagine getting acquainted with yourself at eighty! It's better to learn how to get along on your own when you're young. Later, the only one you can count on for company is yourself. I'm starting to get a kick out of it now, but solitude takes practice.*
>
> —ANNIE BAKERSMITH, in *What's Worth Knowing*

What is your sense of time and aging now? How old do you feel? Is your mental or psychological age different from your physical age? If there is a difference, how has it shown up in your daily life? What is the biggest change brought on by age other than purely physical changes?

What health problems have you faced or do you face? What memories do you have that are related to your health? Were/are you ill? Have you spent time in the hospital? Do any aspects of your medical treatment stand out? Have you lived or do you live with pain and discomfort? How do you find relief? Have these problems required you to show courage, stamina, and determination?

Have you experienced any hardships in this period of your life? Economic? Social? Physical? What circumstances did you have to struggle with?

How have you dealt with the losses that this time of life inevitably involves? As friends and acquaintances die, you must adjust, grieve, and go on somehow. How do you cope? Do you and friends help each other? Do you reach out to new friends?

Do you feel connected to the wider world? Or do you feel isolated? Do you worry about what's going on—disasters, wars, politics, and so on?

Age puzzles me. I thought it was a quiet time. My seventies were interesting, and fairly serene, but my eighties are passionate. I grow more intense as I age. To my own surprise I burst out with hot conviction. Only a few years ago I enjoyed my tranquility; now I am so disturbed by the outer world and by human quality in general that I want to put things right, as though I still owed a debt to life. I must calm down. I am far too frail to indulge in moral fervor.

— FLORIDA SCOTT-MAXWELL, *The Measure of My Days*

What preoccupies you? What do you mostly think about? If you let your mind wander, where does it go? Do you tend to worry about things, or is your mind fairly calm and placid? What upsets you?

Do you often think of the past? If so, what do you think about? Do you tend to remember a wide range of people and events in your life? Or do a few keep coming back? Do you recall good times, or bad times? Mistakes or successes? What do you regret?

Do you think about friends, relatives, and others you've forgiven? Did you reach a point where you no longer wanted to carry ill feelings, and the best way to move beyond them was simply to forgive someone? Did anyone forgive you?

How do you spend your time? What do you do on a typical day? How do you fill your time? What do you like to do? What's a typical morning like? A typical afternoon or evening?

> *As I inch toward eighty, people keep asking me when I'm going to retire. . . .*
>
> *Why retire? I leave my kitchen after breakfast every morning, shuffle a few steps to my studio, lie down in my lounge chair 'til I get an idea, shuffle over to my desk to make a few strokes on a piece of paper, and they send me money. What should I retire to . . . ditch digging?*
>
> *I've been writing and drawing "Beetle Bailey" for over fifty-two years. . . . Recently I brought in a character who is completely immersed in everything technological. He challenges the old general who can't even program his VCR. And he has challenged me to learn more about computers so that I can write gags for him. It's been very exciting for me and given me a new lease on my career.*
>
> — MORT WALKER, in *The Older the Fiddle,*
> *the Better the Tune*

Recall your most intense moments and events in the elder stage.
- When did you feel a sense of *peace* and *contentment*?
- When did you feel *loss* and *grief* most intensely?
- What happened to make you feel *joy, happiness,* or *delight*?
- When have you felt most *lonely*?
- What caused you to feel strong *gratitude*?
- Have you ever felt *useless* and *unvalued*?
- Have you ever felt *valuable* and *valued* as an elder?
- What caused you to feel *embarrassment* and *shame*?
- When did you feel *forgiven*?

- Did you ever feel *angry*?
- When did you feel *loved*?
- When did you feel most *loving*?
- What made you feel *envious* or *jealous*?
- Recall some time when you *laughed* and *laughed*?
- What's made you feel really *frustrated*?
- Is there anything that's made you feel *proud*?
- Was there a time when you felt a *strong connection* and *closeness* with another person or a group of people?
- Have you suffered real *physical pain*?
- What *surprised* or *amazed* you?
- When did you fall under the spell of *despair*—a sense of no hope?
- What's given you the strongest sense of *security* and *safety*?
- Recall some time when you felt *truly disappointed*.
- What's the most *emotional pain* and *hurt* you've felt as an elder?
- What intense experiences have you had in your elder years around your senses: *sight, sound, smell, taste,* and *touch*?

How would you describe your personality—the way others experience you—at this time in your life? Or, how might a good, honest friend describe you at the current time? Think of yourself, your personality, at forty, at sixty, and now. What, if anything, has changed? Has your personality become more sharply defined?

What possessions do you most value now? Do you own anything that has great value to you? It doesn't have to be something worth a lot of money, just something that has meaning and emotional value for you.

What is the source of your greatest fear and anxiety now? Is it something that's actually in your life, or is it something that *might* happen? Why does this frighten you or make you anxious?

What is the source of your greatest pleasure and comfort now? Seeing friends and family? What, if anything, makes you feel the world is right and good? Recall times when you've experienced that feeling. What part of your life do you look forward to most each day? Is it something you do? Something done to you or for you? Is it memories—something in the past?

How would you like to be remembered? Were there themes in your life—helping others, for instance, or designing buildings where people work—that give you satisfaction as you remember what you did? Are there parts of your life story that you regret or feel dissatisfied with? Do you ever think about your legacy, what you will leave behind? If so, what is it? Perhaps it's children, the next generation, or something you created.

> *[I'd like to be remembered] just as a good person, a good friend. I'd like our whole family to remember that I loved them and tried to treat everybody with honesty and goodness. If they do that, they'll have a pretty good life. I think all our children do that. They're good, sound characters, and I think we taught them. And of course, we had good characters because we loved our parents, we respected our parents. And they taught us . . . I think my dad taught me how to be a good father. And I think my kids think that I'm a pretty good guy. What else can I say? That's how I'd like to be remembered.*
>
> —IRA MARKS, in *A Legacy of Love*

Marriage/Partnership

If you're lucky enough to still be with your spouse or partner in these elder years, or were together for at least part of this time, recall your relationship here.

FACTS ABOUT YOUR MARRIAGE/PARTNER RELATIONSHIP

❦ Note any factual turning points, life events, changes, or highlights in the life of your spouse or partner, or in your relationship with your spouse or partner, during this time in your life, such as illness, a change in circumstances, some new interest, and so on.

MEMORIES OF YOUR MARRIAGE/PARTNER RELATIONSHIP

If you lost your spouse or partner during this stage, consider the following questions for the time you had together.

Think about your daily routines together. Did you have any daily rituals? What did you do together? Apart? What did you talk about? What was your social life like as a couple?

How did advancing age affect your relationship? Did you continue to pursue interests that you'd had for a long time? Did you pursue any new interests? Recall ways you helped each other at this time. Did your relationship continue to evolve and grow? Did age bring you closer?

Think about the highlights and turning points during this period of your life. What life events happened to your spouse or partner at this time? What memories do they bring to mind? How were you involved?

Children, Grandchildren, and Great-grandchildren

What memories of your elder years are stirred by thinking of your children and their children?

FACTS ABOUT YOUR CHILDREN

❦ Note the names and ages of each of your children at the beginning of this stage, and the names and ages of your grandchildren and great-grandchildren.

❦ Note for each any significant events that occurred in his or her life during this period—just note the year and the event briefly.

❦ Note the times, if any, that all or most of you got together as a family, for a reunion or for some other family occasion.

MEMORIES OF YOUR CHILDREN, GRANDCHILDREN, AND GREAT-GRANDCHILDREN

For each of your children, grandchildren, and great-grandchildren, consider the following questions.

- *Where does this child live?* What does he or she do? Think of where this child lives and let thoughts of that place bring back memories of what happened there that involved you.
- *Think of times you spend with this child.* When do you see each other? What do you do together? Do you live far apart and see each other rarely, or close by and see each other often? Do you confide in each other? Are you involved in his or her life? Do you want to be? Do you spend holidays together? Recall special moments together.

We have what we call the "command attendance Sunday" when the entire Mancuso clan comes to our home for Sunday dinner and conversation. It also allows us to celebrate special occasions like birthdays and anniversaries together at one of the Sunday dinners. With all the practice, I have noticed how much better the grandchildren have gotten at blowing out candles and singing "Happy Birthday." But, ultimately it is about the conversation with all of them, not only with us, but that which they have with each other that is the most memorable part of our Sunday family dinners. We are never more than seven days behind what goes on in their lives at school, in sports, or who the new best friend is, and it is quite amazing to see how attached the seven cousins have become. These are the things that family traditions are made of.

—ART LINKLETTER, in *If I Knew It Was Going to Be This Much Fun, I Would Have Become a Grandparent First*

- *Recall the events and milestones in the life of this child.* What of significance has occurred in this child's life during this period? Marriage? Divorce? Childbirth? A move? A promotion or job change? Do you have any memories connected with any of those events? Did you participate in any of them? How did each turn out?

Home

Has home changed for you as you've become elderly? Or have you been able to live through this period in the place you've always lived?

FACTS ABOUT YOUR HOME

❦ List the address, town or city, and state (and country, if not the United States) of each place you have lived in this stage.

❦ Provide a brief description of the physical place—house, apartment building, assisted living, retirement home, etc.—and the neighborhood or town.

MEMORIES OF YOUR HOME

If you lived in more than one place as an elder, think of each place prior to your current home. If your home is the same as in previous stages, consider these questions as they apply to the elder stage of your life.

- *Recall the house or building and the yard or grounds around it.* Imagine yourself there, walking from room to room, or around the outside. What happened in those spaces? Who was there?
- *Recall the neighborhood.* Imagine walking around the neighborhood and see what memories come to mind of events and people associated with different places in the neighborhood.
- *Recall the town or city.* Imagine walking around that place—the downtown, parks, buildings, etc.—and see what memories come to mind of events and people associated with those different places.

- *Recall your daily life in all of those places.* Imagine going through a typical morning or afternoon in that home, that yard, that neighborhood, that town. What did you most like to do, places you most liked to visit, in the neighborhood or city?

What memories do you have of your current home? What events have occurred in your home or building, neighborhood, town, or city? What do you like about your current residence? What does it not provide? Do you have friends there? What does it offer of interest or help to you?

Birth Family

Have any members of your birth family—brothers and sisters and cousins—survived with you into these elder years? Do you see each other or talk often? Do you still play a role in each other's lives?

FACTS ABOUT YOUR BIRTH FAMILY

❦ Note the names of those who remain in your birth family at the beginning of this period—mother or father, brothers and sisters, cousins, aunts and uncles, others. Note the ages of each at this time.

❦ Note any factual and significant turning points or life events, with year of occurrence, that happened in their lives during this period—death, illness, accidents, accomplishments, marriage/divorce, and so on.

MEMORIES OF YOUR BIRTH FAMILY

Think of each of the relatives you identified above and for each consider the following:

- *What contact have you had with this relative in your elder years?* When have you seen him or her? Was it daily, often, or infrequently? How has what happened in his or her life touched you and your life? What moments of happiness and pain have been connected with each relative? Has your relationship changed in this period?

When I was a little girl, 5 or 6, my father's gas station and auto repair business was next to the highway that ran between York and Harrisburg, Pennsylvania. There was a beautiful farmhouse and peach orchard across the way. They grew the sweetest Pennsylvania peaches, and I've never tasted one as good since. I always wanted to go across the street to play on the lawn in front of the farmhouse. My mother would take my hand and walk me across. I'd stay and play while she returned to my father's garage. She told me I must call out for her before crossing the highway in return. "Don't forget to yell for me so I can walk you back safely." That's my earliest memory of her telling me what to do. I always listened.

She wasn't always vocal with her orders, but I could tell from her facial expressions and body movements what she expected. She'd give me a look if she disapproved. She'd roll her eyes, and purse her lips. I always knew when things I did either met or didn't meet with her approval. I wanted to please her and make her happy. For the most part I did.

My father adored me and trusted my judgment. My mother did too, but she wouldn't admit it.

My mother died at age 98. I was 76 at the time. When she got close to death, she repeatedly expressed her readiness to go. She didn't want to be a burden to me or my brother any longer. It's sad not having her anymore, but I feel she's in a good place. At age 76, for the first time in my life, I felt a certain freedom in not having to think about her approving or disapproving what I was doing anymore. Even now at age 78, that sense of freedom still feels fresh and wonderful.

—GLORIA SINGER WILLIAMS, personal story

- *Think of the turning points or life events for this person.* What happened? Were you involved in some way? How has it affected you?

Religion or Spirituality

Does your faith continue into your elder years? Do you continue the religious or spiritual practices that were important to you in earlier periods? Do you try to pass on your beliefs and conditions to children and grandchildren and great-grandchildren?

FACTS ABOUT RELIGIOUS OR SPIRITUAL BELIEFS

❧ Name or describe the beliefs that continue to be or have become important to you in your elder stage? Have they changed from your earlier beliefs?

❧ Describe briefly any practices related to your beliefs that you continue to perform, such as attending worship services, prayer, and so on.

❧ Describe any religious or spiritual experiences you've had in your elder years.

MEMORIES OF RELIGIOUS OR SPIRITUAL BELIEFS

Think about your major beliefs and religious or spiritual practices. Are they the same as you've held or followed for a long time? Did you recently adopt them? Have they changed in any way? What have your beliefs and practices led you to do, or not do?

Recall any special moments or experiences around your beliefs. Have there been times when your religious or spiritual life changed or deepened? Has your faith ever helped you through a time of crisis? Have you had any moments of insight or epiphany or deeper understanding?

Has your age affected any of your religious practices? Do you attend church more often, for example?

Friends and Other Memorable People

What individuals have remained or become important to you in your elder years? How many have you lost?

FACTS ABOUT FRIENDS AND OTHER MEMORABLE PEOPLE

❧ List the people who have been your good friends in this time of your life. Note any facts or highlights that have occurred in their lives or in their relationship with you.

❧ Identify any other people who qualify as memorable. Note briefly and factually what they've done, including when and where.

❧ Describe briefly the circle of people with whom you've tended to socialize in your elder years. Note where you've typically gotten together—at a community center or a club, for example—and what you do together.

MEMORIES OF FRIENDS AND OTHER MEMORABLE PEOPLE

Bring to mind each of your good friends and recall moments and occasions you've shared with them. For each, recall why and how you remain close. Have you kept in touch with friends from your past? What events and circumstances led to your closeness? How have they helped you, or you them? What have you done together? Have you confided in them and they in you?

When I get to feeling blue, my neighbor boy Billy is the best company. He's five. We sit out on the curb and play with the ants. We don't kill them, we just give them a little trouble getting back to their nest. We pile up twigs, or put a big shoe in the way.

Billy always knows how I'm feeling, without my saying a word. He doesn't notice I'm an old lady, except for when it's time to get me back on my feet. Then it's a real production. First, I have to roll over onto the grass. Once I get myself onto my hands and knees, he helps me haul myself up the rest of the way. I moan and groan and put on a good show. He thinks it's great. By that time, I'm usually feeling pretty great, too.

— MARIA SANCHEZ, in What's Worth Knowing

Call to mind the other individuals you've identified and think of times and places and moments associated with each. Have you done things together? Have you shared interests, like a hobby? Have you helped this person in some way, or has this person done the same for you? Have you ever sought advice from someone, or someone from you? Has anyone younger sought your counsel or help? What did you do for that person? Has anyone ever caused you to change your mind? Has a professional, like a doctor or minister or rabbi, helped you deal with a problem or get through a difficult time?

For each of your social groups, recall the times and activities you've enjoyed together. What community of people have you felt connected to? What have you and the others in this group usually done together? Played games and socialized? Gone to church together? Watched movies or gone to shows? Has anything unusual happened on those occasions? Who have been the key people in the group—the ones who tend to be more visible and make things happen? Have you been one of them? Has this group changed in any way through this period? Have any members moved away or died? How has that affected the group and what it has done? What sorts of things have happened in the lives of group members and how much have you and other group members gotten involved? Have you traveled together?

What other social occasions do you remember from this time? Recall any other social moments or events that have been especially memorable. What other people have you seen and done things with?

Interests, Causes, and Community

Have you remained in your elder years in touch with, engaged in, any interests and activities, such as community affairs, hobbies, causes, or even work of some kind?

FACTS ABOUT YOUR INTERESTS, CAUSES, AND COMMUNITY

❦ Note any interests you pursue, such as clubs, the arts, hobbies and games, sports, reading, and so on.

❧ Name any programs you've taken in order to learn something new.

❧ Identify any social, political, community, or other causes that you still work to support.

❧ Note any pets that are important parts of your life.

❧ If you still travel, note any memorable trips you've taken in this period—where you went, with whom, when, and briefly what you saw.

❧ Describe what work, if any, you perform.

MEMORIES OF YOUR INTERESTS, CAUSES, AND COMMUNITY

Think of any political or social causes that have taken up your time and effort. What memories of events or occasions or people come to mind around your involvement? How did you become involved? What have you and others hoped to accomplish?

Recall the clubs and other social organizations you belong to. Think of each organization and the people in it and the events and occasions associated with each group.

Do you still do work of some kind? Is it related to the work you've always done, or new work? How does it enrich your life?

What pets have you had or do you have? What happened to each pet? As you think of each pet, what memories come to mind?

Do you still follow the arts in some way? Which arts and what do you do? What events and memories come to mind as you think of each?

Think of each hobby you still pursue. What memories of each hobby do you have from this time in your life?

Think about popular entertainment you enjoy the most now. What television or radio programs do you follow? What actors (male and female)? Do you read? Do you go to the movies? Think of any books or movies or programs that have meant a lot to you.

Do you still love to follow sports? What sports? What teams? How have your teams done? Do you recall any memorable games or events?

Recall any trips you've taken in these years. What struck you about the places you visited? Did you have any travel adventures? With whom did you travel?

Recall each learning program you took. What was the subject? What happened in each course? What did you learn? Who else was there? Who taught it? Why were you interested?

Notable Events

What outside events have touched you in your elder years?

FACTS ABOUT NOTABLE EVENTS

❧ What historical or newsworthy events have touched you in this stage? Describe briefly what happened and when. This includes both great news-making national and world events, and local events too.

MEMORIES OF NOTABLE EVENTS

Bring to mind any notable events in this period that touched your life. Recall moments or people connected with those events.

Other Voices

If you want, contact any people who are or have been a part of your elder life. Ask them to record any memories of you in this important time of your life.

If you want to include other people's memories of you as an elder . . .

1. Make a list of people from your time as an elder and ask them to share their memories with you, in their own words.
2. Record each memory on a separate sheet of paper. Label each memory "A Memory of Me" and include the memory teller's name, as well as the approximate date and location of the memory.
3. Add these memory sheets to your own memories in your *My Life Story* notebook.

THE MEANING OF YOUR ELDER STAGE

Every stage has its particular significance and role in the unfolding of our lives. Though this stage is still ongoing for you, there's still something to be gained by reflecting on your elder years as you've experienced them so far.

Defining Moments

Compare yourself as a person now with the person you were ten or twenty years ago. How have you changed? Where in your elder years did those changes occur? What caused them? Did the changes happen all at once, or in a series of steps? What events, occasions, and moments come to mind when you reflect on how you changed? Those are the defining or pivotal moments you should note here.

Values—What Matters

What do you most value at this time of your life? What part of your life would you least want to lose or give up? Family? Friends? Some hobby? Religious beliefs and practices? Where is the center of gravity of your life now? What keeps you an-chored and steady?

Love

As before, the task here is *not* to identify all members of your family and your clos-est friends—the people you're supposed to love. Don't take that love for granted. But here you should identify the love that has made or is making a real difference in your life. For example, has love repaired a damaged relationship? Have you for-given someone or has someone forgiven you? As you identify each person, think of the relationship between the two of you and the ways you each took care—you of them and they of you.

Learning and Wisdom

Is there anything you've learned in your elder years that you wish you'd known earlier? Have you been surprised by anything in these years? Was there anything you expected to find and didn't, or didn't expect to find and did, that you wish you'd known about in advance?

Think of what you might tell someone else coming along behind you, some-one like your daughter or son. What might make this period happier and more productive for that person?

Based on what you've learned in your elder years, what could you tell someone in much earlier stages that might help them live happier, more satisfying lives?

> *My father-in-law, at age seventy, fell and injured his spine when he started wearing bifocals. He became a quadriplegic and was an inspiration to us all, dying at age ninety-seven. I asked him for advice for the elderly and he said, "Tell them to fall on something soft." A few days later he said, "It doesn't always work. They stood me up in therapy and I fell over on my wife and broke her leg. So tell them to just fall up." I thought that was a joke until the night he told us he was tired of his body and was skipping his vitamins and dinner. He died quietly that evening. By my definition he just fell up and once again became dreamless, unalive, and perfect. . . .*

Now presuming you have accomplished what you came to earth to accomplish, when you get tired of your body, gather your loved ones and tell them to tell stories about your life . . . you will hear things that will allow you to die laughing. So serve the world in your way and when you get tired, go out with a smile.

—Dr. Bernie Siegel, in *The Older the Fiddle, the Better the Tune*

Summing Up

Step back after all your remembering and express now briefly this period of your life thus far, your elder years. How would you characterize it in, say, fifty or one hundred words?

If you want, use this opportunity to do more. In a few words, how would you describe the life you've lived and what it's meant to you? What's your story in a nutshell?

NOTES

PREFACE

"When I was barely a teenager . . ." Kent Lineback, personal story.

TIPS AND ADVICE

"My mother took up two new hobbies . . ." James McBride, *The Color of Water,* 5, 7.

"Thirty years ago . . ." Anne Lamott, *Bird by Bird: Some Instructions on Writing and Life,* 18–19.

FAMILY INFORMATION

"My mother married my father . . ." Robert Graves, *Good-bye to All That,* 12.

STAGE 1—CHILDHOOD

"I did, however, have a fantasy . . ." Neil Simon, *Rewrites,* 193.

"My sister, being not merely the only woman . . ." Laurence Olivier, *Confessions of an Actor,* 14–16.

"I lay alone and was almost asleep . . ." Annie Dillard, *An American Childhood,* 21.

"It was around 3:00 pm . . ." John R. Saunders, "The Perfect Prisoner," unpublished memoir.

"One rainy Sunday morning . . ." Rich Shearer, personal story.

"Jenny, our wonderful cook . . ." Jane Buchsbaum, personal story.

"They must have had a fight last night . . ." Pam Lewis, "A Little Death," in *How I Learned to Cook,* ed. Margo Perin, 194.

"One of my most vivid memories . . ." Jane Fonda, *My Life So Far,* 15–16.

"One day I decided to run away . . ." Toni Sciarra Poynter, personal story.

"As a twin . . ." Deborah Ogawa, personal story.

"The family home of Rock Hill . . ." Michael Ondaatje, *Running in the Family,* 98–99.

"I remain unaware of anyone talking to us . . ." Stephen K. Blumberg, *A Satisfying Life,* 41.

"When I was in the sixth grade . . ." Kent Lineback, personal story.

"My first day at the Walley . . ." Mary Cantwell, *Manhattan Memoir,* 44.

"[The Governess and I] continued to toil . . ." Winston Churchill, *My Early Life,* 3–4.

"Pam McGavin was my best friend . . ." Carol Franco, personal story.

"On a bicycle I traveled . . ." Annie Dillard, *An American Childhood,* 42.

"You begin by bouncing a ball . . ." Bill Bradley, *Values of the Game,* 17.

"I don't recall exactly how old I was . . ." Allen Weitsman, personal story.

"Mrs. Callaway made her own rules . . ." Eudora Welty, *One Writer's Beginnings,* 30.

"While the tornado itself was on . . ." Annie Dillard, *An American Childhood,* 102.

"It was the summer of 1957 . . ." Sandy Rubin, personal story.

"When I was about five or six . . ." Warren Bennis, *Geeks & Geezers,* 34.

"I was a long-legged seven-year-old . . ." Jill Ker Conway, *The Road from Coorain,* 42–43.

"I didn't become an overtly affectionate mother . . ." Ruth Kluger, "Still Alive," in *How I Learned to Cook,* ed. Margo Perin, 72–73.

"Holy Family [School] was at most a mile . . ." Tim Russert, *Big Russ and Me,* 55–56.

STAGE 2—ADOLESCENCE

"In my grandmother's house in Brooklyn . . ." Elizabeth Ehrlich, *Miriam's Kitchen,* 205.

"I was entering the period . . ." Jane Fonda, *My Life So Far,* 65.

"During the summer . . ." Alan Alda, *Never Have Your Dog Stuffed,* 51–52.

"When I was 17 . . ." Susan Huter, personal story.

"When we were girls . . ." Dorothy Allison, *Two or Three Things I Know for Sure,* 78.

"Eventually, we sat down to dinner . . ." Jill Ker Conway, *The Road from Coorain,* 72.

"The next day my mother put vodka . . ." Jamie Callan, "Just Another Movie Star," in *How I Learned to Cook,* ed. Margo Perin, 41–42.

"I remember Dad telling the story . . ." Carol Franco, personal story.

"My house as I grew up . . ." Kent Lineback, personal story.

"When my father was dying . . ." Eudora Welty, *One Writer's Beginnings,* 92–93.

"There was not much grass . . ." Hillary Gamerow, "How I Learned to Cook," in *How I Learned to Cook,* ed. Margo Perin, 136–137.

"Mass, Communion, fish on Fridays . . ." Maureen Howard, *Facts of Life,* 12–13.

"Our team—the Waukegan Township High School Bulldogs . . ." Stephen K. Blumberg, *A Satisfying Life,* 59.

"After mass Sergeant Benet and I drove . . ." Tobias Wolff, *In Pharaoh's Army,* 89–90.

"Goey and I drove to the pier . . ." Jane Fonda, *My Life So Far,* 100.

"In the early '60s . . ." Elsa Pennewell, personal story.

"It is still there, the Pastime Theater . . ." Mary Cantwell, *Manhattan Memoir,* 72.

"Now and then Father put the drafting tools aside . . ." Margaret Bourke-White, *Portrait of Myself,* in *Written by Herself,* ed. Jill Ker Conway, 425.

"I had wanted to escape from my class prison . . ." Vida Dutton Scudder, *On Journey,* in *Written by Herself,* ed. Jill Ker Conway, 341.

"Finally late that spring I saw an amoeba . . ." Annie Dillard, *An American Childhood,* 148–149.

STAGE 3—YOUNG ADULT

"I always wanted to tell my dad . . ." Mildred Potter, in *What's Worth Knowing,* ed. Wendy Lustbader, 208–209.

"My insecurity . . ." Katharine Graham, *Personal History,* 230–231.

"When John and I decided to marry . . ." Jill Ker Conway, *True North,* 132–133.

"Bea Brown was a violist . . ." Alan Alda, *Never Have Your Dog Stuffed,* 73–74.

"I sat at the table . . ." Kent Lineback, personal story.

"It seems to me that we were . . ." Stephen K. Blumberg, *A Satisfying Life,* 99.

"'A boy,' I cried . . ." Erin Cressida Wilson, "Milk Dress: A Nursing Song," in *The May Queen,* ed. Andrea N. Richesin, 217.

"What's for dinner? . . ." Elizabeth Ehrlich, *Miriam's Kitchen,* 295.

"I am a single mother . . ." Elizabeth Cohen, *The House on Beartown Road,* 100.

"I think we must have just finished lunch . . ." Laurence Olivier, *Confessions of an Actor,* 161–162.

"'Come home!' I cried . . ." Kathleen Finneran, *The Tender Land,* 69, 271–272.

"After college I went to work . . ." Deborah Ogawa, personal story.

"Now we come to my editor . . ." Mary Cantwell, *Manhattan Memoir,* 215–219.

"How many prejudices . . ." Yvonne Thornton, *The Ditchdigger's Daughters,* 171–172.

"I'm coming home! . . ." Al Puntasecca, 1953, in *Behind the Lines,* Andrew Carroll, 417–419.

"'I used to baby-sit for Lois . . .'" Maggie Brooke, in *Leadership on the Line,* Ronald A. Heifetz and Marty Linksy, 9–10.

"I had one big problem . . ." Cherry Austin, in *Women Travel,* ed. Natania Jansz, et al., 89–90.

"It was 6:01 a.m. . . ." Carol Franco, personal story.

"I grabbed my sleeping bag . . ." Eric Lineback, personal story.

"I entered every class in existence . . ." Janet Scudder, *Modeling My Life,* in *Written by Herself,* ed. Jill Ker Conway, 350–351.

"'Look at your mom and me' . . ." Yvonne Thornton, *The Ditchdigger's Daughters,* 161.

"It was a caramel-colored, hard-sided suitcase . . ." Elizabeth Ehrlich, *Miriam's Kitchen,* 90–91.

STAGE 4—ADULT

"How did I finally get comfortable . . ." Marisa de los Santos, "Wide Awake," in *The May Queen,* ed. Andrea N. Richesin, 81.

"I am convinced that I have been . . ." Sukey Field, in *Reinvented Lives,* Elizabeth Handy and Charles Handy, 200–201.

"As we grow up . . ." Goldie Hawn, *A Lotus Grows in the Mud,* 379.

"I've been scheming . . ." Elizabeth Cohen, *The House on Beartown Road,* 204.

"Steven and I drove in silence . . ." Marjorie Williams, personal story.

"One day when I was about five months pregnant . . ." Yvonne Thornton, *The Ditchdigger's Daughters,* 208.

"One spring evening in 2003 . . ." Stacy Young, personal story.

"As a parent . . ." Karin Bartow, personal story.

"Zeb and Jake argued . . ." Bret Lott, *Fathers, Sons & Brothers,* 75–77.

"When my two older kids . . ." Sonja Benson, personal story.

"We never thought we'd be here . . ." Amanda Eyre Ward, "To All the Men I've Loved Before," in *The May Queen,* ed. Andrea N. Richesin, 233–234.

"While the circumstances of our life . . ." Jill Ker Conway, *True North,* 102–103.

"Back in 1974 . . ." Zack Gould, personal story.

"When we married . . ." Kathryn Harrison, "Keeping Vigil," in *I Married My Mother-in-Law,* ed. Ilena Silverman, 206.

"In the end . . ." Mary Cantwell, *Manhattan Memoir,* 299.

"When doctors have bad news . . ." Louise Jarvis Flynn, "Plus One, Plus Two, Plus Three," in *The May Queen,* ed. Andrea N. Richesin, 252–253.

"When I was 10 or 11 . . ." Sandy Rubin, personal story.

"I began keeping Passover . . ." Elizabeth Ehrlich, *Miriam's Kitchen,* 213–214.

"Life in an advertising agency . . ." John Fortune, in *Working,* Studs Terkel, 112–113.

"I had seen anti-Semitism . . ." Muriel Siebert, in *Geeks & Geezers,* Warren Bennis and Robert Thomas, 38.

"The other person who stiffened my back . . ." Katharine Graham, *Personal History,* 319.

"Not long ago . . ." Susan Huter, personal story.

"Back in 1974 . . ." Zack Gould, personal story.

"Nowadays my affections . . ." Bill Blass, *Bare Blass,* 99–100.

"My grandmother . . ." Patricia Weitsman, personal story.

"[My] father, Milton . . ." Ronald A. Heifetz, *Leadership on the Line,* 217–218.

"It was still the days . . ." Kent Lineback, personal story.

"When I started out as an actor . . ." Alan Alda, *Never Have Your Dog Stuffed,* 160–161.

STAGE 5—MIDDLE ADULT

"At approximately 3:45 . . ." Elizabeth Cohen, *The House on Beartown Road,* 199.

"I was the youngest . . ." Miriam Reeder, personal story.

"One of the hardest things . . ." Karin Bartow, personal story.

"Mom and Dad picked me up . . ." Carol Franco, personal story.

"So, here we stand . . ." Goldie Hawn, *A Lotus Grows in the Mud,* 408–411.

"*Why do you always . . .*'" Joan Didion, *The Year of Magical Thinking,* 138.

"On Saturday morning . . ." Bill Clinton, *My Life: The Presidential Years,* 444, 458–459.

"The morning was quite cold . . ." Zack Gould, personal story.

"When we worked together . . ." Alan Alda, *Never Have Your Dog Stuffed,* 163.

"When I found out . . ." Stacy Young, personal story.

"The difficulties of my job . . ." Katharine Graham, *Personal History,* 371.

"For years I had thought . . ." Leslie Zheutlin, personal story.

"Just weeks after the milestone . . ." Patricia Weitsman, personal story.

"The lure of the sea . . ." Errol Flynn, *My Wicked, Wicked Ways,* 352.

"On Tuesday . . ." Linda Grabel, personal story.

"My father is not . . ." Lesley Shearer, personal story.

"Isn't one of the difficulties . . ." Jane Fonda, *My Life So Far,* 433–434.

"The three of us were together . . ." Stan Davis, "Three Generations," in *Tall Tales,* unpublished memoir.

"The problem when someone loses . . ." Elizabeth Cohen, *The House on Beartown Road,* 136–137.

STAGE 6—LATE ADULT

"But all the memories . . ." Ellen Anderson Gholson Glasgow, *The Woman Within,* in *Written by Herself,* ed. Jill Ker Conway, 399.

"It is not unusual . . ." Jane Fonda, *My Life So Far,* 315–16.

"When the twilights got long . . ." Joan Didion, *The Year of Magical Thinking,* 163–164.

"I literally cannot take my eyes . . ." Phil Donahue in *If I Knew It Was Going to Be This Much Fun, I Would Have Become a Grandparent First,* Willard Scott and Friends, 82–83.

"I came back from his wedding . . ." Stan Davis, "Guadalajara Wedding," in *Tall Tales,* unpublished memoir.

"It was a Sunday morning . . ." Kent Lineback, personal story.

"I kept my promise . . ." Rick Bragg, *All Over but the Shoutin',* 308–309, 313.

"We got feedback . . ." Leon Gorman, *L.L. Bean: The Making of an American Icon,* 235–236.

"After the speech . . ." Ronald Reagan, *An American Life,* 259–260.

"It was never my intention . . ." Audrey Eyton, in *Reinvented Lives,* Elizabeth Handy and Charles Handy, 55–56.

"We've always been cat people . . ." Jane and Bill Buchsbaum, personal story.

"I have just purchased . . ." Joseph S. Colletto, in *The Older the Fiddle, the Better the Tune,* Willard Scott and Friends, 28–29.

"One fall day . . ." Marcia Keeline, personal story.

"The defining moment . . ." James Botkin, personal story.

"I wanted to speak . . ." Alan Alda, *Never Have Your Dog Stuffed,* 165.

"Sometimes, when life gets too hard . . ." Goldie Hawn, *A Lotus Grows in the Mud,* 296–297.

STAGE 7—ELDER

"I always needed to have people . . ." Annie Bakersmith, in *What's Worth Knowing,* Wendy Lustbader, 18.

"Age puzzles me . . ." Florida Scott-Maxwell, *The Measure of My Days,* 13–14.

"As I inch toward eighty . . ." Mort Walker, in *The Older the Fiddle, the Better the Tune,* Willard Scott and Friends, 49–50.

"[I'd like to be remembered] just as . . ." Ira Marks, in *A Legacy of Love,* Sally Goldin, 148.

"We have what we call . . ." Art Linkletter, in *If I Knew It Was Going to Be This Much Fun, I Would Have Become a Grandparent First,* Willard Scott and Friends, 148.

"When I was a little girl . . ." Gloria Singer Williams, personal story.

"When I get to feeling blue . . ." Maria Sanchez, in *What's Worth Knowing,* Wendy Lustbader, 120.

"My father-in-law . . ." Dr. Bernie Siegel, in *The Older the Fiddle, the Better the Tune,* Willard Scott and Friends, 113–115.

BIBLIOGRAPHY

Alda, Alan. *Never Have Your Dog Stuffed and Other Things I've Learned*. New York: Random House, 2005.

Allison, Dorothy. *Two or Three Things I Know for Sure*. New York: Plume, 1996.

Bennis, Warren G., and Robert J. Thomas. *Geeks & Geezers: How Era, Values, and Defining Moments Shape Leaders*. Boston: Harvard Business School Press, 2002.

Blass, Bill. *Bare Blass*. New York: HarperCollins, 2002.

Blumberg, Stephen K. *A Satisfying Life*. Santa Fe: Authentic Publishing, 2003.

Bourke-White, Margaret. *Portrait of Myself*. New York: Simon & Schuster, 1963.

Bradley, Bill. *Values of the Game*. New York: Artisan/Workman Publishing, 1998.

Bragg, Rick. *All Over but the Shoutin'*. New York: Vintage: 1997.

Cantwell, Mary. *Manhattan Memoir*. New York: Penguin, 2000.

Carroll, Andrew. *Behind the Lines*. New York: Scribner, 2003.

Churchill, Winston. *My Early Life*. New York: Touchstone, 1996.

Clinton, Bill. *My Life: The Presidential Years*. New York: Alfred A. Knopf, 2004.

Cohen, Elizabeth. *The House on Beartown Road*. New York: Random House, 2004.

Conway, Jill Ker. *The Road from Coorain*. New York: Vintage, 1989.

Conway, Jill Ker. *True North*. New York: Vintage, 1994.

Conway, Jill Ker, ed. *Written by Herself: Autobiographies of American Women*. New York: Vintage, 1992.

Didion, Joan. *The Year of Magical Thinking*. New York: Alfred A. Knopf, 2005.

Dillard, Annie. *An American Childhood*. New York: Harper Perennial, 1988.

Ehrlich, Elizabeth. *Miriam's Kitchen*. New York: Penguin, 1998.

Finneran, Kathleen. *The Tender Land: A Family Love Story*. Boston: Houghton Mifflin, 2000.

Flynn, Errol. *My Wicked, Wicked Ways*. New York: A Berkley Book, 1979.

Fonda, Jane. *My Life So Far*. New York: Random House, 2005.

Glasgow, Ellen Anderson Gholson. *The Woman Within*. New York: Harcourt Brace, 1954.

Goldin, Sally. *Ann and Ira Marks: A Legacy of Love*. San Francisco: Tell Me a Story—Oral and Written Histories, 2005.

Gorman, Leon. *L.L. Bean: The Making of an American Icon*. Boston: Harvard Business School Press, 2006.

Graham, Katharine. *Personal History*. New York: Vintage, 1998.

Graves, Robert. *Good-bye to All That*. New York: Anchor, 1998.

Handy, Elizabeth, and Charles Handy. *Reinvented Lives: Women at Sixty*. London: Hutchinson, 2002.

Hawn, Goldie. *A Lotus Grows in the Mud*. New York: G. P. Putnam's Sons, 2005.

Heifetz, Ronald A., and Marty Linsky. *Leadership on the Line*. Boston: Harvard Business School Press, 2002.

Howard, Maureen. *Facts of Life*. New York: Penguin, 1980.

Jansz, Natania, Miranda Davies, Emma Drew, Lori McDougall, eds. *Women Travel: First-hand Accounts from More than 60 Countries*. London: Rough Guides, 1999.

Lamott, Anne. *Bird by Bird*. New York: Pantheon, 1994.

Lott, Bret. *Fathers, Sons & Brothers: The Men in My Family*. New York: Washington Square Press, 2000.

Lustbader, Wendy. *What's Worth Knowing*. New York: Jeremy P. Tarcher, 2001.

McBride, James. *The Color of Water: A Black Man's Tribute to His White Mother*. New York: Riverhead, 1996.

Olivier, Laurence. *Confessions of an Actor*. New York: Touchstone, 1992.

Ondaatje, Michael. *Running in the Family*. New York: Vintage, 1983.

Perin, Margo, ed. *How I Learned to Cook*. New York: Jeremy P. Tarcher, 2004.

Reagan, Ronald, *An American Life*. New York: Simon & Schuster, 1990.

Richesin, Andrea N., ed. *The May Queen*. New York: Jeremy P. Tarcher, 2006.

Russett, Tim. *Big Russ and Me*. New York: Hyperion, 2005.

Scott, Willard and Friends. *The Older the Fiddle, the Better the Tune*. New York: Hyperion, 2003.

Scott, Willard and Friends. *If I Knew It Was Going to Be This Much Fun, I Would Have Become a Grandparent First*. New York: Hyperion, 2004.

Scott-Maxwell, Florida. *The Measure of My Days*. New York: Penguin, 1979.

Scudder, Janet. *Modeling My Life*. New York: Harcourt, Brace, 1925.

Scudder, Vida Dutton. *On Journey*. New York: E. P. Dutton, 1937.

Silverman, Ilena, ed. *I Married My Mother-in-Law*. New York: Riverhead, 2006.

Simon, Neil. *Rewrites*. New York: Simon & Schuster, 1996.

Terkel, Studs. *Working*. New York: Ballantine, 1972.

Thornton, Yvonne S. *The Ditchdigger's Daughters*. New York: Plume, 1996.

Welty, Eudora. *One Writer's Beginnings*. Cambridge: Harvard University Press, 1983.

Wolff, Tobias. *In Pharaoh's Army*. New York: Vintage, 1994.

ACKNOWLEDGMENTS

Many family members, friends, and colleagues made invaluable contributions as we prepared *The Legacy Guide*. Some read and reacted to drafts early and late. Others suggested ways to make the book more useful, or to bring it to the attention of a wider audience. All encouraged us at crucial times. Without their help and support, *The Legacy Guide* would not possess whatever strengths it has. Thanks to: Susan Alvey, Karin Bartow, Mark Bloomfield, James Botkin, Jane Buchsbaum, Marni Clippinger, Sara Cummins, Stan Davis, Mike Fender, Liz Hiser, Kathleen Jordan, Rosalie Kerr, Eric Lineback, Perry McIntosh, Caroline Michel, Sharon Rice, Judy Uhl, Marjorie Williams, Connie Wind, Ellen Wingard, Leslie Zheutlin. They all have our deep gratitude.

Some of these same people and many others allowed us to reproduce here memories and stories from their own lives. Whatever charm *The Legacy Guide* might claim to possess comes directly from their stories. Thanks to: Karin Bartow, Sonja Benson, Stephen Blumberg, James Botkin, Jane and Bill Buchsbaum, Stan Davis, Sally Goldin, Zack Gould, Linda Grabel, Susan Huter, Marcia Keeline, Eric Lineback, Deborah Ogawa, Elsa Pennewell, Miriam Reeder, Sandy Rubin, John Saunders, Toni Sciarra Poynter, Lesley Shearer, Rich Shearer, Allen Weitsman, Patricia Weitsman, Gloria Singer Williams, Marjorie Williams, Stacy Young, Leslie Zheutlin. For their contributions we are especially grateful.

Finally, we'd like to thank our agent, Jim Levine, for his enthusiastic support of our original idea; our editor, Sara Carder, for her encouragement, suggestions, help, and guidance all along the way; and Kat Kimball, whose steady hand smoothed the preparation of the final manuscript.

ABOUT THE AUTHORS

Carol Franco has been a publishing executive for more than twenty-five years. Formerly the director of Harvard Business School Press, she is currently an affiliated agent with Kneerim & Williams. Franco previously was president of Ballinger Publishing Company, at the time a subsidiary of Harper & Row.

Kent Lineback is a professional writer who specializes in collaborating with prominent business thinkers and executives who want to write books. He is the coauthor and author of several books, including the *BusinessWeek* bestseller *The Monk and the Riddle*.

Carol and her husband, Kent, live in Santa Fe.